MW00950880

The Automated Accountant

DAMON L. RUSSEL

ISBN: 979-8-34068161-4

DEDICATION

For Eric, Zax and Doofer, who always make the journey worthwhile.

TABLE OF CONTENTS

ACKNOWLEDGMENTS

I would like to express my heartfelt thanks to the following people for their invaluable contributions to this book:

To Eric, my partner, for his unwavering support, patience, and constant encouragement during this project. Your encouragement and positivity kept me motivated and focused through the many long and late hours of writing, editing and chart-making.

To my colleagues and mentors at Wolters Kluwer, whose guidance and expertise have shaped this book and my understanding of AI and its role in transforming the accounting industry. Your feedback has been instrumental in refining the ideas and concepts presented here.

Special thanks to Zax and Doofer, my loyal companions, for reminding me to take breaks and providing endless entertainment and joy during the writing process.

To the broader community of accounting and AI professionals, whose forward-thinking approaches and openness to technology inspired many of the case studies and examples in this book.

Finally, a sincere thank you to the readers of this book. Whether you're exploring AI for the first time or are well-versed in its applications, I hope this work provides valuable insights to apply to your practices and firms.

If you find value in this book, I hope you will consider leaving a review on Amazon so that others may more easily find it.

INTRODUCTION: THE AI REVOLUTION IN ACCOUNTING

The accounting profession is undergoing a digital transformation unlike anything it has experienced in its long history. Artificial intelligence (AI) was once a futuristic concept, but the wait is over. AI is already here, in use by firms of all sizes, and getting better every day. AI is now a critical tool in modern accounting firms to automate tasks, enhance decision-making, and discover new business insights for the firm and its clients. Whether you are a small firm seeking to streamline your processes or a large multinational firm looking to leverage advanced technologies, or anywhere inbetween, you'll learn how AI can revolutionize accounting.

This book, *The Automated Accountant*, is the first in the *AI-Powered Accounting: Strategies for the Digital Age* series. It's designed to guide accountants, firm leaders, and financial professionals through the practical applications of AI in accounting. The focus is on the real-world impact of AI technologies on tasks like tax compliance, financial reporting, auditing, and advisory services. We'll explore how AI is not just a tool to improve efficiency but a key driver in innovation in accounting today. As you read this book, consider how integrating AI into your practice could transform not just your processes, *but the very value you bring to your clients.*

GreenTree Financial, a mid-sized accounting firm at the core of this revolution, embarked on a journey to integrate AI into its operations. Throughout this book and the *AI-Powered Accounting* series, we'll follow GreenTree's story, learning how the firm successfully navigated the challenges of AI implementation and transformed itself into a modern, tech-forward firm. GreenTree's experience will serve as a case study to show how businesses can use AI to improve client advisory services, streamline processes, and build a more agile, forward-

96%
of accountants believe automation is essential for the profession
Study from CPA Practice Advisor

Figure 1 Majority of Accountants Value Automation

thinking company.

Why AI Matters for Accountants

For decades, accounting has been synonymous with precise, manual work. From balancing ledgers to ensuring compliance with tax regulations, accountants have long been the guardians of financial accuracy and integrity. However, as businesses and financial landscapes have become more complex, the demands on accountants have increased exponentially. Manual processes are no longer sufficient to meet the demands of today's fast-paced, data-driven business environment.

AI enables accountants to automate repetitive tasks such as data entry, reconciliations, and tax calculations, freeing up staff for higher-value work. Additionally, AI provides deep analytical capabilities, allowing firms to offer more strategic advisory services beyond just efficiency. Using AI tools, accountants can now predict future trends, analyze risk more effectively, and help their clients make better business decisions.

How This Book is Structured

The Automated Accountant is divided into three key sections:

1. **Understanding AI in Accounting:** In this section, we'll cover the core AI technologies driving automation in the industry, from optical character recognition to natural language processing. We'll explore how AI is reshaping traditional accounting tasks like financial reporting, audits, and compliance work.

2. **Practical Applications and Case Studies:** This section focuses on real-world applications of AI, using GreenTree Financial as an anchor case study. You'll see how AI has transformed specific areas of accounting, including tax compliance, fraud detection, and business intelligence in firms of all sizes.

3. **Future of AI in Accounting:** We'll close by looking ahead at what the future holds for accountants in the age of AI. From emerging technologies like blockchain and AI ethics to advanced AI-driven strategies for firms of every size, we'll explore how you can stay ahead of the curve and lead your firm into the future.

Who This Book is For

This book is for professionals at all levels of accounting – from accountants to small firm owners to leaders of large CPA firms – looking to understand how to implement AI and drive meaningful change. Whether you're just beginning to explore AI or already using it in your practice, *The Automated Accountant* offers actionable insights, strategies, and practical examples to help you navigate this new era in accounting.

CHAPTER 1: THE DAWN OF AI IN ACCOUNTING

Introduction

The accounting profession has undergone significant changes in technology over the years, but none have had as profound an impact as artificial intelligence (AI). While the initial waves of innovation focused on digitizing manual processes, the rise of AI represents a transformative leap forward. AI automates tasks that your staff may not enjoy—those mundane, repetitive, and error-prone tasks—and enhances decision-making capabilities by analyzing data in previously impossible ways. This chapter explores the evolution of accounting technology, starting with manual bookkeeping and leading to the advanced AI-powered tools that are reshaping the profession today.

AI's impact on accounting goes beyond mere automation. It has the potential to shift accountants' roles from more tactical functions like data processing to more strategic advisory roles. AI provides insights that allow firms to deliver greater value to their clients. As we revisit the evolution of accounting technology in this chapter, we will also examine how AI sets the stage for the profession's future.

Core Concepts

1. **Evolution of Accounting Technology:** The chapter traces the journey of accounting technology, starting from manual bookkeeping and evolving through the digital age. Initially, physical ledgers gave way to spreadsheets like Lotus 1-2-3 and Microsoft Excel, which brought efficiency in calculations. The next phase introduced dedicated accounting software, such as QuickBooks and Sage, designed to automate routine tasks. Today, AI is the most recent advancement, representing a leap toward enhanced automation and strategic capabilities.

2. **AI and Automation**: AI technology has transformed the scope of accounting automation. While early automation focused on routine, rules-based tasks like data entry and invoicing, AI has extended this by incorporating intelligent decision-making and adaptive processes. Modern AI-powered tools can automate not only low-value tasks but also high-value tasks, reducing errors and enhancing productivity across accounting firms.

3. **AI-Enhanced Decision-Making**: AI has taken automation a step further by enabling accountants to make more informed decisions. With tools like predictive analytics, accountants can forecast cash flow, detect anomalies, and anticipate tax liabilities. AI brings real-time insights that allow firms to identify risks early, provide proactive advice, and improve financial outcomes for clients.

4. **The Shift in Accountants' Roles**: AI has changed accountants' responsibilities, moving them from traditional, tactical roles—such as manual data processing and compliance—to more strategic roles. By handling mundane tasks, AI empowers accountants to focus on higher-value services, like advisory and financial planning, ultimately allowing them to deliver greater value to clients and become trusted business advisors.

Early Automation: From Ledgers to Spreadsheets

In the early days of accounting, bookkeepers maintained physical ledger books, recording transactions by hand. These paper-based ledgers were meticulously kept, but they were also prone to errors and required significant time and effort to update and maintain. The introduction of computerized systems in the 1980s marked a monumental shift in the accounting landscape. For the first time, accountants had access to computer software that would change how they worked forever. Computer software like Lotus 1-2-3® and Microsoft Excel® dramatically improved accountants' work by providing nearly instant calculations and a more reliable way to store vast amounts of data electronically, allowing accountants to track transactions more easily. By the mid-1980s, spreadsheet software like Lotus 1-2-3 had become essential tools in accounting, reducing the time for financial modeling from 20 hours to 15 minutes.

Despite the productivity gains, these early tools were still quite limited. They required manual data input and data validation, meaning that while accountants could perform calculations more efficiently, they still spent a lot of their time focused on processing information rather than analyzing it. Automation at

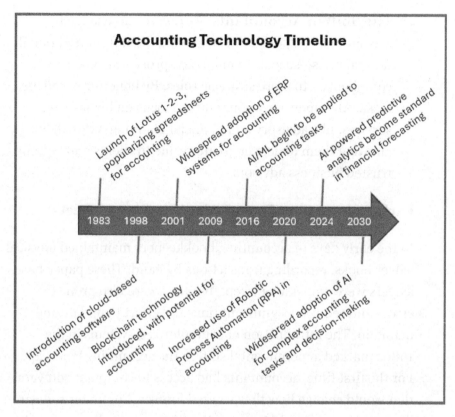

Figure 2 Timeline of Accounting Technology Changes

this time was primarily focused on data storage and calculation. It lacked the intelligence to assist in complex decision-making. Even still, this initial phase laid the groundwork for the more sophisticated technologies of today and the future.

The Software Revolution: Rules-Based Automation

In the early 2000s, dedicated accounting software like Quickbooks®, Peachtree Accounting®, and Sage® began to appear. These software tools were designed for small and medium businesses (SMBs) and automated routine accounting tasks, including payroll, invoicing, and bank reconciliations. Automating these processes freed small business owners and accountants from time-consuming manual work. However, developers of these early solutions were limited to the use of pre-programmed rules. They designed solutions for the most common or straightforward scenarios but could not adapt to irregular scenarios or handle complex decision-making tasks. Rules-based automation helped firms achieve greater efficiency in basic tasks, but it didn't address the strategic needs of accountants who sought more than simple task automation.

Task automation improved productivity significantly; however, accountants' roles remained largely unchanged. They still had to enter data and ensure compliance manually, which left them with limited time for higher-value advisory services. Despite its limitations, rules-based automation paved the way for the introduction of AI in accounting, which promised to go far beyond simple task automation and transform how decisions are made within firms.

AI-Enhanced Decision-Making

The introduction of AI marked a fundamental shift in accounting technology's capabilities. Unlike traditional boxed software, which followed rigid rules, AI allowed accountants to analyze vast amounts of data to detect patterns and predict future outcomes. AI-enhanced decision-making enables accountants to provide more strategic insights, helping businesses optimize operations, manage risk, and improve overall financial performance.

Predictive analytics is a form of AI that analyzes historical data to forecast cash flow, anticipate tax liabilities, and optimize budgets. Using these tools, firms can help their clients avoid financial risk by identifying potential dangers before they materialize. AI models can detect minor differences in financial data that might indicate fraud or errors and offer insights that human accountants might miss. This level of analysis allows accountants to move beyond reporting and focus on strategic planning.

For example, firms using predictive analytics can offer clients more accurate cash flow forecasts, which are critical for businesses navigating uncertain economic times. Instead of relying on static historical reports, AI provides real-time insights that help firms adjust their strategies on the fly. This capability is particularly valuable in today's fast-paced business environment, where firms must make data-driven decisions quickly.

56% of organizations report that AI-powered business intelligence tools have improved their decision-making processes. Additionally, AI can improve forecasting accuracy in financial predictions by up to 82%.

AI Today: Beyond Basic Automation

Today, AI has advanced far beyond its initial role of automating repetitive tasks. While early AI applications focused on automating data entry or document processing, modern AI systems are used for more complex functions such as financial forecasting, fraud detection, and even client engagement. AI tools like machine learning (ML) and natural language processing (NLP) enable accountants to automate both low-value and high-value tasks. For example, today firms can use these technologies for everything from tax preparation to real-time financial advice.

The global market for AI in accounting is projected to reach $12.52 billion by 2031, with a 34.51% CAGR from 2024 to 2031, as reported by SNS Insider. Additionally, 73% of organizations currently utilize AI for automation in accounting processes.

Kount® is a tool that specializes in fraud detection and uses machine learning algorithms to analyze transactional data and identify patterns that suggest potential fraud. Botkeeper® is another platform that similarly offers AI-powered bookkeeping services, automating tasks like reconciliation while providing real-time financial insights to businesses. These advanced AI tools not only free accountants from routine work but also enable them to deliver deeper insights into their clients' financial health.

The shift from basic automation to AI-driven decision-making is one of the most significant changes the accounting industry has seen. Accountants are no longer limited to processing numbers—they are now equipped with tools that allow them to predict trends, manage risks, and guide their clients' financial futures with greater accuracy.

REAL-WORLD EXAMPLES/CASE STUDIES

GreenTree Financial Case Study:

Throughout this book and the entire *AI Powered Accounting* series, we will delve into the world of GreenTree Financial to gain valuable insights and expertise that will complement our understanding of the real-world uses of AI in accounting. GreenTree Financial is a fictional mid-sized firm in Denver that struggled with hiring and retaining top talent, had inefficiencies in its tax preparation and financial reporting processes, and could not meet its economic goals. Much of the work relied on manual data entry and reconciliation, which consumed valuable time and led to frequent errors.

To address these challenges, the firm integrated AI-powered tools such as Optical Character Recognition (OCR) to automate the extraction and classification of financial data. This automation cut processing times in half and significantly reduced the margin for error. With AI handling routine tasks for the firm, GreenTree Financial's staff could now focus on more strategic activities, such as advising clients on tax planning and optimizing their financial strategies.

CCH® ProSystem fx® Scan and AutoFlow Technology:

A real-world example comes from firms that adopted CCH ProSystem *fx* Scan with AutoFlow Technology. This AI-driven solution automates the extraction of tax data from scanned tax source documents and financial documents, creates a consistently organized workpaper PDF, and reduces the need for manual data entry. By automating the document processing workflow, firms could push more work to lower-level staff and prepare taxes more quickly and with fewer errors. This technology can reduce data entry time by up to 70% compared to manual methods. Time saved using these solutions allows these accountants to focus on tasks that require critical thinking skills, such as providing strategic tax advice to clients.

Actionable Insights

If your firm plans to integrate AI into your accounting processes, there are several practical steps you can follow:

1. **Assess Your Firm's Readiness for AI:** Start with an internal review of the firm's key processes to identify bottlenecks in existing workflows. Look for areas where manual data entry or repetitive tasks impede productivity or where detecting data anomalies can be especially helpful during analysis. These are areas in which AI excels particularly well, making these processes ideal candidates for automation using AI-powered tools. As we have seen, tasks like data reconciliation, document classification, and tax preparation can often be automated, freeing up time for higher-value services.

2. **Leverage AI Tools for Predictive Analytics:** After deciding on areas for automation, you should next consider how AI tools can enhance your firm's decision-making processes. AI-driven predictive analytics tools can help firms forecast cash flow, detect fraud, and analyze financial data in real time. Solutions like CCH Axcess™ iQ use predictive analytics to review recent tax law changes and then find clients who may be affected. It also helps draft a letter to each client about the impact on their tax situation or their business.

3. **Automate Low-Value Tasks:** While AI can enhance decision-making, its immediate value often comes from automating low-value, repetitive tasks. By automating data entry, invoice processing, and document management, firms

can redirect their efforts toward advisory services, tax strategy, and financial planning. This shift allows accountants to focus on delivering higher-value services to their clients, enhancing overall firm profitability.

AI-powered accounting systems can reduce human error rates by up to 90%, drastically improving the reliability and accuracy of financial data. Moreover, 93% of accountants agree that artificial intelligence is positively impacting their work by providing more actionable insights, allowing them to spend less time on mundane tasks and more time on strategic advisory roles. These insights enable accountants to better understand financial trends, identify potential issues before they become significant

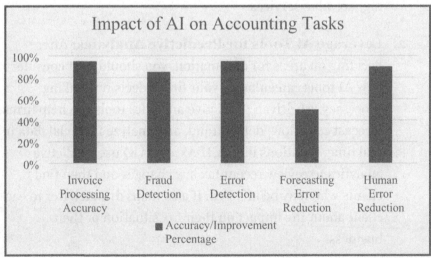

Figure 3 Impact of AI on Accounting Tasks

problems, and proactively advise their clients, enhancing the overall value they provide. As AI technology continues to evolve, the potential for even greater efficiency gains and deeper insights into financial data will only increase.

Conclusion/Takeaways

Artificial intelligence is rapidly changing the accounting landscape. From automating routine tasks to enhancing strategic decision-making, AI is enabling accountants to deliver more value to their clients. As we've seen with firms like GreenTree Financial, AI tools can streamline workflows, reduce errors, and provide critical insights that help businesses thrive. Firms that embrace AI now will be prepared to lead in the future as AI becomes an indispensable tool for modern accounting practices.

As we have seen, AI is fundamentally transforming the accounting profession, moving beyond simple automation to enhanced decision-making and strategic advisory roles. But how exactly does this technology work, and what are the driving forces behind this transformation? In the next chapter, we will dive deeper into the specific AI technologies—such as Optical Character Recognition (OCR), Robotic Process Automation (RPA), and Machine Learning (ML)—that are powering the automation revolution. These technologies are streamlining accounting processes and providing accountants with tools to deliver more value to their clients. Let's explore these key innovations and how they are shaping the future of accounting.

References

Botkeeper, Inc. (2024). *Botkeeper Automated Bookkeeping Platform.* https://www.botkeeper.com

Kount, Inc. (2024). *Kount Fraud Prevention and Risk Management Platform*. https://www.kount.com

IBM. (2024). *Lotus 1-2-3 Spreadsheet Software*. https://www.ibm.com

Intuit Inc. (2024). *QuickBooks Online Accounting Software*. https://quickbooks.intuit.com

Sage Group plc. (2024). *Sage Accounting Cloud*. https://www.sage.com

Wolters Kluwer. (2024). *CCH ProSystem fx Scan and AutoFlow Technology*. https://www.wolterskluwer.com

CHAPTER 2: KEY AI TECHNOLOGIES DRIVING ACCOUNTING AUTOMATION

Introduction

Artificial Intelligence (AI) has become a driving force in the transformation of the accounting industry, reshaping how firms approach everything from data extraction to financial reporting. As businesses move towards greater automation, AI technologies enable firms to streamline workflows, reduce human error, and enhance overall efficiency. In this chapter, we will explore the key AI technologies that are revolutionizing accounting, like Optical Character Recognition (OCR), Robotic Process Automation (RPA), Machine Learning (ML), Natural Language Processing (NLP), and more. These innovations are automating routine tasks and providing actionable insights, allowing firms to deliver more value to clients.

Core Concepts

The rise of AI in accounting is fueled by a diverse set of technologies, each bringing unique capabilities to the table. These core AI technologies are transforming everything from data processing to decision-making, helping firms streamline operations and enhance client service. Let's take a closer look at 13 key technologies driving this revolution.

1. **Optical Character Recognition (OCR) for Data Extraction**: One of the earliest and most impactful AI technologies in accounting is Optical Character Recognition (OCR). OCR automates the conversion of scanned documents—such as invoices, tax forms, and financial statements—into structured, meaningful data. Before OCR, manual data entry was the norm, which was time-consuming and prone to human error. Now, AI-powered OCR solutions can swiftly extract data, categorize it, and even populate tax or accounting software with minimal human intervention.

OCR can reduce data entry time by up to 80%, significantly improving efficiency in accounting processes (Grand View Research). A notable example of this is Wolters Kluwer's CCH ProSystem *fx* Scan, which uses OCR to automatically pull data from tax forms and input it into tax compliance software. This technology has transformed the tax preparation process, reducing the need for manual data entry and increasing overall accuracy. OCR also supports scalability by allowing firms to process large volumes of documents efficiently, which is particularly valuable during tax season. OCR has streamlined the accounting workflow, reducing bottlenecks and enhancing efficiency while allowing firms to focus on more strategic tasks.

2. **Robotic Process Automation (RPA): Automating Repetitive Tasks:** Robotic Process Automation (RPA) automates repetitive tasks such as data entry, invoice processing, and reconciliations. RPA systems function like digital assistants, carrying out routine tasks that once consumed valuable staff hours. This automation frees up accountants to focus on more strategic activities like advising clients or analyzing financial data.

The global RPA market in financial services is projected to reach $1.12 billion by 2025, with a compound annual growth rate (CAGR) of 24.9% from 2020 to 2025 (Gartner, 2025). RPA can potentially decrease processing costs by up to 80% and reduce turnaround times by 80-90% in accounting operations (Hyland, 2020). Leading RPA platforms such as UiPath and Automation Anywhere are widely used in the industry to automate workflows. These platforms allow firms to significantly reduce manual workloads, minimize errors, and improve the speed at which financial data is processed. RPA also enhances consistency by ensuring that processes are carried out the same way each time, reducing the risk of human error. The actual value of RPA lies in its ability to integrate with other AI technologies, such as machine learning, to extend automation into more complex decision-making areas. By using RPA combined with different tools, accounting firms can automate both mundane and sophisticated tasks, driving efficiency and adding greater value to their services.

3. Machine Learning (ML): Enhancing Decision-Making: Machine Learning (ML) is a subset of AI that enables systems to learn from data and improve their performance over time. In accounting, ML models can analyze large datasets, detect patterns, and offer previously hidden insights. This technology is especially valuable for fraud detection, expense classification, and predictive analytics, where patterns in data can help forecast future trends and financial outcomes.

The global machine learning market is projected to grow from $21.17 billion in 2022 to $209.91 billion by 2029, at a CAGR of 38.8% (Fortune Business Insights, 2022). ML algorithms can improve forecasting accuracy in financial predictions by up to 82% (Aspire Systems, 2022). A real-world application can be seen in Xero®, which uses ML to classify expenses and forecast cash flow. This allows businesses to manage their finances more effectively, reducing the need for manual categorization and ensuring that financial forecasts are based on real-time data. ML is also used to identify anomalies in financial transactions, helping firms detect fraud before it becomes a significant issue. The ability of ML to evolve and adapt means that its value to accounting firms will only grow as more data becomes available. Firms investing in ML now will be better positioned to provide predictive insights to help their clients navigate financial uncertainties.

4. Natural Language Processing (NLP) and AI-Enhanced Communication: Natural Language Processing (NLP) is an AI technology that enables computers to understand, interpret, and respond to human language. In accounting, NLP can automate routine communication tasks, process legal contracts, and analyze unstructured data such as emails and financial statements. This allows firms to improve client communication, automate reporting, and extract insights from vast amounts of text data.

The global NLP market is projected to experience substantial growth, from $11.6 billion in 2020 to $35.1 billion by 2026, representing a remarkable CAGR of 20.3% (MarketsandMarkets, 2026). NLP has shown the potential to slash data analysis time in accounting by up to 50%, enabling accountants to devote their energies to more strategic pursuits (Tungsten Automation, 2022). Virtual assistants powered by NLP are adept at handling basic client inquiries, guiding users through tax-filing procedures, and producing simple financial reports. Additionally, NLP facilitates sentiment analysis, offering firms valuable insight into client concerns through the analysis of communication tone and content.

As this technology continues to improve, NLP will play a larger role in automating communication tasks that previously needed human intervention. The ability to extract valuable insights from unstructured data, such as emails and documents, gives accounting firms a competitive advantage by providing deeper understanding and more personalized client interactions.

REAL-WORLD EXAMPLES/CASE STUDIES:

GreenTree Financial Case Study: Implementing AI for Predictive Analytics

GreenTree Financial, a mid-sized firm based in Denver, was looking for ways to enhance decision-making processes and improve efficiency in its advisory services. The firm faced several challenges, including managing increasing client demands, dealing with complex financial data, and providing prompt and accurate financial advice. By integrating AI-powered tools such as predictive analytics, the firm was able to forecast tax liabilities, improve cash flow, and give more tailored financial advice to clients. The AI tools enabled the firm to find trends in client data, predict financial challenges, and proactively offer solutions. Additionally, the automation of mundane data processing tasks allowed staff to focus more on strategic client engagement and business development. The implementation of AI not only reduced the time spent on manual data processing but also gave the firm a strategic advantage by offering real-time insights that helped clients make better financial decisions, especially during critical periods like tax season or economic downturns. This shift positioned GreenTree Financial as a more proactive and trusted advisor to their clients.

Wolters Kluwer's CCH® ProSystem fx® Scan

Wolters Kluwer's CCH ProSystem *fx* Scan and AutoFlow work together to streamline tax preparation processes. First, CCH ProSystem *fx* Scan uses AI-driven OCR technology to extract data from scanned tax source documents. It finds relevant fields within documents like W-2s, 1099s, and other tax forms and converts this information into structured, digital data. Then, AutoFlow technology seamlessly integrates with tax compliance software to import the extracted data, reducing the need for manual input. This automation ensures consistency and accuracy, significantly reducing errors while also speeding up the overall tax preparation process for accounting firms. For example, a mid-sized firm in California, featured in a Wolters Kluwer whitepaper, reported a 40% reduction in the time spent on tax preparation after implementing Scan and AutoFlow. By automating data extraction and entry, the firm was able to allocate more resources to higher-value activities, such as tax advisory and client engagement, improving both productivity and client satisfaction.

5. **Deep Learning:** Deep learning, a subset of machine learning, is particularly useful in accounting for tasks that require recognizing patterns in vast, unstructured datasets. This technology is applied in fraud detection, where it can analyze large volumes of financial transactions to identify anomalies and suspicious behavior in real-time. For example, systems using deep learning models, such as IBM Watson, can recognize complex patterns of fraudulent activity that simpler algorithms might miss. Firms that integrate deep learning into their fraud detection processes have reported a reduction in false positives by up to 60% (Deloitte).

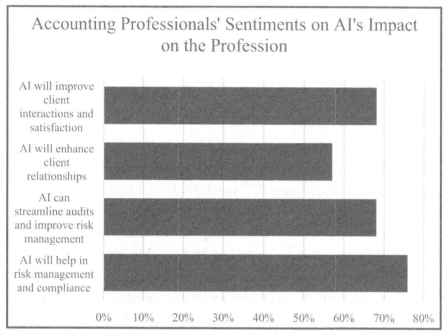

Figure 4 Accounting Professionals' Sentiments on AI's Impact

6. Neural Networks: Neural networks are designed to mimic the way the human brain processes information, making them powerful tools in predictive analytics and financial forecasting. These systems can identify non-linear relationships between variables in financial data, leading to more accurate predictions in areas such as budgeting, cash flow management, and revenue forecasting. For instance, neural network-based tools can analyze historical financial data to help firms anticipate market shifts and adjust financial strategies accordingly, with studies showing a 25% improvement in forecast accuracy (McKinsey).

7. Computer Vision: Although primarily used in fields like healthcare and security, computer vision is increasingly being applied in accounting to automate document processing. It goes beyond traditional OCR by enabling systems to interpret visual data, such as handwritten notes, diagrams, or scanned images that are harder to recognize. Computer vision tools, such as Microsoft's Azure Computer Vision, can analyze scanned invoices or receipts and accurately extract data even when the quality of the document is poor. This can enhance the document intake process, especially for firms that deal with paper-heavy workflows.

8. Cognitive Computing: Cognitive computing uses AI to simulate human thought processes, aiding accountants in analyzing vast amounts of financial data and making informed decisions. Cognitive systems like IBM Watson for Financial Services assist by processing complex regulatory documents, identifying relevant information, and offering insights on how firms should comply with evolving regulations. Cognitive computing platforms can also assist in strategic planning by recommending optimal investment or tax strategies based on historical performance data and market conditions, which can improve decision-making speed and accuracy by up to 70% (Forrester).

9. Chatbots: Chatbots powered by AI are increasingly being utilized in client-facing roles within accounting firms. These virtual assistants can handle routine client queries, such as answering tax questions, providing updates on tax return statuses, or guiding clients through the process of submitting documents. Platforms like Intuit's TurboTax employ chatbots to automate basic customer service functions, reducing the need for human interaction. Firms that implement chatbot technology can handle up to 50% more client inquiries without increasing headcount, significantly improving service capacity (Gartner).

10. Expert Systems: Expert systems, which use predefined rules to emulate the decision-making ability of a human expert, are useful in providing advisory services within accounting.

These systems can assist with complex tax planning or compliance scenarios by offering recommendations based on coded tax laws and regulations. For example, systems like Wolfram Alpha can suggest optimal tax strategies by interpreting rules and best practices. Expert systems are known to reduce errors in tax preparation by up to 30%, especially in highly specialized cases (ACCA Global).

11. Decision Management: AI-powered decision management systems streamline the decision-making processes within accounting by automating routine approvals and rejections, such as those involved in expense report reviews, loan applications, or even vendor selection. Tools like FICO's Decision Management Suite can analyze predefined criteria and make instant decisions on financial matters, improving efficiency and reducing processing times. These systems have been shown to cut decision-making time by up to 90% in accounting and finance operations (FICO).

12. Virtual Agents: Virtual agents go beyond simple chatbots, functioning as full-scale virtual assistants that can manage more complex client interactions. For instance, virtual agents powered by AI can proactively gather missing documents from clients, schedule appointments, or remind clients of deadlines. In accounting, virtual agents integrated with platforms like Salesforce Einstein can track client interactions, follow up on pending tasks, and ensure client satisfaction. Firms employing virtual agents report an average 40% increase in client engagement and satisfaction (Salesforce).

13. AI in Predictive Analytics: AI-driven predictive analytics tools analyze historical financial data and forecast future trends in areas such as revenue, expenses, and investment returns. By employing algorithms to assess market conditions, client behavior, and transactional data, predictive analytics systems like SAP Analytics Cloud can help firms anticipate future financial outcomes with high accuracy. Firms leveraging AI for predictive analytics have seen forecasting error rates drop by as much as 50%, leading to more informed strategic planning (PwC).

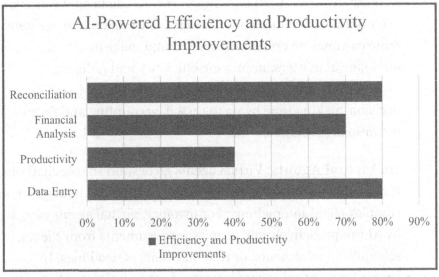

Figure 5 Efficiency and Productivity Improvements with AI-Powered Technologies

With so many AI technologies now available, it's clear that firms of any size can find at least one solution to begin their journey into AI-driven accounting. The sheer power and versatility of these tools—from automating routine tasks to making complex predictions—show that AI isn't just a futuristic concept; it's reshaping the industry right now. But with all these options, where do you start? How can you make sure you're choosing the right technology for your firm? Whether you're looking to automate document processing, enhance fraud detection, or improve client engagement, there's an AI tool ready to fit your needs. The key is taking that first step. In the next section, we'll explore actionable insights that will guide you in not just understanding these technologies but also in implementing them effectively. It's time to move from learning about AI to experiencing its real-world benefits for your practice.

Actionable Insights

1. Leverage OCR to Automate Data Extraction: If your firm is still manually entering data from financial documents, it's time to consider OCR. AI-powered tools like CCH ProSystem fx Scan can handle this task with speed and precision, allowing your team to focus on more important work. OCR doesn't just reduce data entry time—it can also boost accuracy. Imagine cutting your data entry workload by 80%, freeing up your staff to focus on client relationships and strategic tasks.

2. Use RPA to Automate Routine Accounting Tasks: RPA is a game-changer for repetitive, rule-based tasks. Think about how much time your team spends on tasks like processing invoices or reconciling accounts. Automating these with tools like UiPath won't just save time; it can also reduce errors. Less human involvement means fewer mistakes, and that translates into better results for your clients. Plus, when you integrate RPA with other AI technologies like machine learning, the potential for even greater efficiency is huge.

3. Adopt Machine Learning for Predictive Analytics: Machine learning isn't just for tech giants. Any firm can use ML to improve financial forecasts. Imagine being able to predict cash flow issues before they arise or spot potential fraud before it hits your bottom line. Platforms like Xero use ML to analyze historical data and predict outcomes—giving your team a powerful tool for making informed decisions. Don't just invest in technology, though. Invest in your team's ability to interpret these insights. A well-informed team is your greatest asset when communicating complex data to clients.

4. Utilize NLP and LLMs for Enhanced Client Communication: We've all had those days where client questions pile up. Enter NLP and large language models (LLMs). These tools can automate responses to common client inquiries and even draft reports or advisory notes in real time. Virtual assistants powered by NLP can take some of that load off your team, answering routine questions quickly and efficiently. And don't overlook sentiment analysis. It can help you get a pulse on how clients are feeling, allowing you to adjust services when needed. The real win? More time for your team to focus on the advisory work that clients value most.

5. Explore Deep Learning for Fraud Detection: Fraud detection doesn't have to be a reactive process. With deep learning, you can analyze large volumes of financial transactions in real time, spotting anomalies before they become major problems. Platforms like IBM Watson use deep learning to pick up on patterns that might fly under the radar with traditional methods. This technology is especially valuable for larger firms dealing with high volumes of transactions, but it's adaptable enough for smaller firms, too. Reducing false positives while catching real threats? That's a win every accountant can get behind.

6. Utilize Neural Networks for Improved Financial Forecasting: Neural networks go beyond standard financial models by identifying complex patterns in data. These patterns can help firms forecast revenue, manage cash flow, and even anticipate market shifts. Ever wonder why some firms always seem to be ahead of the curve? Neural networks might be the answer. By digging deeper into the data, you can make better predictions and smarter decisions, especially in uncertain market conditions.

7. Adopt Computer Vision for Document Processing: If your firm deals with a lot of paper—whether it's receipts, invoices, or financial statements—computer vision might be your new best friend. Unlike traditional OCR, it can handle more complex visual data, like handwritten notes or poorly scanned documents. Ever had to manually input data from a blurry receipt? Computer vision can handle that for you. It takes document processing to the next level, saving time and improving accuracy.

8. Leverage Cognitive Computing for Strategic Insights: Cognitive computing goes beyond number-crunching. Tools like IBM Watson for Financial Services help firms navigate complex regulatory landscapes by processing and analyzing vast amounts of data. Imagine a system that could sift through mountains of regulatory documents, highlighting what's most relevant to your firm's compliance needs. Whether it's tax planning or investment strategy, cognitive computing can offer insights that speed up decision-making while keeping your firm on the right side of regulations.

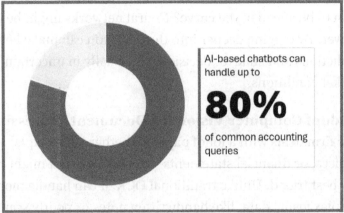

AI-based chatbots can handle up to

80%

of common accounting queries

Figure 6 AI-based Chatbots in Accounting

9. Implement Chatbots to Improve Client Service: Chatbots aren't just for customer service in retail. They can take over routine tasks in accounting too, such as answering tax questions or updating clients on the status of their returns. I've seen firms that use AI chatbots handle double the client inquiries without increasing headcount. Clients appreciate quick, accurate responses, and your staff will appreciate having more time to focus on higher-value services. It's a win-win.

10. Deploy Expert Systems for Advisory Services: If your firm offers advisory services, expert systems could be the tool you didn't know you needed. These systems mimic the decision-making process of a human expert, offering recommendations based on complex tax codes and financial regulations. Picture an expert system offering your clients fast, accurate tax planning advice based on up-to-the-minute rule changes. It's like having a tax expert on call, 24/7, ready to help you deliver faster results.

11. Use AI for Decision Management in Routine Approvals: Tired of reviewing the same types of expense reports or loan applications over and over? AI-driven decision management systems can take those tasks off your plate.

Platforms like FICO's Decision Management Suite use predefined criteria to automate decisions, improving speed and consistency. The result? Less time spent on routine approvals and more time for your team to focus on complex, strategic issues.

12. Utilize Virtual Agents for Client Engagement: Virtual agents do more than just answer basic client questions—they can manage entire workflows. Imagine a system that not only gathers missing documents from clients but also schedules meetings and sends reminders about upcoming deadlines. Firms using AI-driven virtual agents often see a big boost in client satisfaction. After all, a client who feels supported and informed is more likely to stick around for the long haul.

13. Enhance Predictive Analytics with AI: Predictive analytics isn't just a buzzword. It's a game-changer. AI models, like those found in SAP Analytics Cloud, analyze historical data and help firms forecast future trends, whether it's revenue, expenses, or cash flow. Firms that embrace predictive analytics often find themselves ahead of the competition, spotting trends and addressing potential issues long before they become problems. The key? Putting those insights to work in strategic planning and decision-making.

Conclusion/Takeaways

AI isn't just a future trend—it's here, and it's reshaping accounting in ways that matter today. From automating data extraction with OCR to predicting financial trends with machine learning, AI is doing more than just speeding things up. It's making processes smarter and more accurate. These technologies allow firms to reduce human error, make data-driven decisions, and ultimately provide more value to clients.

Whether you're a small or large firm, adopting AI tools will keep you ahead of the curve in an industry that's evolving faster than ever. Firms that take the leap into AI aren't just keeping up— they're setting the pace.

Now that we've explored how these technologies are revolutionizing core accounting processes, let's dive into a crucial area: tax preparation. If you've ever been through tax season manually, you know how time-consuming it can be. But AI is poised to change that, making real-time tax filing and fully automated tax prep a reality. In the next chapter, we'll break down these advancements and see how firms can use them to streamline operations and reduce manual effort during tax season. AI is proving itself as a powerful ally in tackling one of the most complex and tedious aspects of accounting.

References

ACCA Global. (n.d.). *Expert Systems in Tax Preparation.* ACCA - AI in Tax. https://www.accaglobal.com

Aspire Systems. (n.d.). A Closer Look at the Technologies Behind Document Processing.

Automation Anywhere. (2024). *Automation Anywhere RPA Platform.* https://www.automationanywhere.com

Deloitte. (n.d.). *Deep Learning for Fraud Detection.* Deloitte - AI in Fraud Detection. https://www2.deloitte.com

FICO. (n.d.). *Decision Management Systems in Finance and Accounting.* FICO - Decision Management. https://www.fico.com

Fortune Business Insights. (n.d.). Machine Learning Market Size, Share & COVID-19 Impact Analysis.

Forrester. (n.d.). *Cognitive Computing in Financial Decision-Making*. Forrester - Cognitive Computing. https://www.forrester.com

Gartner. (n.d.). *Chatbots in Accounting: Improving Client Engagement*. Gartner - Chatbots in Finance. https://www.gartner.com

Gartner. (n.d.). Forecast Analysis: Robotic Process Automation, Worldwide.

Grand View Research. (n.d.). Intelligent Document Processing Market Size Report, 2030.

MarketsandMarkets. (2024). Natural Language Processing Market - Global Forecast to 2026.

McKinsey. (n.d.). *Neural Networks for Financial Forecasting*. McKinsey - AI in Finance. https://www.mckinsey.com

PwC. (n.d.). *Predictive Analytics in Financial Forecasting*. PwC - AI in Forecasting. https://www.pwc.com

Salesforce. (2024). *Virtual Agents in Client Engagement*. Salesforce - Virtual Agents. https://www.salesforce.com

UiPath. (2024). *UiPath Automation Platform*. https://www.uipath.com

Wolters Kluwer. (2024). *CCH ProSystem fx Scan*. https://www.wolterskluwer.com

Xero Ltd.. (2024). *Xero Accounting Software.*
https://www.xero.com

CHAPTER 3: AUTOMATION AND FULLY AUTOMATED TAX PREPARATION

Introduction

Tax preparation has long been one of the most labor-intensive processes within the accounting profession. From gathering client documents to reviewing new or updated tax regulation changes, accountants have traditionally devoted considerable time and resources to ensure compliance. However, the rise of Artificial Intelligence is dramatically improving this process. Automation tools like OCR, Robotic Process Automation (RPA), Machine Learning, Natural Language Processing, and Large Language Models are enabling fully automated tax workflows.

The future of tax preparation will bring more automation with increased accuracy and efficiency. This chapter explores the key technologies driving this revolution and examines the potential for real-time tax filing in the not-too-distant future.

Core Concepts

1. The Road to Full Automation: Historically, tax preparation has always been a time-consuming, manual process involving the input and review of large amounts of data from various financial documents. These workflows were time-consuming and prone to human error, particularly during peak tax seasons when staff worked longer hours and were under added pressure to deliver on time.

AI has transformed this landscape by enabling firms to automate nearly every stage of tax preparation, from data gathering and extraction to filing submission. As firms move closer to fully automated workflows, the prospect of real-time tax filing—where returns are prepared and submitted without the need for human reviews—comes into view. We have seen AI's capability to streamline tax processes, reducing the time and effort required for tax compliance while increasing accuracy.

The global business intelligence market, which includes tax automation tools, is projected to reach $43.03 billion by 2028, growing at a CAGR of 8.7% from 2021 to 2028 (Thomson Reuters). Additionally, 73% of organizations utilize AI to automate accounting processes, including tax preparation (AI Journal).

2. Key AI Technologies Enabling Tax Automation: Several advanced AI technologies are pushing the boundaries of automation in tax preparation.

- **Optical Character Recognition (OCR):** OCR tools like Wolters Kluwer's CCH® ProSystem *fx*® Scan are essential to automating data extraction. These AI-powered systems efficiently read and extract data from tax forms, financial statements, and invoices and then can import that data into tax preparation software. This technology significantly reduces the time spent on manual data entry, ensures consistency in preparation and review practices, and ensures higher accuracy. OCR can minimize data entry time by up to

80%, significantly improving efficiency in accounting processes (Grand View Research).

- **Robotic Process Automation (RPA):** RPA technology manages repetitive and rule-based tasks like document categorization, invoice matching, and tax form processing. Tax filings can be completed more accurately and quickly without adding human labor. Platforms like UiPath help firms scale operations by automating high-volume, low-complexity tasks, thereby reducing errors. RPA can reduce processing costs by up to 80% and turnaround times by 80-90% in accounting operations (Hyland).

- **Machine Learning (ML):** ML models have proven valuable in tax automation. They learn from historical tax filings to suggest the best deductions and credits. Tools like SurePrep's 1040Scan leverage ML to categorize tax forms, predict outcomes, and show data trends, all while ensuring compliance with tax regulations. Machine Learnng algorithms can improve forecasting accuracy in financial predictions by up to 82% (Aspire Systems).

- **Natural Language Processing (NLP) and Large Language Models (LLMs):** AI advancements in natural language processing and LLMs, such as OpenAI's GPT-4, are transforming tax preparation workflows in ways that are still being understood. By automating complex decision-making and interpreting tax regulations, firms can provide more value for their clients. NLP can read and analyze large volumes of unstructured text, such as tax codes, legal documents, and client communications.

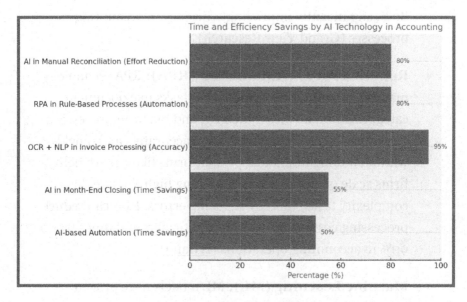

Figure 7 Time and Efficiency Savings

At the same time, LLMs can assist in generating tax reports, drafting advisory notes, and even answering tax-related queries from clients in real time. As a result, accountants can devote more time to providing higher-value advisory services instead of interpreting regulations or drafting reports.

REAL-WORLD EXAMPLES/CASE STUDIES OF NLP AND LLMS:

Intuit's TurboTax and KPMG's Clara Platform

Intuit's TurboTax® has implemented NLP technologies in its tax preparation software for taxpayers through tax preparation and filing. Using NLP technology, TurboTax automatically extracts essential information and recommends tax deductions. Another LLM in use today is KPMG's Clara platform, which can analyze large datasets, offer real-time insights, ensure accurately filed returns, and refine client tax strategies.

Deloitte's CognitiveTax Insight (CTI) Platform: Revolutionizing Multinational Tax Compliance

In today's increasingly complex global tax environment, firms operating across multiple jurisdictions often struggle to comply with evolving regulations. Deloitte recognized this challenge and developed its proprietary CognitiveTax Insight (CTI) platform to offer a solution. The platform streamlines multinational corporations' tax compliance by integrating machine learning, big data analytics, and natural language processing.

CTI automatically analyzes large datasets frequently sourced from nations with distinct tax codes. It continuously monitors changes in tax laws and regulatory updates, ensuring that Deloitte's clients are always compliant in real-time. One of CTI's key advantages is its ability to detect discrepancies and outliers in tax filings, which might indicate non-compliance or potential fraud. By analyzing historical tax data, CTI can predict areas of risk and suggest corrective actions before issues arise, effectively preventing costly penalties.

The platform's real-time capabilities have reduced tax compliance processing times for Deloitte's clients by over 50%. This automation reduces human error and allows the firm's tax professionals to focus on strategic advisory services, such as cross-border tax planning and optimization strategies, rather than mundane compliance checks. Deloitte's CTI platform exemplifies how AI can handle complex, high-volume tasks quickly and precisely, dramatically improving large firms' operational efficiency.

GreenTree Financial Case Study: Automating Tax Preparation for Strategic Gains

GreenTree Financial, a mid-sized accounting firm, faced a recurring challenge every tax season. Like other firms its size, their staff felt buried with a surge of manual tax preparation tasks, from collecting client documents to entering financial data into tax software. With a growing client base, the firm's workflow became inefficient, and human error was increasingly concerning. To address these challenges, GreenTree adopted AI-powered tools such as CCH® ProSystem fx® Scan and AutoFlow to automate data extraction and processing.

The Optical Character Recognition (OCR) integration allowed GreenTree to digitize and extract information from scanned tax forms like W-2s, 1099s, and other client documents. Because manual data entry was eliminated, preparing tax filings took much less time. The process was sped up by 40% thanks to automatically populating the firm's tax software with precise, categorized data.

Additionally, GreenTree implemented Machine Learning (ML) models to analyze historical tax data. Using clients' prior year returns as a basis, these models offered real-time recommendations for credits and deductions, further optimizing tax strategies. For instance, GreenTree's AI-driven system flagged potential deductions that human accountants had previously overlooked, leading to an average of 15% in tax savings for clients.

GreenTree transformed its tax preparation process, allowing its staff to redirect their efforts toward providing higher-value advisory services. Client satisfaction increased as the firm offered personalized tax-saving advice in a fraction of the time. By automating the most time-consuming tasks, GreenTree improved operational efficiency and boosted its bottom line by taking on more clients during busy seasons without hiring additional staff.

The Future of Tax Automation: Real-Time Tax Filing

One of the most exciting possibilities on the horizon is real-time tax filing. As AI technologies continue to evolve, the idea of automatically processing tax returns in real time is becoming more feasible. Instead of the traditional annual rush to prepare taxes, AI-powered systems can continuously monitor financial transactions throughout the year, automatically classifying and preparing tax returns without human intervention.

Real-time tax filing would allow businesses and individuals to stay compliant all year round rather than scrambling to gather documents and file returns once a year. By automating this process, firms can reduce errors, improve cash flow management, and provide clients with ongoing, up-to-date tax advice.

PwC's TaxVision AI: A Leader in Automated Tax Processing

PwC has long been a leader in leveraging new technology to simplify tax processes. Its TaxVision AI platform is at the forefront of automated tax preparation. TaxVision AI is an advanced automated tax preparation solution that uses AI algorithms, including Natural Language Processing (NLP) and Machine Learning (ML), to automate everything from document review to regulatory compliance monitoring. The platform extracts relevant information from tax documents and scans for regulatory changes that might impact a client's tax obligations.

Keeping up with local tax laws and staying compliant across different jurisdictions can be overwhelming for large, multinational corporations. TaxVision AI constantly scans for changes in tax regulations, flagging potential issues before they become problems. This proactive approach helps companies reduce the risk of costly errors or penalties for non-compliance.

One of the most compelling aspects of PwC's platform is its ability to process unstructured data, such as emails or contracts, using NLP. TaxVision AI can handle more complex tax scenarios, such as international tax agreements or multi-jurisdictional reporting, with minimal human intervention. As a result, PwC has cut tax preparation times nearly in half while providing clients with more accurate, data-driven insights. The system's ability to learn and adapt means that PwC continuously improves its tax services, keeping it ahead of the curve in the rapidly evolving tax landscape.

AI-Enhanced Accuracy and Efficiency

AI's role in tax preparation is not just about automating repetitive tasks—it's also about enhancing accuracy and efficiency. AI systems can process large volumes of data much faster and more accurately than humans. With the ability to cross-reference data from multiple sources, AI can detect inconsistencies and anomalies, reducing the likelihood of errors in tax filings.

Machine learning algorithms, for example, continuously improve over time by learning from past filings and adjustments, enhancing accuracy. This allows firms to reduce the time spent on revisions and amendments, providing more reliable results to clients. AI-driven accuracy is a game-changer in a tax landscape where even minor errors can have significant consequences.

The Human Element in a Fully Automated World

As tax workflows become more automated, one question remains: what role will human accountants play in a fully automated tax preparation process? The answer lies in the evolving nature of the profession. While AI will handle most repetitive, low-value tasks, human accountants will shift toward more strategic roles, focusing on interpreting AI-generated insights, advising clients, and navigating complex, non-standard tax issues that require professional judgment.

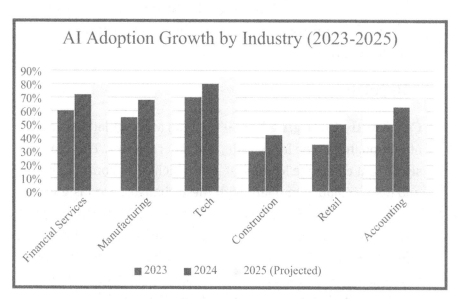

Figure 8 AI Adoption Growth Across Industries

93% of accountants agree that artificial intelligence and automation positively affect their work, helping them transition from data processors to trusted advisors who provide value-added services and insights to their clients (AI Journal). Accountants will continue to be indispensable in providing personalized service, especially in areas where the application of tax law is subjective or ambiguous. Furthermore, clients will still value human interaction and trust accountants to give tailored advice that AI may not yet be able to deliver. In this sense, automation will free accountants from mundane tasks, allowing them to engage more deeply with their clients and offer higher-value advisory services.

Challenges in Fully Automating Tax Compliance

While a fully automated tax compliance process may sound like a dream come true, it presents unique challenges that must be addressed. Below is a more detailed look at these challenges, including examples and insights into how they impact accounting firms:

1. Regulatory Complexity

Constantly Changing Law—Tax laws and regulations are often updated at the local, state, and federal levels. This creates a significant challenge for AI systems, which must continually update to remain compliant with these changes. For instance, a firm operating in multiple states must ensure its AI-driven tax software is aware of and updated for the latest regulatory differences across jurisdictions. The dynamic nature of tax laws requires ongoing investment in AI training and data updates to avoid potential penalties due to outdated information.

Jurisdictional Variations – Tax rules vary significantly across countries, states, and municipalities. AI-based systems must account for these variations and apply the correct rules based on jurisdiction. For example, multinational firms face other complexities when dealing with international tax laws, VAT, and other localized tax requirements. These jurisdictional differences mean that AI systems need to be highly flexible and adaptable to correctly interpret and apply the relevant tax codes in each location.

2. Data Quality and Integration

Diverse Data Sources – Tax compliance requires information from various sources, including financial records, payroll systems, and third-party reports. Integrating and standardizing this diverse data can be challenging, particularly if the data formats are inconsistent or if data is missing. Poor data quality can lead to errors in AI processing, affecting the accuracy of tax filings. For example, a firm might pull data from multiple software systems, each with different data structures, which complicates the integration process—The quality of input data is crucial for accurate tax compliance. Errors or inconsistencies in source data can lead to incorrect tax calculations and filings. Accounting firms must ensure that the data used by AI systems is correct, clean, and up-to-date. Validating data before it is fed into AI systems may require more resources, which could offset some of the efficiency gains from automation.

3. Interpretational Challenges

Complex Scenarios – Some tax situations require a nuanced interpretation of laws and regulations. AI systems may struggle with unique or complex scenarios that don't fit standard patterns. For instance, tax implications for mergers, acquisitions, or cross-border transactions often require sophisticated analysis and judgment that AI alone cannot provide. Human accountants must step in during such scenarios to ensure compliance and the best tax outcomes.

Ambiguity in Tax Code – Tax laws often contain ambiguities that require human judgment. Automated systems may have difficulty interpreting these gray areas. For example, determining the eligibility for certain tax credits may depend on subjective criteria that require professional judgment. In these cases, the limitations of AI become apparent, and human expertise is needed to make the final decision.

4. Technological Limitations

AI Reliability – Ensuring the reliability and accuracy of AI decisions in high-stakes tax matters is crucial. Errors can result in significant financial and legal consequences. Accounting firms must have mechanisms to verify AI-generated outputs and correct discrepancies. This may include periodic audits of AI systems to ensure they function as intended and produce accurate results.

Explainability – The "black box" nature of some AI algorithms can make it difficult to explain how decisions were reached, which is problematic in tax audits or disputes. Clients and regulators may demand a clear explanation of how tax calculations were performed, which can be challenging if the AI model's decision-making process is not transparent. To address this, firms need to invest in explainable AI solutions that provide insight into how decisions are made.

5. Security and Privacy Concerns

Data Protection – Handling sensitive financial information requires robust security measures to protect against data breaches and unauthorized access. AI systems used in tax preparation must comply with data protection regulations, such as GDPR, to ensure that client information remains confidential. Firms must implement robust encryption protocols, access controls, and regular security audits to safeguard data.

Compliance with Privacy Laws – Automated systems must comply with various data protection regulations, which can be challenging across different jurisdictions. For example, privacy laws in the European Union may differ significantly from those in the United States, requiring AI systems to be configured differently depending on where the data is processed. This adds a layer of complexity to implementing fully automated tax compliance systems.

6. Human Factors

Resistance to Automation – There may be resistance from tax professionals and organizations that are accustomed to traditional methods or concerned about job displacement. Implementing AI and automation can be met with skepticism, particularly among staff who fear that their roles may become redundant. To mitigate this, firms need to focus on change management, emphasizing that AI is a tool to enhance productivity and allow professionals to focus on higher-value tasks rather than a replacement for human judgment and expertise.

Trust and Acceptance – Building trust in fully automated tax compliance systems among taxpayers, businesses, and regulatory bodies is a significant challenge. Trust in AI systems is critical, especially when dealing with sensitive financial information and tax compliance. Clients, regulators, and employees must feel confident that the AI systems are accurate, secure, and unbiased. Firms must prioritize transparency and provide thorough documentation to help stakeholders understand how AI-driven decisions are made. Conducting training sessions to educate staff and clients about how AI works and its benefits can also foster greater acceptance and trust.

Addressing these challenges will require ongoing collaboration between tax experts, AI developers, and regulatory bodies to create robust, reliable, and adaptable automated tax compliance systems.

Actionable Insights

1. Adopt OCR for Efficient Data Extraction:

Firms should adopt OCR technology to automate data extraction from tax forms and reduce the burden of manual data entry. AI-powered OCR tools such as CCH® ProSystem fx® Scan enable seamless data import into tax software, improving accuracy and turnaround times. This can be particularly helpful during busy tax seasons, ensuring accountants can focus on more strategic tasks rather than being bogged down by manual data entry.

2. Leverage RPA to automate repetitive tasks:

RPA can streamline the processing of tax forms, from categorizing documents to submitting returns. Platforms like UiPath can handle high volumes of transactions, allowing firms to scale without adding staff. RPA bots can work around the clock, ensuring tasks are completed faster and with fewer errors. This enhances overall productivity and allows accountants to focus on advisory roles and client engagement.

3. Implement ML for Optimized Tax Strategies:

ML tools like SurePrep's 1040Scan can help firms find deductions and enhance tax strategies based on historical data, improving accuracy and compliance. By using ML for predictive analytics, firms can also predict tax liabilities and offer proactive strategies to clients. Firms should consider integrating ML models with existing systems to enhance their capabilities and contribute deeper insights into client finances, delivering better and more strategic tax planning.

4. Utilize NLP and LLMs for Enhanced Tax Reporting:

Firms should explore using NLP and LLMs to automate the interpretation of tax regulations and generate client-ready tax reports. These technologies not only save time but also improve the quality of client interactions by providing more personalized and insightful recommendations. By using NLP to process unstructured text, such as client communications or changes in tax law, firms can ensure that they are providing the most up-to-date and relevant information to their clients, enhancing trust and client satisfaction.

5. Be Prepared for Challenges:

Understanding the challenges you might face while implementing a fully automated tax compliance process will help you prepare to handle them better. Identify the risks and challenges that are most likely to occur, then plan mitigation measures to solve them effectively. Develop a robust change management strategy to address employee concerns and ensure buy-in from all stakeholders. By preparing for potential hurdles, firms can create smoother transitions and maximize the benefits of AI-driven tax compliance.

Conclusion/Takeaways

The automation of tax preparation through AI is transforming the accounting profession. OCR, RPA, ML, and NLP/LLMs enable firms to automate tax preparation, providing consistent accuracy and faster turnaround times. As tax technology evolves, real-time tax filing is becoming a reality, allowing firms to streamline tax workflows and deliver higher-value client services. However, while automation will take over many routine tasks, human accountants will still play a crucial role in providing strategic advice and navigating complex tax scenarios. Firms that embrace AI for tax preparation now will gain a strategic advantage in the future of tax compliance.

As tax preparation becomes fully automated, AI's capabilities are expanding into other areas of accounting. For instance, generative AI enables firms to deliver more accurate and insightful financial reports faster than ever before in financial reporting. In the next chapter, we will explore how generative AI is revolutionizing financial reporting by automating the generation of financial statements, conducting complex audits, and predicting future financial performance. The same AI technologies driving tax automation are now helping firms streamline reporting processes and deliver enhanced value to clients. Let's dive into how generative AI is shaping the future of financial reporting.

References

AI Journal. (n.d.). Tips on How AI is Automating Tax Preparation.

Aspire Systems. (n.d.). A Closer Look at the Technologies Behind Document Processing.

Deloitte. (2024). CognitiveTax Insight (CTI) Platform. https://www2.deloitte.com

Grand View Research. (n.d.). Intelligent Document Processing Market Size Report, 2030.

Hyland. (n.d.). Robotic Process Automation in Accounting.

KPMG. (2024). KPMG Clara Platform. https://home.kpmg.com

OpenAI. (2024). GPT-4. https://openai.com

PwC. (2024). AI for Automated Tax Processing. https://www.pwc.com

Thomson Reuters. (n.d.). Exploring the Future of Tax Automation.

Wolters Kluwer. (2024). CCH ProSystem fx Scan and AutoFlow. https://www.wolterskluwer.com

CHAPTER 4: GENERATIVE AI IN FINANCIAL REPORTING

Introduction

Technology is reshaping the evolving financial reporting landscape, and generative AI is at the forefront of this transformation. Once reliant on manual labor and prone to human error, financial reports are becoming more automated, precise, and dynamic. Generative AI allows firms to streamline the creation of financial statements, analyze unstructured data, and deliver personalized insights to stakeholders. This chapter will examine how generative AI transforms financial reporting, from producing predictive insights to automating compliance procedures and assisting companies in navigating a more complicated regulatory landscape. We will learn about these subjects and how AI enables accounting professionals to concentrate on high-value, strategic decision-making instead of manual tasks.

Core Concepts

1. Automating Financial Statement Creation

Generative AI is revolutionizing financial statement creation. Preparing balance sheets, income statements, and cash flow reports previously required accountants to consolidate data from multiple sources manually. With AI, this process is now automated, drastically reducing the time it takes to compile these critical reports.

Generative AI systems analyze and process large volumes of financial data in real-time. AI can autonomously generate up-to-date financial statements by continuously tracking and classifying transactions, allowing firms to maintain accurate and timely records without manual intervention. This ensures consistency in reporting and frees accountants to focus on strategic decision-making rather than repetitive data entry. AI can reduce the time spent on data analysis in accounting by up to 50%, and 73% of organizations currently utilize AI for automation in accounting processes.

2. Generating AI-Driven Narratives for Stakeholders

Beyond simply producing financial statements, advanced AI systems offer a more nuanced approach to financial reporting. By leveraging natural language processing, these systems can craft detailed narratives that breathe life into raw financial data. Natural Language Generation (NLG) technologies now automatically produce standardized financial reports, including income statements, balance sheets, and cash flow statements. Narrative Science's Quill leverages advanced technology to transform complex financial data into tailored reports for different audiences, such as shareholders, management teams, and government agencies. This improvement in financial reporting significantly enhances stakeholder communication. Instead of presenting stakeholders with a wall of numbers, firms can now provide insightful, context-rich reports they can understand.

These narratives go beyond just data presentation. They also explain revenue fluctuations or highlight emerging risks based on current trends. This approach not only makes financial information more accessible but also more actionable. It enables business owners to understand the complete picture of their company's financial health and future prospects.

The Clara platform from KPMG is an excellent example of the increasing potential of generative AI in financial reporting. By using machine learning and natural language processing, Clara improves the clarity of economic narratives and automates the creation of financial statements. Its algorithms can detect financial data trends, risks, and anomalies, offering clients detailed analyses alongside traditional reports.

For example, a large multinational client used Clara to generate quarterly financial reports. Clara produced real-time income statements, balance sheets, and cash flow reports while generating narratives explaining shifts in revenue, expenses, and cash flow. This automation reduced the time spent on report generation by 50%, allowing the client's financial team to focus on strategic forecasting and decision-making. Clara's ability to flag potential risks improved the firm's decision-making, providing early warnings of possible issues that might impact future performance.

3. Analyzing Unstructured Data for Financial Insights

One of generative AI's fundamental advantages is its ability to efficiently process and analyze unstructured data, which is often essential in financial reporting. Traditionally, reviewing sources like emails, contracts, and regulatory filings was a time-consuming task that required extensive time and manual effort. Now, with the integration of AI models enhanced by natural language processing (NLP), these insights can be automatically extracted from unstructured data. This allows firms to incorporate a broader range of information into their financial reports, resulting in more comprehensive insights and improved decision-making.

AI tools can review contracts, identify critical financial terms, and even forecast the potential impact of specific clauses on future financial performance, enabling more informed and strategic business decisions. AI-powered accounting systems can also reduce human error rates by up to 90%.

REAL-WORLD EXAMPLE: NARRATIVE SCIENCE'S QUILL

A mid-sized technology company employed Narrative Science's Quill to generate quarterly financial narratives for its executive team and board of directors. Before Quill, the finance team spent hours drafting reports summarizing the company's financial performance and explaining the underlying drivers. Adopting AI-generated narratives reduced the time required for this task so that finance professionals could focus on more critical analysis.

The AI system not only generated accurate financial summaries but also included context-aware explanations for material changes in revenue, expenses, and profit margins. The ease of understanding these AI-generated narratives improved communication across the company, ensuring that even non-financial stakeholders could understand the firm's performance at a glance.

4. Compliance and Regulatory Reporting

Compliance and regulatory reporting are critical components of financial reporting, but they are often time-consuming and subject to constant regulation changes. AI continuously updates its database with the latest tax regulations, automatically applying these updates to the financial reporting process. This ensures that firms remain compliant with ever-evolving standards without manually adjusting their reports.

For instance, AI systems can scan new tax regulations or changes in accounting standards and instantly apply these updates to financial statements, saving firms the effort of manual research and updates. This improves the accuracy of reports and reduces the risk of non-compliance.

5. Predictive Analytics and Forecasting with Generative AI

One of the most effective applications of generative AI is its ability to predict future financial performance. AI can forecast potential risks and opportunities by analyzing historical financial data and current market conditions, providing firms with actionable insights.

Generative AI tools like SAP's Predictive Analytics offer real-time forecasting models that allow businesses to anticipate cash flow challenges, revenue fluctuations, and expense trends. These predictions enable firms to make informed decisions about resource allocation, investments, and cost-cutting measures, improving their financial resilience. AI can improve forecasting accuracy in financial forecasts by up to 82%, and 56% of organizations report that AI-powered business intelligence tools have improved their decision-making processes.

A large manufacturing company implemented SAP's AI-driven financial reporting tools to generate customized reports for its financial team and executive leadership. The AI-driven system automated the creation of detailed financial statements for the accounting department while generating high-level summaries for the executive team.

By automating these processes, the company reduced the time spent preparing reports by 40%. The AI system also offered predictive insights into future financial performance, allowing the company to recognize upcoming cash flow issues and adjust its strategy accordingly. This improved the company's financial planning and enhanced its ability to communicate effectively with stakeholders.

6. Enhancing Stakeholder Communication with AI-Generated Reports

Generative AI doesn't just automate report creation—it also enhances communication with stakeholders. AI-generated reports can be customized for different audiences, from detailed financial analyses for internal accounting teams to executive summaries for leadership and shareholders. This flexibility ensures that all stakeholders receive the right level of detail, improving engagement and decision-making.

With AI, firms can automatically generate tailored reports that explain key metrics, highlight risks, and suggest actionable insights, fostering more straightforward communication across the board. In a fast-paced business environment, where timely and accurate information is crucial, AI-enhanced reporting ensures that stakeholders always stay informed. 93% of accountants agree that artificial intelligence positively impacts their work by providing more actionable insights.

7. Ethical Considerations in AI-Driven Financial Reporting

The use of generative AI in financial reporting raises important ethical considerations that organizations must address:

- **Transparency and Explainability**: AI systems used in financial reporting must be transparent and explainable. Stakeholders must clearly understand how AI-generated reports are created and which data sources are utilized. This level of transparency is essential for upholding trust in financial reporting processes.

- **Human Oversight**: While AI can automate many aspects of financial reporting, human oversight remains essential. Accountants and financial professionals should review AI-generated reports to ensure accuracy and identify potential errors or biases. This human-in-the-loop approach helps maintain the integrity of financial reporting.

- **Mitigating AI Biases**: AI models can inadvertently perpetuate biases present in training data. Organizations must actively identify and mitigate these biases to ensure fair and accurate financial reporting. This may involve:

  - Regularly auditing AI models for bias ensures they operate fairly and without skewed outcomes. For example, firms can establish periodic reviews where a diverse team of experts assesses the AI's predictions and decisions to ensure no bias has crept in over time.

o   Diversifying training data sources to provide a broader, more representative sample of financial scenarios. This diversity helps reduce the risk of certain groups or situations being misrepresented or overlooked by the AI system.

o   Implementing bias detection algorithms that can flag potential biases within the AI's operations. These algorithms serve as a proactive measure, helping to identify subtle biases before they impact financial reporting, thus maintaining objectivity and fairness.

8. Integration with Blockchain Technology

The combination of generative AI and blockchain technology offers exciting possibilities for enhancing financial reporting:

Enhanced Security and Traceability: Blockchain's immutable ledger can provide an additional layer of security for AI-generated financial reports. Each report can be recorded on the blockchain, creating an unalterable audit trail. This integration enhances the credibility of AI-generated reports and makes tracking any changes or updates easier.

o   **Smart Contracts in Financial Reporting**: Smart contracts on blockchain platforms can automate various aspects of financial reporting. For example:

  ▪ Triggering report generation automatically based on predefined conditions

  ▪ Ensuring compliance with reporting deadlines

- Enabling authorized stakeholders to receive and share financial reports securely

By 2025, 70% of organizations are expected to have operationalized AI architectures, up from 10% in 2020.

9. Regulatory Challenges

As generative AI becomes more prevalent in financial reporting, regulators face new challenges:

- **Jurisdictional Approaches**: Different countries and regions are taking varied approaches to regulating AI in financial reporting:

    - The European Union is developing comprehensive AI regulations impacting financial reporting practices.

    - The United States SEC is considering modifying current laws to include financial reports produced by AI.

    - Some Asian countries, like Singapore, are adopting a more flexible, principles-based approach to AI regulation.

- **Need for New Regulations**: Existing financial reporting regulations may not adequately address the unique challenges posed by AI. New regulations may be needed to cover:

    - Standards for AI model transparency and explainability

- Requirements for human oversight of AI-generated reports

- Guidelines for auditing AI systems used in financial reporting

Real-World Applications of Generative AI

Generative AI is not a theory; numerous organizations leverage its capabilities to enhance their financial reporting processes. Here are three notable examples:

Small and Medium-Sized Enterprise: AI-Driven Financial Reporting

A growing e-commerce company with 50 employees implemented an AI-powered financial reporting system. Because the system automatically generated monthly financial statement reports, staff members spent 70% less time on them. It also provided predictive analytics, helping the company anticipate cash flow issues and adjust inventory levels accordingly. The small finance team was able to concentrate more on strategic decision-making, leading to a 25% increase in profitability the following year.

Non-Profit Organization: Enhancing Donor Reporting

A large international non-profit organization adopted an AI-driven reporting system to improve donor communications. The system generated customized reports for different donor segments, highlighting the impact of their contributions. By automating this process, the organization reduced reporting time by 60% and saw a 15% increase in donor retention rates. The AI system also helped identify potential major donors by analyzing giving patterns, leading to a 30% increase in large donations.

Government Agency: Improving Financial Transparency

A state-level government agency implemented an AI-based financial reporting system to enhance transparency and efficiency. The system automated the creation of comprehensive financial reports, making it easier for citizens to understand how public funds were used. It also generated real-time dashboards for internal use, allowing officials to make more informed budgetary decisions. As a result, the agency reduced its reporting costs by 40% and improved its transparency rating in citizen surveys by 25%.

Actionable Insights

1. **Automate Financial Statement Creation with Generative AI**: Firms should adopt generative AI tools to automate financial statement creation, including balance sheets, income statements, and cash flow reports. Tools like KPMG's Clara Platform can drastically reduce the time and manual effort needed to prepare financial reports, allowing financial teams to focus on more strategic activities.

2. **Leverage AI-Driven Narratives for Enhanced Stakeholder Communication**: Use AI tools such as Narrative Science's Quill to generate detailed financial narratives for stakeholders. Tailored reports that explain complex financial data in simple terms improve engagement and understanding, enabling stakeholders to make more informed decisions.

3. **Integrate Unstructured Data for Comprehensive Financial Insights**: Adopt AI models that analyze unstructured data, such as contracts, emails, and regulatory

filings. This ensures that your financial reports encompass broader insights, providing a more complete and strategic view of economic health.

4. **Implement Compliance Automation to Ensure Regulatory Adherence**: Utilize generative AI systems to automate compliance and regulatory reporting. These systems can automatically track changes in accounting standards and tax regulations and apply them to financial reports. This reduces the risk of non-compliance and ensures accuracy in reporting.

5. **Use Predictive Analytics for Strategic Forecasting**: Implement generative AI solutions like SAP's Predictive Analytics to forecast financial outcomes based on historical data and market trends. These predictions can help anticipate cash flow challenges, enabling firms to proactively adjust strategies and improve economic resilience.

6. **Enhance Stakeholder Communication with Tailored AI Reports**: Use generative AI tools to create tailored reports for different audiences. This approach ensures that the right level of detail reaches each stakeholder, improving engagement and decision-making. Customizing reports allows firms to present complex financial data in a clear, accessible manner that addresses the specific needs of each group.

7. **Address Ethical Considerations and Ensure Transparency**: Organizations should actively address ethical concerns when implementing generative AI in financial reporting. Establish clear guidelines for transparency and explainability and maintain human oversight of AI-generated reports. By doing so, firms can

uphold trust in financial reporting and ensure that the information provided is accurate, unbiased, and aligned with professional standards.

The Future of Generative AI in Financial Reporting

As generative AI continues to evolve, its role in financial reporting will expand. Soon, we can expect AI to take on even more complex tasks, such as real-time financial reporting, automated audits, and more advanced forecasting.

- **Real-Time Reporting**: AI's ability to process and analyze data in real-time means that firms will soon be able to generate up-to-date financial reports at any moment, offering continuous insight into a company's performance. This will enable faster decision-making and more proactive responses to market changes.

- **Automated Audits**: AI will have a more significant role in the audit process, generating reports and identifying potential discrepancies or risks to improve accuracy and speed. Automated audits will reduce the time and cost associated with traditional auditing while enhancing the quality and reliability of audit outcomes.

- **Advanced Predictive Analytics**: As AI models improve, they will better predict financial outcomes, offering firms a more comprehensive view of potential risks and opportunities. This enhanced forecasting capability will allow firms to make more informed strategic decisions, helping them navigate uncertainties and capitalize on emerging trends.

Generative AI's ability to create detailed reports, narratives, and forecasts will soon become an indispensable tool in the financial reporting toolkit, providing firms with greater accuracy, efficiency, and insight.

Conclusion/Takeaways

Generative AI sets a new standard in financial reporting by automating processes, improving accuracy, and enhancing how firms communicate financial insights. Transforming raw data into financial statements, AI-driven narratives, and predictive models enables firms to stay ahead of regulatory changes and respond to real-time market shifts. As we look to the future, firms that embrace generative AI will benefit from real-time reporting, advanced forecasting capabilities, and more efficient compliance measures. With AI handling routine tasks, accounting professionals can focus on strategic, value-added activities. Embracing these advancements will boost operational efficiency and give firms a solid competitive advantage in the dynamic accounting industry.

While generative AI has proven invaluable in financial reporting, its applications extend beyond this domain. In the next chapter, we'll explore how AI is used across the accounting profession, from automating tax preparation to enhancing fraud detection and client advisory services. As AI continues to shape the future of accounting, we'll examine its impact across various functions, helping firms optimize workflows, reduce costs, and deliver more value to their clients.

References

CPA Australia. (2019). The Impact of Artificial Intelligence on the Accounting Profession. Melbourne: CPA Australia Ltd. Retrieved from https://www.cpaaustralia.com.au/

Deloitte. (2024). *AI in Financial Reporting: Transforming the Finance Function.* Retrieved from https://www2.deloitte.com/us/en/pages/audit/articles

IEEE Global Initiative on Ethics of Autonomous and Intelligent Systems. (2019). Ethically Aligned Design: A Vision for Prioritizing Human Well-being with Autonomous and Intelligent Systems. IEEE. Retrieved from: IEEE SA - The IEEE Global Initiative 2.0 on Ethics of Autonomous and Intelligent Systems

KPMG. (2024). *KPMG Clara Platform.* Retrieved from https://home.kpmg.com/xx/en/home/services/audit/kpmg-clara.html

Marr, B.. (2018, June 25). The Future of Financial Reporting: How AI Is Changing the Game. Forbes. Retrieved from: https://www.forbes.com

Narrative Science. (2024). *Quill: Natural Language Generation Platform.* Retrieved from https://narrativescience.com/products/quill/

SAP. (2024). *SAP Predictive Analytics.* Retrieved from https://www.sap.com/products/technology-platform/predictive-analytics.html

Vasarhelyi, M. A., Kogan, A., & Tuttle, B. M.. (2015). *Big Data in Accounting: An Overview. Accounting Horizons*, 29(2), 381-396.

World Economic Forum. (2020). *AI in Financial Services.* Geneva: World Economic Forum.

CHAPTER 5: GENERATIVE AI ACROSS THE ACCOUNTING PROFESSION

Introduction

Generative AI (Gen AI) is reshaping the accounting profession, with its applications extending far beyond traditional automation. From tax preparation to fraud detection, auditing, client advisory services (CAS), and compliance, AI is driving transformative innovation. This chapter explores how Generative AI is automating complex tasks, delivering real-time insights, and enhancing the strategic value firms provide to clients.

Core Concepts

1. Generative AI in Tax Preparation: Automating Complex Processes

Generative AI is like the accounting industry's Swiss Army knife, simplifying even the most intricate aspects of tax preparation. It automates form recognition, deduction analysis, and tax strategy optimization processes, turning what once seemed overwhelming into a seamless experience. AI's ability to interpret changing tax laws and apply them automatically to client data ensures compliance and reduces the risk of errors.

However, the ethical implications of relying heavily on AI are significant. For example, if AI makes an error in tax calculations due to misinterpreted data, who is held responsible? Should it be the firm, the software developers, or a shared accountability model? These questions have sparked debates across the industry, underscoring the importance of establishing a clearer framework for AI accountability.

Despite its versatility, Generative AI cannot replace the human experience, especially when it comes to nuanced, complex scenarios requiring professional judgment. While AI handles repetitive tasks with remarkable efficiency, it lacks the creativity and ethical consideration needed for complex decision-making. For instance, it automates form recognition, deduction analysis, and tax strategy optimization, but will it ever replace the personal touch in tax preparation? Or will there always be aspects that demand human oversight?

Generative AI can be used in diverse types of tax preparation, including:

- **Income Tax (Individual and Business)**: AI automates data extraction, classifies deductions, and generates tax strategies based on historical data and changing regulations.

- **Sales and Use Tax**: AI monitors changes in tax rates and rules across different jurisdictions, ensuring accurate tax filings.

- **VAT/Global Taxes**: AI updates international tax regulations and refines filing approaches for multinational clients.

Firms can find more use cases by examining their existing tax workflows and identifying tasks that are repetitive, data-intensive, or require cross-referencing complex information. Generative AI can reduce manual efforts and improve accuracy in these areas, allowing tax professionals to focus on higher-value advisory services.

According to a recent survey, 73% of organizations are currently utilizing AI for automation in accounting processes, including tax preparation, and AI can reduce the time spent on data analysis in accounting by up to 50% (AI Journal).

REAL-WORLD EXAMPLE: SUREPREP'S AI-POWERED TAX SOLUTIONS

SurePrep uses Generative AI to streamline tax preparation. Its flagship product, 1040Scan, automatically recognizes and categorizes tax forms, reducing accountants' time on manual input. By learning from prior year returns, the AI also suggests deductions and credits, helping accountants deliver strategic value to their clients.

Case Study: A mid-sized accounting firm in New Jersey adopted SurePrep's solution and reduced tax preparation time by 40%, allowing staff to focus on high-value activities like advisory services. This improved client satisfaction and reduced employee burnout during peak tax season.

At Brightstone Accounting, Monday mornings used to be daunting, starting with a mountain of tax documents scattered across desks. Junior accountants spent hours sorting, organizing, and inputting data, often feeling like they were drowning before the week even began. Now, thanks to Generative AI, the morning begins with a simple upload. Watching the AI-powered scanner work is almost hypnotic—like seeing an entire day's worth of manual sorting unfold in seconds.

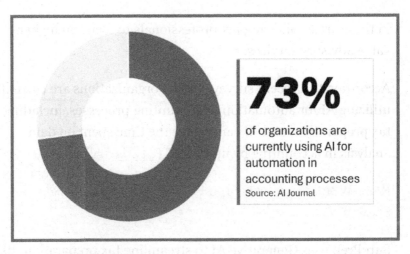

Figure 9 AI in Accounting Automation

Junior accountants now review the AI's output with their mentors, discussing tax strategies and learning the rationale behind various deductions. "It's like we finally have the time to focus on what really matters—helping clients strategize, rather than just crunching numbers," says Emily, a junior accountant at the firm. AI has transformed the workflow from mundane data handling to meaningful, client-focused discussions, providing junior staff the opportunity to grow into advisory roles.

2. Generative AI in Fraud Detection: Real-Time Anomaly Identification

Generative AI is increasingly vital in fraud detection. AI models continuously monitor financial transactions, looking for unusual spending patterns, transfers from unknown accounts, or signs of unauthorized access. Generative AI's ability to learn from historical data allows it to adapt and improve fraud detection capabilities over time, making it more effective than traditional rule-based systems.

However, AI's effectiveness comes with some ethical challenges. If AI wrongly flags a transaction as fraudulent, it could cause significant disruptions for a business. This raises additional questions about accountability: Who is responsible for errors—the software developer, the compliance officer, or both? AI's detection capabilities are only as good as the data it has been trained on, and without human oversight, it may miss subtle, context-specific cues that experienced fraud analysts would catch.

Use cases for Generative AI in fraud detection include monitoring accounts payable for duplicate or unusual payments, identifying unusual vendor activity, and analyzing employee expense reports for irregularities. Firms can identify other use cases by assessing areas where fraud risk is high, such as cash transactions, third-party payments, or cross-border transactions. AI's ability to learn and adapt can significantly reduce false positives, allowing auditors to focus on genuine threats and reduce the workload of compliance teams.

Additionally, AI enhances firms' compliance with anti-money laundering (AML) regulations by scanning financial records and identifying suspicious activities that might indicate money laundering schemes. AI-powered accounting systems can reduce human error rates by up to 90% (AI Journal).

REAL-WORLD EXAMPLE: KOUNT'S AI FRAUD DETECTION

Kount's AI fraud detection platform acts as a vigilant sentinel, constantly checking financial transactions for irregularities. In one instance, Kount flagged suspicious wire transfers at a logistics company, preventing a $200,000 fraud attempt. Further investigation revealed a phishing attack targeting the company. Without AI, this activity could have gone unnoticed, potentially causing severe damage to the business.

Fraud detection use cases for Generative AI include monitoring accounts payable for duplicate or unusual payments, analyzing employee expense reports for irregularities, and identifying unusual vendor activity. Firms can use AI to significantly reduce false positives, allowing auditors to focus on genuine threats.

3. AI-Enhanced Client Advisory Services (CAS): Driving Deeper Insights

Generative AI transforms CAS by enabling accountants to generate real-time financial forecasts and deliver more strategic advice. AI's ability to analyze large datasets allows firms to offer deeper insights into a client's business performance, such as identifying cost-saving opportunities, investment strategies, and long-term financial planning. AI-driven CAS also enables firms to tailor their services to individual client needs, offering advice on liquidity optimization, debt management, and operational expansion.

REAL-WORLD EXAMPLE: BOTKEEPER

Botkeeper combines Generative AI with bookkeeping services, automating routine tasks while offering strategic financial advice. A retail company using Botkeeper's AI-driven insights optimized its purchasing strategy, identifying vendor price fluctuations and saving 15% on operating costs. This demonstrates AI's potential to deliver actionable insights that extend far beyond traditional bookkeeping.

A survey found that 93% of accountants agree that artificial intelligence positively impacts their work by providing more actionable insights. (AI Journal).

4. Generative AI in Auditing: Enhancing Accuracy and Efficiency

Auditing is one of the most time-consuming aspects of accounting, but Generative AI is streamlining the process. AI can automate the examination of large volumes of financial records, quickly cross-checking transaction histories and flagging potential issues for further review. This not only enhances accuracy but also speeds up the auditing process, freeing auditors to focus on more complex areas that require human judgment.

Generative AI can also be used in continuous auditing, providing real-time assessments of financial data. This allows firms to offer continuous audit support rather than periodic audits, reducing the risk of fraud and ensuring ongoing compliance. An EY pilot program using Generative AI for sales-and-use tax audits reduced the audit cycle from four years to one month (EY).

5. Real-Time Client Insights and Forecasting with Generative AI

Generative AI's ability to analyze structured and unstructured data makes it invaluable for real-time insights and forecasting. AI models can track client performance metrics, analyze financial statements, and generate real-time reports, offering firms immediate insights into their clients' financial health.

Revenue forecasting, expense tracking, and cash flow management are among the use cases for real-time insights. AI-powered forecasting tools help firms better predict seasonal fluctuations, assess the impact of changing market conditions, and offer proactive advice to clients. Firms looking to implement Generative AI for real-time insights should evaluate areas where rapid decision-making is critical, such as working capital management or investment decisions.

AI can improve forecasting accuracy in financial predictions by up to 82%, and 56% of organizations report that AI-powered business intelligence tools have improved their decision-making processes (AI Journal).

6. Generative AI in Financial Compliance: Ensuring Regulatory Adherence

Compliance with financial regulations is one of the most critical functions within accounting firms, and the complexity of these regulations continues to grow. Generative AI can keep firms compliant by automatically updating financial reports in line with evolving regulatory requirements. It scans through economic data and ensures adherence to tax codes, international financial reporting standards (IFRS), and other industry regulations.

AI's ability to interpret complex regulatory texts and apply them to client data means that firms can remain compliant without manually adjusting their processes each time new regulations are introduced. For instance, AI can help manage compliance with local tax regulations, VAT filings, and cross-border tax issues. This reduces the risk of penalties and improves overall compliance accuracy.

AI continuously updates its database with the latest tax regulations, automatically applying these updates to the financial reporting process (EY).

Natural Language Generation (NLG): AI also enhances compliance and reporting with NLG technologies, which automatically generate standardized financial reports such as income statements, balance sheets, and cash flow statements. This improves report accuracy and speeds up delivery, ensuring that stakeholders always receive up-to-date and clear financial information.

7. Enhancing Stakeholder Communication with AI-Generated Reports

Generative AI doesn't just automate financial tasks—it also enhances communication with stakeholders by generating clear, understandable reports that can be customized for different audiences. Whether providing high-level executive summaries or detailed breakdowns for financial analysts, AI can generate real-time stakeholder-specific reports communicating vital metrics, trends, and risks.

Use Case: AI-generated reports for investors, management teams, or regulatory bodies transform raw financial data into compelling narratives. AI simplifies complex data for executives while delivering detailed analysis for financial analysts, ensuring all stakeholders receive the insights they need.

Natural Language Generation (NLG): In addition to compiling financial data, NLG enhances these reports by automatically creating narratives tailored to each audience, improving accessibility and comprehension. NLG technologies now automatically produce standardized financial reports, including income statements, balance sheets, and cash flow statements (Tipalti).

8. Predictive Analytics and Forecasting with Generative AI

One of Generative AI's most powerful applications is in predictive analytics. AI models analyze historical data to predict future outcomes, allowing firms to forecast revenue, expenses, and market trends. These forecasts help firms provide more strategic guidance to clients, enabling better decision-making on investments, budgeting, and growth strategies.

Generative AI also aids in financial scenario planning, helping firms simulate various market conditions and predict their impact on a client's business. These insights are invaluable for long-term planning and risk management. Firms can use predictive analytics to anticipate cash flow shortages, identify potential investment opportunities, and proactively adjust business strategies in response to economic changes.

Actionable Insights

1. Adopt AI for Complex Tax Strategies: Accounting firms that handle complex tax filings should implement AI-powered tools like SurePrep's 1040Scan, Wolters Kluwer's CCH ProSystem *fx* Scan, and AutoFlow. These solutions can automate data extraction from tax forms, recognize and categorize tax documents, and optimize deductions. This helps firms reduce manual work, improve compliance, and deliver more personalized tax-saving strategies to their clients.

2. Utilize AI-Enhanced Fraud Detection: Firms should leverage tools like Kount to monitor financial transactions in real-time, preventing fraud before it becomes a costly problem. AI's ability to continuously learn from transaction data helps reduce false positives, allowing auditors to focus on genuine threats. AI systems can also scan for suspicious vendor activities, reducing the risks of fraudulent practices.

3. Expand CAS with Generative AI: Firms looking to expand into Client Advisory Services should adopt AI-driven platforms like Botkeeper to provide their clients with more proactive, data-driven advice. AI can generate real-time financial insights, such as cash flow projections, investment recommendations, and cost-saving opportunities. These insights go beyond traditional accounting services, adding significant value for clients.

4. Implement AI for Real-Time Insights and Auditing: Incorporate AI-driven auditing tools to increase accuracy and enhance real-time client reporting and forecasting. AI tools can perform continuous auditing, allowing firms to provide ongoing compliance checks rather than periodic reviews. This proactive approach reduces the risk of fraud and helps firms find financial misstatements early.

5. Focus on Financial Compliance with Generative AI: Leverage AI's ability to keep up with regulatory changes, ensuring your firm stays compliant without the risk of human error. AI systems like those used in EY's pilot program for sales-and-use tax audits automatically update compliance requirements and apply them to financial reports, reducing the need for manual adjustments and ensuring accuracy.

6. The Future of Generative AI in Accounting

As Generative AI continues to evolve, its applications in accounting will expand further. Future advancements may include fully automated audits, more precise real-time reporting, and increasingly sophisticated predictive analytics that will allow firms to make even more informed decisions on behalf of their clients.

By 2025, 70% of organizations are expected to operationalize AI, up from just 10% in 2020. Moreover, 85% of business leaders believe AI will significantly change how they operate in the next five years, and 86% of accounting professionals expect AI to have a major impact on the profession within the next decade (AI Journal).

Conclusion/Takeaways

Generative AI is revolutionizing the accounting profession by automating complex tasks, improving fraud detection, enhancing advisory services, and delivering real-time insights. Firms that embrace these technologies are better positioned to provide high-value services to their clients, improve operational efficiency, and stay competitive in an increasingly complex regulatory landscape.

As we've explored in this chapter, Generative AI is transforming a wide range of accounting functions, but its impact doesn't stop there. The next chapter will delve deeper into how Predictive Analytics and Business Intelligence enable firms to forecast financial outcomes, make data-driven decisions, and drive future growth. These tools are shaping the future of accounting, allowing firms to plan strategically and stay ahead of the competition.

References

Botkeeper. (n.d.). *AI-powered bookkeeping and financial insights.* Retrieved from https://www.botkeeper.com

EY. (n.d.). *How generative AI might help tax functions tackle challenges.* Retrieved from https://www.ey.com/en_us/insights/tax/how-generative-ai-might-help-tax-functions-tackle-challenges

Kount. (n.d.). *AI-driven fraud detection platform.* Retrieved from https://www.kount.com

SAP. (n.d.). *Predictive analytics.* Retrieved from https://www.sap.com

SurePrep. (n.d.). *1040Scan: AI-powered tax preparation solution.* Retrieved from https://www.sureprep.com

Tipalti. (n.d.). *Accounting hub and AI in accounting.* Retrieved from https://tipalti.com/accounting-hub/ai-accounting/

AI Journal. (n.d.). *Tips on how AI is automating tax preparation.* Retrieved from https://aijourn.com/tips-on-how-ai-is-automating-tax-preparation/

CHAPTER 6: PREDICTIVE ANALYTICS, BUSINESS INTELLIGENCE, AND INTELLIGENT AUTOMATION IN ACCOUNTING

Introduction

In today's rapidly changing financial landscape, accounting firms face increasing demands for faster, more accurate decision-making. Predictive Analytics (PA), Business Intelligence (BI), and Intelligent Automation (IA) are becoming indispensable tools for achieving these goals. These technologies not only help firms forecast future trends and optimize resource allocation but also automate repetitive tasks, enabling accountants to focus on delivering more strategic value.

Predictive Analytics (PA) uses historical data and statistical algorithms to make predictions about future outcomes, allowing firms to anticipate challenges and opportunities before they arise.

Business Intelligence (BI) involves the use of tools and technologies to gather, analyze, and visualize financial data. BI turns raw data into actionable insights, empowering firms to make better, data-driven decisions.

Intelligent Automation (IA) combines automation technologies like Robotic Process Automation (RPA) and artificial intelligence to streamline processes, such as data entry or report generation, reducing the time spent on manual tasks.

Throughout this chapter, we'll explore how PA, BI, and IA reduce errors, improve accuracy, and drive operational efficiency. By following GreenTree Financial's journey, we'll see how these technologies were leveraged to enhance decision-making, improve client offerings, and avoid common implementation challenges.

Core Concepts

1. Predictive Analytics: Leveraging Historical Data for Forecasting

Predictive Analytics (PA) uses historical data to forecast future trends and identify potential opportunities or risks. In accounting, this might mean predicting cash flow, revenue, expenses, or even identifying potential financial risks before they materialize. With this forward-looking insight, firms can advise clients on how to stay ahead of challenges.

GreenTree Financial Case Study: GreenTree Financial implemented a predictive analytics tool that allowed them to anticipate cash flow shortfalls for clients. By analyzing historical cash flow data, the firm was able to forecast potential shortages. For example, they flagged a potential shortfall for a key client 60 days in advance, giving the client ample time to secure funding. This early warning system improved client retention and reduced disruptions by 25%.

2. Business Intelligence: Turning Data into Actionable Insights

Business Intelligence (BI) leverages data tools to help firms gather, analyze, and visualize complex financial data. BI provides real-time insights, helping firms make informed, data-driven decisions that optimize operations and strengthen client relationships.

Real-World Example: Microsoft Power BI for Financial Insights A mid-sized accounting firm integrated Microsoft Power BI into their client advisory services, creating interactive dashboards that tracked performance indicators in real-time. The firm was able to provide clients with deeper insights into their revenue trends and cash flow forecasts, resulting in proactive decision-making that saved clients up to 15% on operational costs.

Real-World Example: Tableau in Accounting A large accounting firm used Tableau to create dynamic, customizable financial dashboards for their clients. The firm visualized key metrics like profitability and cash flow, making it easier for clients to make informed decisions quickly. Internally, they used Tableau to track their own performance, which helped increase resource efficiency by 20%.

3. Expense Management and Cost Optimization

Expense management is another area where predictive analytics delivers value. By examining historical spending data, firms can find inefficiencies and recommend cost-saving measures. Predictive tools can detect patterns of overspending and suggest adjustments, such as renegotiating vendor contracts or improving procurement strategies.

Real-World Example: Expensify and Concur Expense

Expensify and Concur are AI-powered tools that automate expense management. For instance, a small accounting firm reduced manual expense entry time by 40% with Expensify, while Concur helped improve policy compliance by 35%, ensuring that expenses were tracked and managed more effectively across departments.

4. Reducing Errors and Enhancing Accuracy

One of the key benefits of AI and Intelligent Automation is the reduction of human errors, especially in tasks like data entry and financial reporting. AI models excel in handling large volumes of data with precision, cross-referencing entries and finding discrepancies in real-time.

For example, GreenTree Financial's intelligent automation system reconciled data from multiple sources with 99% accuracy, helping the firm streamline processes and reduce compliance errors. This led to a more efficient tax filing process and higher client satisfaction.

5. Cash Flow Forecasting for Financial Stability

Cash flow forecasting is critical for ensuring a firm's financial stability, and predictive analytics enables firms to predict challenges before they arise. By analyzing payment trends and market fluctuations, firms can gain visibility into future cash flow issues and make adjustments to avoid shortfalls.

GreenTree Financial Case Study (Continued): In one instance, GreenTree used predictive analytics to advise a client who was planning a major equipment purchase. By forecasting cash flow needs, they recommended adjusting the timing of the

purchase, which helped the client maintain liquidity without
sacrificing growth opportunities. This strategic insight helped
the client avoid a 10% liquidity shortfall.

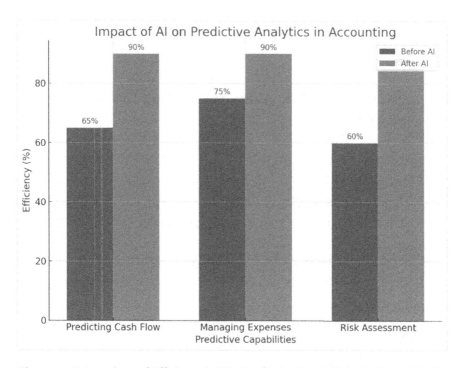

Figure 10 Comparison of Efficiency in Key Predictive Capabilities Before and After
AI Implementation

6. Predictive Tax Compliance: Proactive Tax Planning

AI-powered predictive models are transforming tax compliance
by allowing firms to forecast liabilities and identify tax-saving
opportunities in advance. These models analyze historical tax
data and anticipate changes in tax laws, ensuring that firms stay
compliant and avoid penalties.

Example: GreenTree Financial's Predictive Tax Compliance

GreenTree Financial used AI models to optimize their clients' tax positions, reducing the average tax liability by 15%. By analyzing historical tax data and forecasting upcoming liabilities, they were able to recommend strategies for maximizing deductions and taking advantage of overlooked tax credits, saving clients thousands of dollars.

7. Intelligent Automation: Automating Tax Compliance with RPA and AI

Intelligent Automation, which combines Robotic Process Automation (RPA) with AI, is revolutionizing tax compliance. RPA automates repetitive tasks like data entry, while AI ensures that tax filings adhere to current regulations.

GreenTree Financial Case Study (Continued): Before implementing RPA, GreenTree's tax compliance process was labor-intensive, with staff manually gathering sales data and preparing compliance reports. After deploying RPA, the process became seamless—sales data was collected, tax calculations were automated, and reports were generated without manual intervention. This reduced tax compliance time by 50%, allowing staff to shift their focus to more complex advisory services.

Benefits of Predictive Analytics, BI, and Intelligent Automation in Accounting

1. **Proactive Client Management**: Predictive models help firms identify financial risks early, allowing clients to take preventative measures.

2. **Enhanced Financial Forecasting**: Firms can create accurate forecasts that help clients plan ahead, minimizing financial surprises.

3. **Better Resource Allocation**: BI tools provide insights into resource use, allowing firms to optimize operational efficiency.

4. **Improved Client Relationships**: BI visuals simplify complex financial data, making it easier for clients to understand and act on.

5. **Reduced Errors and Enhanced Accuracy**: Intelligent Automation minimizes human error, increasing the accuracy of reporting and compliance.

Selecting the Right AI Tools for Your Firm

Choosing the right AI tools is crucial to your firm's success. Consider the following factors when evaluating AI solutions:

- **Scalability**: The tool should grow with your firm, handling increasing data volumes without compromising performance.

- **Integration Capabilities**: Seamless integration with your current systems is essential for minimizing workflow disruptions.

- **Ease of Use**: A user-friendly interface ensures that both tech-savvy and non-tech-savvy team members can use the tool effectively.

- **Customization**: Look for solutions that can be tailored to meet the unique needs of your firm, maximizing their value and adaptability.

Conclusion/Takeaways

The integration of Predictive Analytics, Business Intelligence, and Intelligent Automation is reshaping the accounting profession. These tools enable firms to forecast financial trends, provide real-time insights, optimize resource use, and automate tedious tasks, freeing accountants to focus on higher-value advisory services. Firms that embrace these technologies will not only improve their efficiency but also offer more strategic value to their clients, ensuring they stay competitive in an evolving marketplace.

Through GreenTree Financial's journey, we've seen how these tools help firms proactively manage client challenges, streamline operations, and deliver strategic insights. Predictive analytics and intelligent automation have revolutionized how accounting firms manage data, anticipate trends, and streamline operations. These advanced capabilities empower accountants to proactively drive value, harnessing insights that were once hidden in complex data sets. However, with greater access to data and automated processes also comes the need for enhanced vigilance. One area where AI has proven invaluable is in fraud detection—a critical function as firms strive to protect both their integrity and their clients' assets. In the next chapter, we'll delve into how AI's advanced algorithms and machine learning models are being leveraged to identify and mitigate fraud risks, enabling

accountants to detect anomalies and irregularities in real-time
with unprecedented precision.

References

EY. "How Generative AI Might Help Tax Functions Tackle
      Challenges." Retrieved from
      https://www.ey.com/en_us/insights/tax/how-
      generative-ai-might-help-tax-functions-tackle-challenges

AI Journal. "Tips on How AI is Automating Tax Preparation."
      Retrieved from https://aijourn.com/tips-on-how-ai-is-
      automating-tax-preparation/.

Tipalti. "AI in Accounting Hub." Retrieved from
      https://tipalti.com/accounting-hub/ai-accounting/

Microsoft Power BI. Retrieved from
      https://www.powerbi.microsoft.com

CHAPTER 7: AI IN FRAUD DETECTION AND AUDITING

Introduction:

Running an accounting firm today is a lot like driving on a long, complex road trip. In the past, you'd rely on paper maps and manual directions, which often left room for error. You wouldn't realize you'd missed a turn or hit a roadblock until you were already far off course. By the time you figured out what went wrong, it took a lot of extra time, effort, and resources to get back on track.

Now, imagine having a GPS that not only provides directions but also actively scans the road ahead. It alerts you to traffic jams, reroutes you around roadblocks, and warns you about hazards before you even see them. With this system, you don't have to wait until you're lost or stuck to realize something's gone wrong—you get real-time updates, allowing you to make quick adjustments and avoid unnecessary detours.

This is exactly what AI is doing for fraud detection and auditing. Just like a GPS helps you navigate the road, AI continuously monitors financial transactions, detecting irregularities and fraud in real time. Instead of waiting for year-end audits or manual reviews to uncover issues—often when it's too late—AI helps firms stay ahead, identifying risks before they turn into major problems.

In this chapter, we'll explore how AI is transforming fraud detection and auditing, giving firms the ability to detect and respond to potential threats before they cause serious damage—much like a GPS guiding you on a smooth, problem-free journey.

Core Concepts

1. AI-Powered Fraud Detection: Spotting Red Flags in Real Time

AI is transforming how we detect financial fraud. The market for AI-powered fraud detection is set to grow from $12.1 billion in 2023 to over $108 billion by 2033 (HighRadius, 2024). Organizations using AI report a 98% success rate in detecting fraud, cutting fraud exposure time by half, and reducing financial losses by 40%.

What makes AI so effective? It learns from past data and evolves—getting smarter with each new case, making it harder for fraudsters to outwit the system.

2. AI Application Across Firm Sizes

AI's transformative impact on fraud detection and auditing extends across firms of all sizes, from small businesses to global enterprises. While each firm may have different needs, AI technology offers scalable solutions that can be tailored to specific requirements.

Small Accounting Firms: For small firms, AI offers cost-effective, cloud-based tools that help monitor transactions, detect anomalies, and ensure compliance without the need for large IT investments. Small firms can use AI to automate manual processes, allowing staff to focus on higher-value tasks like client engagement. A small firm using AI might see a reduction in fraud losses by up to 60% (Juniper Research, 2023), a significant benefit for firms operating on tight margins.

Mid-Sized Accounting Firms: Mid-sized firms benefit from custom AI models tailored to their industry and client base. With AI, these firms can implement more efficient fraud detection systems and predictive analytics to identify emerging risks. Mid-sized firms, which typically lose $200,000 per fraud incident (PwC, 2022), have experienced a 95% improvement in fraud detection rates thanks to AI (Deloitte, 2023). This level of accuracy helps firms save time and money while improving client trust.

Large or Global Accounting Firms: For large, multi-office firms, AI enables the use of big data analytics and advanced machine learning to detect complex fraud schemes. These firms can take advantage of AI's natural language processing (NLP) capabilities to analyze unstructured data, such as emails or contracts, for signs of fraud. AI systems can reduce false positives by up to 80%, allowing auditors to focus on real risks, while saving millions annually in fraud-related costs (McKinsey & Company, 2023).

3. Automating Audit Tasks with AI: Making Audits Smarter and Faster

Audits have always been labor-intensive, but AI is changing that. Nearly 50% of financial institutions have already integrated AI, and 93% plan to expand usage over the next few years (SafeBooks AI, n.d.). By automating routine tasks like data extraction and validation, AI allows auditors to focus on higher-value work that requires human insight.

For small firms, AI can be a game changer. Cloud-based AI tools can be implemented with minimal cost and effort, offering immediate fraud detection without needing an IT department. These solutions start providing benefits—like reducing fraud risks and freeing up staff time—almost right away.

4. Continuous Auditing and Real-Time Insights: Catching Problems Before They Escalate

Gone are the days of waiting for year-end audits to find out if something went wrong. AI is making continuous auditing the new normal. Instead of reviewing data once or twice a year, AI tools monitor transactions 24/7, flagging potential risks as they arise.

For mid-sized firms, AI can be customized for industry-specific needs. Whether it's fraud detection in healthcare or manufacturing, AI integrates into existing workflows, reducing time spent on repetitive tasks while giving auditors the freedom to focus on client relationships.

5. Risk-Based Auditing with AI: Prioritizing Where It Matters

Fraud costs the global economy a staggering $10 trillion annually, and that doesn't account for the $600 billion lost to cybercrime (Crowe, 2023). AI-powered auditing tools help firms focus on the areas where they're most vulnerable, prioritizing resources in the places that matter most.

For global firms, AI's advanced capabilities—like natural language processing (NLP) and machine learning (ML)—help manage vast datasets across offices and continents. AI ensures compliance with diverse regulatory standards and offers real-time insights for large, cross-border audits.

REAL-WORLD EXAMPLE 1: KPMG CLARA

KPMG's Clara platform is a clear example of AI's power in auditing. Using machine learning, Clara analyzes financial transactions in real time, flagging patterns that don't add up—whether it's an unusually high payment or discrepancies in vendor invoicing.

Over time, Clara has evolved to become even more effective:

- **2017**: Launched as a smart audit platform.

- **2020**: Added predictive analytics for better fraud detection.

- **2022**: Integrated cloud technology for enhanced data analysis.

- **June 2024**: Partnered with Databricks for deeper analysis of billions of transactions.

- **July 2024**: Added generative AI capabilities, making fraud detection smarter and faster.

This progression illustrates Clara's increasing ability to find fraud and help auditors with more complex tasks as AI technologies have evolved.

Practical Application:

One of KPMG's retail clients was facing a growing risk of internal fraud, with thousands of transactions processed across multiple locations daily. After deploying Clara's real-time fraud detection, the company saw its financial losses from fraud drop by 30% within a year. Clara's ability to flag unauthorized payments allowed the audit team to investigate issues before they spiraled into major problems.

This improvement not only reduced financial losses but also improved internal controls, fostering a culture of accountability within the organization.

6. Automating Audit Tasks with AI: Enhancing Accuracy and Speed

The traditional auditing process, based on manual sampling, often involves reviewing a small subset of transactions—a process that's effective but limited in scope. With AI, the entire auditing landscape changes. AI tools allow firms to automate many of the repetitive, time-consuming tasks associated with audits, such as data extraction, validation, and report generation. This shift enhances both accuracy and speed.

For instance, AI systems can analyze complete datasets, ensuring that no discrepancies go unnoticed. By automating routine tasks, auditors can dedicate more time to higher-value activities like strategic planning and risk management. AI not only reduces the risk of human error but also accelerates the audit process, enabling firms to deliver insights more quickly.

REAL-WORLD EXAMPLE 2: PWC'S HALO AI PLATFORM

PwC's Halo AI platform is a prime example of how automation is reshaping the audit landscape. By automating data extraction and validation, Halo reduces the manual workload involved in auditing financial statements. The platform leverages AI to analyze entire datasets, detecting inconsistencies or irregularities that could indicate fraud or mismanagement.

Practical Application:

A major financial services firm used PwC's Halo platform during its annual audit, which involved reviewing millions of transactions across multiple business units. Halo's AI-driven data validation process reduced the time required for this audit by 45%, saving the firm hundreds of hours in manual labor. Additionally, Halo detected several irregular transactions that had gone unnoticed in previous manual audits, helping the firm recover over $500,000 in lost revenue due to internal errors. The firm's leadership praised the platform for its ability to improve both audit accuracy and efficiency, reducing the risk of financial misstatements.

7. Continuous Auditing and Real-Time Insights: Shifting to Proactive Audits

Traditional audits are periodic, usually conducted annually or semi-annually, which leaves gaps in fraud detection and compliance monitoring. AI is changing this approach by enabling continuous auditing. Instead of reviewing financial data once or twice a year, AI tools monitor transactions and activities in real-time, offering proactive insights into potential risks.

Continuous auditing ensures that financial issues can be addressed as they arise rather than after the fact. This shift significantly improves transparency and reduces the risk of financial misstatements. Moreover, real-time insights help firms stay ahead of emerging risks, enabling faster decision-making and improving overall financial health.

REAL-WORLD EXAMPLE 3: DELOITTE'S CORTEX AI FOR
CONTINUOUS AUDITING

Deloitte's Cortex AI platform is a leader in continuous auditing, providing firms with real-time insights into their financial activities. By continuously monitoring transactions and comparing them against historical data, Cortex identifies potential risks and irregularities that would otherwise be missed in periodic audits.

Practical Application:

A multinational corporation implemented Cortex to continuously audit its global supply chain transactions. The AI platform identified several inconsistencies in vendor payments and flagged anomalies in currency conversion rates across its different regions. By catching these issues early, the company prevented what could have been a multi-million-dollar loss due to mismanaged contracts and overpayments. Deloitte's platform not only saved the firm from financial loss but also helped refine its payment processes, improving overall operational efficiency.

8. Risk-Based Auditing with AI: Prioritizing High-Risk Areas

Risk-based auditing focuses on the areas of a business that are most susceptible to fraud, financial misstatements, or compliance violations. AI enhances this process by analyzing vast amounts of data to find patterns that suggest higher risk. By comparing historical data, market trends, and industry-specific risks, AI can predict where fraud is most likely to occur.

For firms, this means audits can be more targeted and efficient, with resources distributed to the areas that need the most attention. AI's ability to highlight high-risk transactions or activities helps auditors prioritize their efforts, ensuring that the most vulnerable aspects of a firm's financial operations are thoroughly examined.

REAL-WORLD EXAMPLE 4: EY'S HELIX AI PLATFORM

EY's Helix AI platform leverages predictive analytics to enhance risk-based auditing. By analyzing client financial data, market trends, and industry-specific risks, Helix helps auditors prioritize their efforts on the areas most vulnerable to fraud or mismanagement.

Practical Application:

A large pharmaceutical company used Helix to streamline its audit process by focusing on high-risk areas, such as R&D spending and international sales. The AI platform predicted that certain regions were more prone to financial irregularities due to fluctuating currency rates and inconsistent invoicing practices. Armed with this insight, the auditors were able to identify and resolve discrepancies in the company's revenue recognition practices, saving the firm millions of dollars in potential fines and penalties. The firm's CFO praised Helix for its ability to "predict the unpredictable," enabling the audit team to mitigate financial risks before they escalated.

9. Challenges in Adopting AI for Fraud Detection and Auditing

While AI offers great advantages in fraud detection and auditing, its adoption also presents challenges for firms of all sizes:

1. **Data Privacy and Security**: AI systems require access to vast amounts of sensitive financial data, raising concerns

about data security and compliance with regulations such as the General Data Protection Regulation (GDPR). Firms must invest in secure AI systems that ensure client data is protected.

2. **Training AI Models**: AI systems are only as effective as the data they are trained on. To develop accurate fraud detection models, firms must provide high-quality, diverse datasets. This can be a challenge, particularly for firms in niche industries with limited data availability.

3. **Human Oversight**: AI can flag suspicious activities, but human auditors are still needed to interpret the results and decide whether a flagged transaction truly indicates fraud. AI should complement human expertise, not replace it, making it important for firms to retain a balance between automated processes and human judgment.

The Future of AI in Fraud Detection and Auditing

As AI continues to evolve, its role in fraud detection and auditing will expand, offering even more advanced capabilities. Here are some key future trends:

AI-Driven Forensic Audits: In the future, AI will play a larger role in forensic audits by reconstructing entire financial histories, identifying inconsistencies, and providing detailed analyses of potential fraud or mismanagement. These audits will be more precise and faster than manual forensic audits, allowing firms to resolve issues more efficiently.

Real-Time Fraud Prevention Systems: AI systems will soon be able to prevent fraud in real-time by blocking suspicious transactions as they occur. These systems will integrate with broader financial security platforms, using predictive algorithms to detect and halt fraudulent activities before they can cause harm.

AI and Blockchain Integration: Combining AI with blockchain technology can improve fraud detection by creating clear, unchangeable records of financial transactions. AI can monitor blockchain transactions for irregularities, adding another layer of security. While blockchain brings its own challenges, such as data storage costs and interoperability between platforms, the potential for a more transparent and secure financial system is immense.

Actionable Insights

1. Real-Time Fraud Detection: Use Platforms Like KPMG Clara to Continuously Monitor Transactions

- **For Small Firms:** Start with cloud-based AI tools that offer fraud detection features. Leverage MSPs if internal IT support is limited.

- **For Mid-Sized Firms:** Integrate AI tools into existing systems and customize fraud alerts for high-risk transactions.

- **For Large Firms:** Scale AI to handle global transactions and use predictive analytics to forecast potential fraud.

2. Automate Audit Tasks: Use Tools Like PwC's Halo to Free Up Time for Auditors

- **For Small Firms:** Use affordable cloud-based automation tools and train staff to handle automated tasks.

- **For Mid-Sized Firms:** Deploy AI across multiple clients and create an AI audit playbook to standardize processes.

- **For Large Firms:** Automate entire sections of the audit and build AI-driven dashboards for real-time audit oversight.

3. Continuous Auditing: With Tools Like Deloitte's Cortex, Firms Can Monitor Transactions in Real Time

- **For Small Firms:** Set up continuous monitoring for high-risk transactions and gradually expand to other areas.

- **For Mid-Sized Firms:** Implement real-time dashboards and establish a continuous improvement process.

- **For Large Firms:** Use AI to handle big data across regions and manage compliance in real time.

4. Risk-Based Auditing: Platforms Like EY's Helix Allow Firms to Focus Audits on High-Risk Areas

- **For Small Firms:** Prioritize audits based on key risk areas and develop a risk-based audit plan for clients.

- **For Mid-Sized Firms:** Leverage AI's predictive analytics to adjust audit plans dynamically.

- **For Large Firms:** Build a global risk model integrated with AI, focusing audits on multi-region high-risk areas.

Conclusion/Takeaways

Just as a GPS guides you through difficult roads by providing real-time updates and rerouting you around obstacles, AI helps firms navigate the complex world of fraud detection and auditing. The days of relying solely on manual audits and post-event checks are behind us. With AI, firms can detect irregularities and fraudulent activity as they happen, allowing for immediate action to keep things on track.

In today's fast-paced financial environment, where small missteps can quickly escalate into significant problems, firms that utilize AI's real-time monitoring and predictive capabilities will stay ahead of the curve. By treating AI like your fraud detection GPS, you can avoid costly mistakes and ensure that your financial path remains clear and secure. As we've explored in this chapter, AI's ability to detect fraud and enhance auditing processes offers unprecedented accuracy and efficiency for accounting firms. But as firms continue to expand into global markets, they face a new challenge: navigating an increasingly complex web of international compliance regulations. Staying up to date with constantly evolving laws, tax codes, and industry-specific standards across multiple jurisdictions is no small task. In the next chapter, we'll dive into how AI is helping firms tackle these global compliance challenges—automating regulatory reporting, ensuring adherence to local laws, and reducing the risk of costly compliance failures. With AI, firms can manage global compliance with the same precision and real-time monitoring they've come to expect from their fraud detection systems.

References

Crowe. (2023, March 14). The role of artificial intelligence (AI) and data analytics in auditing. Crowe. https://www.crowe.com/mv/insights/the-role-of-artificial-intelligence-and-data-analytics-in-auditing

HighRadius. (2024, January 29). How AI is helping in automating the audit process. HighRadius. https://www.highradius.com/resources/Blog/leveraging-ai-in-accounting-audit/

Juniper Research. (2023). AI for fraud detection: A comprehensive market analysis. Juniper Research. https://www.juniperresearch.com/researchstore

KPMG. (2024, July 29). KPMG announces AI integration into global smart audit platform, KPMG Clara. KPMG. https://home.kpmg/xx/en/home/media/press-releases/2024/07/kpmg-announces-ai-integration-into-global-smart-audit-platform-kpmg-clara.html

McKinsey & Company. (2023). The state of AI in risk management and fraud detection. McKinsey & Company. https://www.mckinsey.com/business-functions/risk/our-insights/the-state-of-ai-in-risk-management

SafeBooks AI. (n.d.). How AI audit tools are changing the financial landscape. SafeBooks AI. https://safebooks.ai/resources/financial-audit/how-ai-audit-tools-are-changing-the-financial-landscape/

Trellis AI. (2024, September 3). AI-powered audits: Transforming efficiency and accuracy in financial review. Trellis AI. https://runtrellis.com/blog/ai-powered-audits-for-accounting-firms

CHAPTER 8: AI IN GLOBAL COMPLIANCE

Introduction

As globalization continues, accounting firms are increasingly challenged to ensure compliance across different jurisdictions. Global compliance involves navigating a complex web of tax regulations, data privacy laws, and financial reporting standards, all of which vary from country to country. Firms must stay abreast of this ever-evolving regulatory landscape while mitigating the risks of non-compliance, penalties, and reputational damage. Thankfully, AI offers a way to tackle these challenges by automating compliance processes, monitoring regulatory updates in real time, and ensuring adherence to regional data privacy laws.

This chapter examines how AI is transforming global compliance, the challenges firms face, and practical steps for implementing AI-driven compliance solutions that work for firms of all sizes.

Core Concepts

To understand how AI can enhance global compliance, it's important to be familiar with some key concepts and technologies that are transforming the way firms operate in this area. Below are the core AI technologies that are driving efficiency and accuracy in global compliance:

1. **Machine Learning (ML)**: Machine learning is used to identify patterns in compliance-related data, predict future compliance issues, and recommend actions. ML models continuously improve by learning from new data, making them effective in adapting to evolving regulations.

2. **Natural Language Processing (NLP)**: NLP enables AI systems to understand and process human language, which is especially useful for scanning regulatory documents, extracting relevant updates, and making compliance suggestions.

3. **Robotic Process Automation (RPA)**: RPA automates repetitive, rules-based tasks such as data entry and report generation. This is particularly valuable for reducing manual errors in tax filings and compliance reporting.

4. **Predictive Analytics**: Predictive analytics uses historical data and statistical algorithms to forecast future events. In compliance, predictive tools can alert firms to potential risks or changes in regulation, enabling proactive measures.

5. **Data Classification and Privacy Management Tools**: These AI tools classify data based on privacy sensitivity, ensuring compliance with data protection laws like GDPR and CCPA. Automating data classification helps firms avoid breaches and adhere to privacy regulations.

To illustrate the distinct roles that these technologies play in enhancing global compliance, the following comparison table breaks down each core AI technology by its specific function, practical use in compliance, and associated benefits. This table provides a clearer understanding of how each tool can be applied effectively to meet the demands of global compliance.

Technology	Function	Example in Compliance	Benefits
Machine Learning (ML)	Identifies patterns in compliance data, predicts issues, and recommends actions.	Analyzing historical tax data to identify irregularities.	Reduces human error and speeds up the identification of potential risks.
Natural Language Processing (NLP)	Processes regulatory documents, extracts updates, and provides suggestions.	Extracting relevant updates from government regulatory announcements.	Helps firms stay updated on regulatory changes efficiently.
Robotic Process Automation (RPA)	Automates repetitive tasks like data entry and report generation.	Automating the generation of compliance reports for tax filings.	Minimizes manual labor, ensuring consistent compliance processes.
Predictive Analytics	Uses historical data to forecast compliance risks and regulatory changes.	Forecasting potential compliance issues based on changing regulations.	Enables proactive adjustments to stay ahead of regulatory changes.
Data Classificatio n & Privacy Management	Classifies data to ensure adherence to GDPR, CCPA, and other privacy laws.	Classifying client data based on privacy sensitivity to ensure proper handling.	Ensures data privacy compliance, reducing risk of legal issues.

Table 1 Comparison of core AI technologies used in global compliance, including their functions, practical examples, and benefits for accounting firms.

Challenges of Global Compliance

Global compliance is a complex and dynamic task for firms of all sizes. Below are some of the most pressing challenges that firms encounter:

Challenges of Global Compliance

Regulatory Complexity
- 34% of firms outsource all or part of their compliance functionality due to increasing complexity.

Cross-Border Issues
- Each jurisdiction has unique rules, complicating global operations.

Data Privacy and Cybersecurity
- Reliance on digital technologies continues to increase cybersecurity risks.

Resource Limitations
- 47% of firms expect the cost of senior compliance staff to rise in the next 12 months.

Technology and AI Integration
- 48% of financial institutions struggle with outdated AML compliance technology.

Environmental, Social, and Governance (ESG) Compliance
- ESG assets are projected to exceed $53 trillion by 2025, making up more than one-third of assets under management.

Figure 10 Key challenges firms face in managing global compliance, including regulatory complexity, cross-border issues, data privacy, and resource limitations.

1. Complex and Evolving Regulatory Landscape

The regulatory environment changes constantly as governments introduce new tax policies, data privacy laws, and financial reporting standards. Each jurisdiction has its own rules, which can shift often—especially in emerging markets or regions undergoing legal reform. Firms need not only to understand the current regulations but also to stay ahead of upcoming changes to remain compliant.

For instance, value-added tax (VAT) regulations differ significantly across the European Union, with frequent updates to the rules. This requires constant vigilance, which can be overwhelming for firms without sophisticated compliance tools.

Personal Perspective from an Accountant

"Every time new tax regulations were introduced, it felt like we were playing catch-up," says Amanda Foster, a senior tax accountant at a mid-sized firm. "There was a period when our team spent days deciphering changes just to ensure we didn't miss anything. The adoption of AI tools has helped us drastically reduce that stress and make sure we are always on top of these updates."

2. Managing Cross-Border Transactions

Cross-border transactions bring added layers of complexity, such as differing tax rates, compliance requirements, and customs duties depending on the country of operation. Proper management of these transactions is crucial to avoid tax penalties—particularly on issues like transfer pricing or VAT.

Without real-time visibility into these transactions, firms risk misreporting tax obligations, which can lead to costly fines or legal consequences. This challenge is even greater for firms dealing with multiple currencies, contracts, and varied fiscal policies.

Accountant's Experience with Cross-Border Challenges

"Cross-border transactions are always a tough nut to crack," explains Brian Lee, an accountant at a multinational firm. "Before implementing AI, we had multiple instances where tax obligations were misreported due to manual errors. Now, with real-time AI insights, those issues have become far less frequent, and the whole team feels more confident about compliance."

3. Data Privacy and Security Concerns

Data privacy laws, such as the General Data Protection Regulation (GDPR) in Europe and the California Consumer Privacy Act (CCPA), add complexity to cross-border data management. Firms operating internationally must ensure compliance with the privacy regulations in each area they serve.

For example, GDPR mandates that personal data be stored within the EU or in countries with adequate privacy protections. Firms must track where data is transferred to ensure these rules are followed.

Personal Story from Data Management Team

"There was a time when we nearly faced a serious GDPR violation simply because we couldn't track the movement of client data accurately," recalls Jessica Allen, who works in data management for an accounting firm. "Since integrating AI-driven tracking tools, our team has far greater control, and incidents like that are no longer a concern."

4. Resource Limitations

Smaller and mid-sized firms often lack the resources to manage global compliance effectively. Without dedicated compliance teams or advanced technology, these firms face a higher risk of non-compliance, which could lead to penalties, reputational damage, and inefficiencies.

A Perspective from a Small Firm Owner

"We simply didn't have the capacity to keep up with changing regulations across different regions," says Martin Clarke, owner of a small accounting firm. "AI tools have been a game-changer for us—they help streamline what used to be an overwhelming workload, allowing us to compete with larger firms more effectively."

How AI Helps Ensure Global Compliance

AI offers solutions to many of these challenges by automating processes, tracking regulatory changes in real time, and reducing the risk of human error. Here are the primary ways AI helps ensure global compliance:

1. Automating Compliance Tasks

AI can automate repetitive and time-consuming compliance tasks, including tax calculations, VAT filings, customs duties management, and regulatory reporting. By automating these processes, AI minimizes human errors, helping firms meet compliance obligations across different authorities.

For example, an AI platform can automatically calculate VAT rates for transactions across EU countries and generate reports that follow each country's tax regulations, reducing the need for manual data entry and significantly decreasing administrative burden.

AI systems can also categorize, process, and store data efficiently, ensuring compliance with regulations like GDPR and CCPA. A study by IDC predicts that AI-powered data classification tools will automate 70% of tasks related to

Personally Identifiable Information (PII) by the end of 2024 (Compunnel, 2024).

EY's compliance technology, which leverages Microsoft Azure, offers businesses seamless outsourcing capabilities with enhanced global visibility, data analytics, and improved tax governance, all of which reduce compliance risks significantly (EY, 2024). The EY Global VAT Reporting Tool automates the production of VAT/GST returns globally, ensuring compliance by keeping current with VAT law changes and providing powerful dashboards for risk management (EY, 2024).

2. Tracking Real-Time Regulatory Updates

AI can monitor regulatory changes by scanning legal databases, government websites, and tax authority publications, providing firms with real-time updates. These platforms allow compliance processes to be automatically adjusted as regulations change, ensuring firms stay compliant without needing to manually track updates across multiple regions.

For instance, an AI platform could alert a firm to an upcoming change in U.S. tax policies, allowing it to adjust its strategy well ahead of the change.

AI tools also monitor data flows in real time, quickly flagging non-compliance issues and generating reports for regulatory bodies. For example, a major international retailer implemented an AI-driven data management system that checked data transactions in real time, helping the firm identify compliance issues more swiftly (Compunnel, 2024).

3. Improving Cross-Border Data Management

Managing data across borders while following privacy regulations can be daunting. AI tools help firms by identifying risks associated with cross-border data transfers and ensuring compliance with laws like GDPR and CCPA. AI can flag transactions that may violate privacy regulations and suggest corrective actions, helping firms avoid costly penalties.

For instance, an AI tool might flag a transfer of customer data from Europe to the United States, prompting the firm to ensure the U.S. recipient meets GDPR requirements.

In the healthcare sector, an AI system was used to manage patient data, ensuring HIPAA compliance and identifying potential data breaches, which enhanced overall data security (Compunnel, 2024).

4. Enhancing Accuracy and Reducing Costs

By automating compliance tasks and monitoring updates, AI significantly reduces the costs associated with global compliance. Firms can allocate fewer resources to manual compliance tasks and minimize the risk of penalties due to errors. AI's ability to handle complex data sets with precision improves the accuracy of compliance reporting.

For example, a firm using AI-driven tax compliance tools can reduce costs by automating VAT filings across multiple jurisdictions, thus improving accuracy and reducing the risk of penalties for incorrect filings.

AI's predictive capabilities also help firms stay ahead of regulatory changes. For instance, an international retailer used an AI system to provide predictive alerts on potential future compliance conflicts, enabling proactive adjustments (Compunnel, 2024).

Adoption of AI in Compliance

AI adoption in compliance is growing as firms recognize the benefits of automation and predictive analytics for managing complex regulations. A 2023 Gartner survey found that 60% of compliance officers plan to invest in AI-powered RegTech solutions by 2025 (Thomson Reuters, 2024). Additionally, 78% of professionals believe AI is a force for good in their profession, and 75% of risk management professionals were already using AI as a starting point for many processes (Thomson Reuters, 2024).

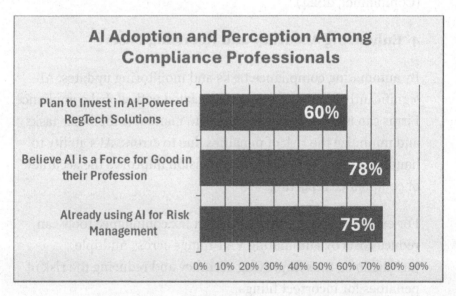

Figure 11 AI Adoption and Perception Among Compliance Professionals

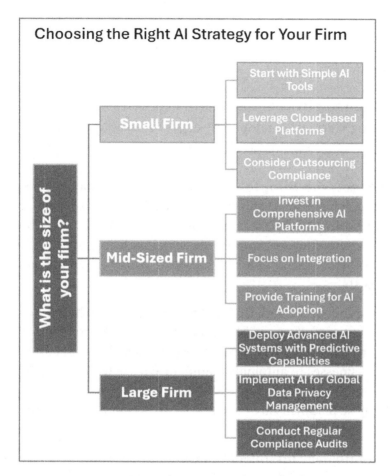

Figure 12 Use this guide to identify the most suitable AI compliance strategy for your firm based on its size and resources.

Steps for Implementing AI for Global Compliance

Successful implementation of AI for global compliance requires thoughtful planning, considering the firm's size, resources, and specific compliance needs. Below, we've included reflections and rhetorical questions to help guide firms on their journey:

"How much time would your team save if they didn't have to manually enter tax data for every jurisdiction?" This kind of reflection can help smaller firms recognize the practical benefits

of even the simplest AI implementations. Here are tailored strategies for small firms, medium-sized firms, and large enterprises:

For Small Firms Small firms usually have limited resources, making it critical to adopt cost-effective, easy-to-use AI tools that address their specific needs.

1. **Start with Simple AI Tools**: Small firms should consider implementing AI solutions for specific tasks like tax reporting or document management. Tools like QuickBooks or Xero offer AI-powered features that help manage tax compliance and financial reporting without high upfront costs.

2. **Leverage Cloud-Based Platforms**: Cloud-based AI solutions offer scalability, making them ideal for small and growing firms. Cloud platforms like Sage Intacct enable small businesses to automate compliance tasks without needing significant IT infrastructure investments. As the firm grows, these platforms are easy to scale to accommodate more complex needs.

3. **Consider Outsourcing Compliance**: Small firms lacking internal expertise can outsource compliance to third-party providers who use AI-driven tools, allowing them to benefit from advanced technologies without the overhead.

For Medium-Sized Firms Medium-sized firms have greater resources, enabling them to invest in more sophisticated AI solutions to handle broader compliance needs across multiple jurisdictions.

1. **Invest in Comprehensive AI Platforms**: Medium-sized firms should consider AI platforms that offer diverse compliance functions, from tax automation to real-time updates. Solutions like Thomson Reuters ONESOURCE or

CCH Axcess™ iQ help firms stay current with evolving tax regulations and privacy laws.

2. **Focus on Integration**: It is crucial for medium-sized firms to choose AI platforms that integrate smoothly with their existing financial systems, such as ERP software. Proper integration helps ensure compliance processes run seamlessly, minimizing data synchronization errors.

3. **Provide Training for AI Adoption**: To maximize the benefits of AI, firms should invest in training programs for staff to learn how to use these tools effectively, ensuring they are equipped to troubleshoot and make the most of AI-driven compliance solutions.

For Large/Enterprise Firms Large enterprises have complex needs, often operating in multiple countries with extensive regulatory requirements. AI can streamline compliance, but implementation must be strategic.

1. **Deploy Advanced AI Systems with Predictive Capabilities**: Large firms should invest in predictive AI platforms that not only automate tasks but also forecast regulatory changes, allowing proactive strategy adjustments. These systems offer real-time insights into compliance risks, enabling preventive measures.

2. **Establish a Dedicated Compliance Team**: Large firms should establish dedicated teams to manage AI-driven compliance processes. These teams ensure the AI tools are used effectively and compliance strategies align with global regulations.

3. **Implement AI for Global Data Privacy Management**: With data privacy laws becoming more critical, large firms must invest in AI tools to monitor data transfers and ensure compliance with GDPR and CCPA. AI tools can track data movement across borders, flag violations, and recommend corrective actions.

4. **Conduct Regular Compliance Audits Using AI**: AI-driven audit tools can help large firms conduct regular audits, automate the process, and identify potential risks, ensuring compliance with global standards.

REAL-WORLD EXAMPLES AND CASE STUDIES

1. Thomson Reuters ONESOURCE for Global Compliance Automation

Thomson Reuters ONESOURCE is a comprehensive AI platform that helps multinational firms manage tax compliance across multiple jurisdictions by automating calculations and providing real-time regulatory updates.

Case Study: Global Accounting Firm Automates VAT Compliance

A global accounting firm operating in 15 countries used ONESOURCE to automate VAT compliance for its clients. Before adoption, the firm struggled with frequent errors and penalties related to manual VAT processing. By implementing ONESOURCE, they reduced compliance workload by nearly 50% and eliminated VAT-related penalties by staying up-to-date with changing regulations. This allowed their accountants to focus more on strategic advisory services rather than routine compliance tasks.

2. GreenTree Financial: Streamlining Global Compliance with AI

GreenTree Financial faced significant challenges while expanding into Europe and Asia. Using AI-driven compliance tools for tax reporting and GDPR tracking, GreenTree cut down manual compliance work by 35%, avoiding data privacy penalties.

Chapter 8: AI in Global Compliance

A Personal Perspective from GreenTree's CFO

"When we first entered the European market, compliance was a huge roadblock," says Susan Michaels, CFO of GreenTree Financial. "Our team was overwhelmed trying to understand the different requirements in each country. AI tools have really helped us simplify this process. We've been able to focus more on growth rather than worrying about regulatory issues."

3. AI Adoption by Mid-Sized Accounting Firms

A mid-sized accounting firm implemented an AI platform for regulatory updates and tax compliance. Before AI adoption, the firm faced frequent challenges in staying updated with shifting compliance regulations across different regions. With the AI solution, the firm automated compliance tracking and reduced manual errors significantly.

Employee Insights on AI Integration

John Davis, a compliance manager at the firm, shares,"Initially, there was some hesitation around adopting AI, but after seeing how much time it saved us by automating mundane tasks, the whole team got on board. It gave us more time to concentrate on client services and improving our advisory offerings."

Expert Commentary

"AI in accounting is not just about compliance—it's about transforming how teams operate," says Carla Nguyen, a financial technologies strategist. "The time saved through automation is invaluable, especially when it allows accountants to focus on value-added services rather than rote tasks."

4. CCH Axcess for Accounting Compliance

A regional accounting firm used CCH Axcess™ to streamline client tax compliance. By adopting AI-driven tools, the firm was able to automate much of its compliance workload, including calculating tax liabilities across different jurisdictions and generating compliant reports for their clients. The adoption of CCH Axcess led to a 40% reduction in manual processes, freeing up staff time for more valuable activities, such as client consulting.

Insights from Firm Leader

"We used to spend countless hours on manual tax calculations, which were prone to human error," says George Howard, a partner at the firm. "With CCH Axcess, we've streamlined our processes significantly, allowing us to focus on delivering deeper insights and value to our clients instead of getting lost in spreadsheets.".

Actionable Insights

1. **Leverage AI for Cross-Border Tax Compliance:** Implement AI tools like Thomson Reuters ONESOURCE or CCH Axcess to automate tax compliance processes across different jurisdictions, ensuring accuracy and reducing the risk of penalties.

2. **Adopt Real-Time Compliance Monitoring Systems:** Use AI platforms that provide real-time updates on regulatory changes, enabling your firm to stay compliant with the latest tax laws, financial reporting standards, and data privacy regulations.

3. **Tailor AI Solutions to Your Firm's Size and Needs:**
   Smaller firms should start with simple, cost-effective AI
   tools, while larger firms should invest in advanced, predictive
   AI platforms. Each firm should choose tools that align with
   its specific compliance requirements and business goals.

4. **Conduct Regular AI-Driven Audits:** Large and mid-
   sized firms should use AI to conduct regular compliance
   audits, ensuring that all operations adhere to local and global
   regulatory standards.

The Future of AI in Global Compliance

AI's role in global compliance is poised to expand as regulatory
environments become more complex and businesses
increasingly operate across borders. Here are a few trends to
watch for in the future:

1. Predictive Compliance

AI platforms will soon incorporate predictive analytics, allowing
firms to anticipate upcoming regulatory changes based on
historical trends and patterns. This will enable firms to
proactively adjust their compliance strategies before new laws
come into effect.

2. Automated Regulatory Filings

In the near future, AI systems will be able to generate, submit,
and track regulatory filings in real time, reducing the
administrative burden on firms and ensuring timely compliance
with global regulations.

3. AI-Driven Data Protection

As data privacy laws continue to evolve, AI tools will play a critical role in ensuring compliance with regional and international data protection standards. AI-driven solutions will help firms manage data privacy risks, flag potential violations, and provide corrective actions before issues arise.

Conclusion: AI as a Future Driver of Compliance

As firms face increasing global compliance challenges, AI offers an effective solution for automating compliance tasks, ensuring accuracy, and staying updated with ever-changing regulations. By implementing AI-driven compliance tools, firms of all sizes can navigate complex regulatory environments with ease, reducing the risk of penalties and improving operational efficiency. As global regulations continue to evolve, AI will become an indispensable tool for maintaining compliance and staying ahead of potential risks.

In this chapter, we explored how AI is transforming global compliance by automating complex regulatory tasks and providing real-time insights across multiple jurisdictions. Now, we turn our attention to small firms. While small firms face unique challenges due to limited resources, AI offers affordable, scalable solutions that allow them to automate processes, reduce errors, and compete with larger firms. In the next chapter, we'll examine how small firms can leverage cost-effective AI tools and strategies to drive efficiency and growth.

References:

Compunnel. (2024). The Intersection of AI and Data Security Compliance in 2024. Retrieved from https://www.compunnel.com/blogs/the-intersection-of-ai-and-data-security-compliance-in-2024/

International Compliance Association. (2024). The rise of AI and its impact on compliance. Retrieved from https://www.int-comp.org/insight/the-rise-of-ai-and-its-impact-on-compliance/

HighRadius. (2024). How AI is helping in automating the Audit Process. Retrieved from https://www.highradius.com/resources/Blog/leveraging-ai-in-accounting-audit/

Long Island Business News. (2024). KPMG adds AI into its audit and workflow platforms. Retrieved from https://libn.com/2024/07/30/kpmg-adds-ai-into-its-audit-and-workflow-platforms/

Thomson Reuters. (2024). Many risk and compliance professionals see AI as a "force for good" in their industry. Retrieved from https://legal.thomsonreuters.com/blog/many-risk-compliance-professionals-see-ai-as-a-force-for-good-in-their-industry/

CHAPTER 9: AI FOR SMALL FIRMS: COST-EFFECTIVE SOLUTIONS AND STRATEGIES

Introduction

The Evolution of AI for Small Firms

Historically, artificial intelligence (AI) seemed out of reach for small firms due to high costs, complexity, and the need for dedicated IT resources. As we move forward, it's important to understand how these challenges have evolved and how recent advancements have made AI far more accessible to small firms. For example, in the early 2000s, a small accounting firm in New York struggled to afford AI-powered data analytics tools that were only accessible to larger enterprises, making it challenging to compete with bigger firms that could automate complex processes and improve efficiency. Large companies were the primary beneficiaries of early AI systems, leveraging them for operational efficiency and advanced analytics.

However, advancements in cloud computing, subscription-based services, and Software-as-a-Service (SaaS) models have changed the game, making AI tools accessible even to the smallest firms. These advancements allow small firms to leverage automation to save time, reduce costs, and improve efficiency, providing specific efficiency gains that were previously only available to larger enterprises. These advancements have allowed small businesses to access powerful AI tools without needing substantial upfront investments, bridging the gap and leveling the playing field with larger enterprises. For example, tools like QuickBooks Online were affordable and easy to use, allowing small firms to access AI-driven financial management features without significant upfront costs. Today, AI is no longer just a luxury for large enterprises—it has become an essential tool for small businesses to compete and thrive. A 2024 survey by BPC-Morning Consult revealed that 57% of small business owners and executives were incorporating AI to some extent in their operations, and 64% of them believe that the benefits of increased AI adoption outweigh the drawbacks. This chapter explores how AI has become a cost-effective solution for small accounting firms, allowing them to streamline operations and stay competitive.

Core Concepts

To better understand how small accounting firms can leverage AI, we'll explore several key concepts highlighting the practical benefits and strategic advantages of adopting AI-driven tools and processes.

1. Automating Repetitive Tasks to Boost Efficiency

The most immediate benefit of AI for small firms is its ability to automate repetitive, time-consuming tasks. This includes activities like bookkeeping, invoicing, and parts of the tax preparation process. For example, a small accounting firm in Ohio adopted automation for their payroll and tax preparation tasks, which helped them cut down on administrative workload by 30%, allowing their team to dedicate more time to personalized client services and strategic financial planning.

Chapter 9: AI for Small Firms:
Cost-Effective Solutions and Strategies

Tools such as Botkeeper, QuickBooks Online, and Xero provide automation features that reduce manual effort in bookkeeping while minimizing errors. This allows firms to focus more on strategic tasks, improving both efficiency and client service.

To assist with tax preparation, CCH ProSystem *fx* Scan (SaaS) with AutoFlow is a cloud-based tool that helps small firms quickly input tax data by automatically reading and extracting information from client source documents. For example, it allows accountants to scan and process client tax forms in minutes, significantly reducing manual data entry time and improving accuracy. This simplifies data entry and improves accuracy, saving time for accountants. Professionals in smaller firms appreciate using technology that reduces their manual work, so they can use their professional skills more effectively to help their clients and the firm. Small firms that adopt AI-driven solutions like these can reduce administrative burdens while enhancing accuracy and client and staff satisfaction. One small firm shared, "After implementing AI, we not only cut down on manual tasks but also saw a noticeable increase in client satisfaction due to faster turnaround times and improved accuracy. Staff now had the opportunity to collaborate more closely with clients directly, resulting in higher client retention." Specifically, the firm reported a 25% improvement in accuracy and a noticeable boost in client satisfaction. One client noted, "The new system is much faster, and I feel more confident knowing our data is handled accurately," highlighting the value of automation in delivering better service. In fact, a Small Business Entrepreneurship Council (SBEC) survey found that AI tools saved small business owners an average of 13 hours a week, and 76% of small business owners reported that AI is freeing both themselves and their employees to focus on high-value tasks.

Real-World Example: A small CPA firm in Texas implemented AI tools like Gusto and Botkeeper to automate payroll and bookkeeping functions. Within six months, the firm cut administrative time by 40%, allowing it to focus more on tax advisory services and attract new clients. This automation improved accuracy and reduced errors, contributing to a 20% increase in client retention.

Automation is like having an extra set of hands that never gets tired—it's key for small firms needing to save time and redirect their energy toward value-driven services like advisory and strategic planning. By automating repetitive tasks, small firms can avoid the mundane work that slows them down and instead concentrate on delivering high-impact services to their clients. AI tools like QuickBooks, Botkeeper, and Gusto help automate repetitive tasks such as bookkeeping and payroll, minimizing manual errors and reducing the need for manual data entry.

2. Affordable AI Tools for Small Firms

There are numerous AI tools on the market today that cater specifically to the needs of small accounting firms. To help small firms get started, below are some popular AI tools in use today. These tools are designed to be affordable, scalable, and easy to integrate into your existing workflows, providing automation and insights without requiring a massive investment. For small firms, these tools offer simplicity and cost-effectiveness, while mid-sized firms may benefit from their scalability. Larger firms can take advantage of advanced features that support more complex processes and integration needs. Below are some common AI tools that small firms can take advantage of:

- **FreshBooks**: A cloud-based accounting software tailored for small businesses and freelancers, FreshBooks uses AI to automate invoicing, expense tracking, and time tracking. It offers real-time reporting, enabling small firms to gain deeper insights into their financial performance with minimal effort.

- **Receipt Bank (Dext)**: This AI-powered tool automates expense management by scanning and categorizing receipts and invoices, making bookkeeping easier for smaller firms. Dext integrates with popular accounting platforms like QuickBooks and Xero to streamline data entry and reporting.

- **Zoho Books**: Zoho Books is an AI-powered accounting solution for small businesses that automates key processes such as invoicing, inventory management, and tax preparation. It includes real-time financial reporting and integrates with the broader Zoho ecosystem for CRM and other business functions.

- **Fathom**: Fathom provides advanced financial reporting and analysis tools that are especially useful for small firms looking to offer advisory services. The platform uses AI to help accountants deliver data-driven insights and visual performance reports.

- **Bill.com**: Bill.com uses AI to automate bill payment workflows and approvals, reducing the time spent on manual processes. It integrates with major accounting software platforms and simplifies vendor management, making it easier for small businesses to manage accounts payable.

- **Plooto**: Plooto is a cloud-based payment solution that automates accounts payable and receivable workflows. It helps small businesses streamline their payment processing and approval workflows, minimizing the time spent on financial management tasks.

- **CCH ProSystem *fx* Scan (SaaS) with AutoFlow**: ProSystem *fx* Scan (Saas) with AutoFlow is a cloud-based solution that scans tax source documents, extracts key data, and imports it directly into the client's 1040 or 1041 tax return, significantly streamlining the data entry process for small accounting firms.

- **ChatGPT**: A conversational AI tool that supports content creation and customer communication, helping firms draft emails, create documents, and respond to client inquiries more efficiently.

- **DALL·E 2**: An AI tool that assists with visual content creation, making it easy to generate graphics for marketing materials or visual reports without needing a dedicated graphic designer.

- **Grammarly**: An AI-powered writing assistant that helps firms improve the clarity and professionalism of their written communication, ensuring all client-facing documents are polished and error-free.

- **Notion AI**: A project management and collaboration tool that uses AI to help teams organize their tasks, track progress, and manage client projects seamlessly.

- **QuickBooks Intuit Assist**: An AI assistant embedded within QuickBooks that helps small firms manage their finances by automating tasks such as expense tracking, invoicing, and providing financial insights.

Chapter 9: AI for Small Firms:
Cost-Effective Solutions and Strategies

These tools allow small firms to automate critical financial processes and gain access to real-time financial data without the need for expensive software or complex IT infrastructure.

The following chart demonstrates how several small firms are saving time using AI-powered tools.

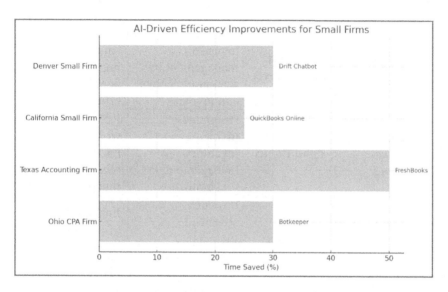

Figure 13 AI Tools Driving Efficiency in Small Firms

AI-powered tools have never been so accessible to small firms as they are today. A small accounting firm in California started using Zoho Books, and within three months, they saw a 30% reduction in manual data entry time, allowing them to focus more on advisory services, which led to increased client satisfaction. Whether it's managing finances, automating expense tracking, or improving client communication, tools like FreshBooks, Zoho Books, and Bill.com offer practical solutions that are both scalable and easy to implement.

The following table outlines several use cases with the AI tools meant for the job, along with the key features and benefits of each tool.

The Automated Accountant

Use Case	AI Tool	Key Features	Benefits
Financial Management & Accounting	**FreshBooks**	Automates invoicing, expense tracking, time tracking	Saves time, improves financial reporting accuracy
Financial Management & Accounting	**Receipt Bank (Dext)**	Automates expense management by scanning receipts and invoices	Reduces manual data entry, improves bookkeeping efficiency
Financial Management & Accounting	**Zoho Books**	Automates invoicing, inventory management, tax preparation	Reduces manual workload, integrates with other CRM functions
Financial Advisory & Reporting	**Fathom**	Provides advanced financial reporting and analysis tools	Enables delivery of data-driven insights for clients
Accounts Payable & Receivable	**Bill.com**	Automates bill payment workflows and approvals	Simplifies vendor management, saves time on manual processes
Accounts Payable & Receivable	**Plooto**	Automates accounts payable and receivable workflows	Streamlines payment processes, reduces administrative workload
Tax Data Automation	**CCH ProSystem *fx* Scan with AutoFlow, SurePrep 1040San**	Scans and extracts tax source data for direct import	Significantly reduces data entry time, improves accuracy, and processes

Use Case	AI Tool	Key Features	Benefits
Content Creation & Client Communication	**ChatGPT, CoPilot, Gemini, etc.**	Supports content creation, drafting documents, client communication	Speeds up client communication, supports content quality
Visual Content Creation	**Canva, DALL·E 2, MidJourney**	Assists with visual content creation for marketing and reports	Enhances visual marketing efforts without graphic designer
Writing Assistance	**Grammarly**	Improves clarity and professionalism of written communication	Polishes client-facing documents, ensures professional tone
Project Management & Collaboration	**Notion AI**	Helps teams organize tasks, track progress, manage projects	Improves project management efficiency, collaboration
Financial Management Assistant	**QuickBooks Intuit Assist**	Automates expense tracking, invoicing, provides financial insights	Provides automated financial insights, saves time on tracking tasks

Table 1 AI Tools Available to Small Firms

3. Real-World Examples of AI Adoption in Small Firms

AI adoption in small firms has produced tangible results, from reducing costs to improving client satisfaction. Below are some examples of firms leveraging AI to drive operational improvements:

- *CPA Practice Advisor Case Study*: A small firm used Botkeeper to automate its bookkeeping processes, saving 15 hours per week and significantly reducing manual errors.

- *Xero Case Study*: A mid-sized firm utilized Xero's AI-powered financial reconciliation and forecasting tools, cutting the time spent on manual data entry in half and improving cash flow forecasting accuracy.

According to a survey by BPC-Morning Consult, 48% of small businesses use AI-based technology for accounting, such as QuickBooks, and 48% use AI for customer management and communication, such as Microsoft Office and Mailchimp. These examples illustrate the growing reliance on AI to improve efficiency and deliver value to clients.

4. Best Practices for AI Implementation in Small Firms

Implementing AI in small firms requires careful planning and execution to ensure the best results. Following these best practices is essential to maximize the benefits of AI, reduce potential challenges, and ensure a smooth transition for both staff and clients. By focusing on high-impact areas, involving your team early, and continuously measuring ROI, firms can achieve greater efficiency and accuracy while maintaining data security and compliance. For example, a small accounting firm in Denver successfully integrated AI by first identifying key pain points, such as manual bookkeeping tasks, and then selecting cloud-based tools to address those areas. The firm involved all team members in training sessions and measured the impact over three months, ultimately seeing a 35% reduction in administrative hours and improved staff satisfaction.

Here are a few best practices firms should consider when integrating AI tools into their workflows:

Start with High-Impact Areas: Identify the areas of your practice that are the most time-consuming or prone to error (e.g., invoicing, payroll, or data entry) and prioritize those for AI automation. By starting with processes that have the highest impact, you'll see immediate benefits in terms of time saved and error reduction.

Involve Your Team Early: Ensure that your team is part of the AI implementation process from the start. Involving team members in selecting the right tools and providing training ensures smoother adoption and minimizes resistance to new technologies. Regularly seek feedback from staff to refine the use of AI tools and ensure they are maximizing productivity.

Leverage Cloud-Based AI Solutions: Cloud-based AI tools like QuickBooks Online or Zoho Books are cost-effective and scalable, allowing firms to start small and expand their AI usage as their needs grow. Cloud solutions also reduce the need for in-house IT support and offer automatic updates, ensuring that your firm always has access to the latest technology.

Measure Performance and ROI Regularly: Track key performance indicators (KPIs) such as time saved, reduction in manual errors, or client satisfaction improvements after implementing AI tools. Regular performance measurement helps you gauge the effectiveness of AI and make data-driven decisions on whether to expand its use.

Ensure Data Security and Compliance: As AI tools handle sensitive financial data, it's important to ensure they comply with data security regulations. Choose AI platforms that offer built-in encryption and privacy features to protect client information and maintain compliance with data protection laws such as GDPR.

Stay Agile and Ready for Upgrades: AI technologies are constantly evolving, and small firms should stay agile by being open to upgrading or switching tools as better solutions emerge. By periodically reviewing the available AI tools on the market, small firms can ensure that they are using the most efficient and effective technologies for their needs.

5. The Future of AI in Small Firms

As AI technologies continue to evolve, small firms will have access to more sophisticated tools that enable them to compete on a more level playing field with larger firms. For example, emerging AI technologies like machine learning-based predictive analytics and natural language processing are allowing small firms to better anticipate client needs and automate customer communications. A small firm in Chicago used predictive analytics to identify seasonal cash flow patterns and proactively offered tailored financial planning services to clients, resulting in a 20% increase in client retention. The future of AI in small firms will include advanced features like:

Predictive Analytics: AI will provide small firms with the ability to analyze historical data and predict future outcomes, such as cash flow issues or tax liabilities.

AI-Enhanced Client Advisory Services: By automating data analysis and report generation, small firms can offer personalized financial advice without increasing their workload.

Real-World Example: A small firm in San Francisco adopted predictive analytics tools to forecast tax liabilities and recommend tax-saving strategies to clients. By using AI to analyze historical data, the firm was able to proactively identify opportunities for tax savings, improving client satisfaction and boosting revenue by 15%. Clients noted that the proactive approach made them feel more informed and supported, enforcing their trust in the firm's services.

Actionable Insights for Small Firms

1. **Adopt Scalable AI Tools**: Begin with affordable, scalable AI tools like QuickBooks Online, Dext, or FreshBooks, which provide immediate time savings and increased accuracy without a large upfront investment.

2. **Automate Routine Tasks**: Use AI to automate repetitive tasks such as invoicing, payroll, and bookkeeping. This frees up accountants to focus on higher-value services such as tax planning and client advisory.

3. **Measure ROI and Adjust Accordingly**: Regularly assess the return on investment by tracking time saved, error reduction, and client satisfaction improvements. Use these metrics to guide decisions on where to further expand AI usage.

4. **Stay Informed About Emerging Tools**: As AI continues to evolve, keep track of new and emerging AI tools that can further streamline processes and enhance your firm's capabilities.

Conclusion/Takeaways

AI has opened up significant opportunities for small accounting firms to enhance efficiency, accuracy, and client satisfaction. By leveraging affordable AI tools, firms can automate repetitive tasks, provide more value-driven services, and stay competitive in a rapidly evolving market. Implementing best practices, such as focusing on high-impact areas and involving the entire team, ensures that AI adoption is both effective and sustainable. Looking forward, small firms that remain agile and informed about emerging AI technologies will be well-positioned to continue thriving and expanding their service offerings.

As small firms continue to integrate AI into their workflows, the next natural step is to explore how these technologies can further enhance client relationships. AI is not only transforming back-office efficiency but also how accountants deliver value through personalized client advisory services (CAS). In the following chapter, we will delve into how AI-powered tools are changing the dynamics of client interactions, enabling firms to provide more proactive, data-driven advice, and improve overall client satisfaction.

Chapter 9: AI for Small Firms: Cost-Effective Solutions and Strategies

References

Bipartisan Policy Center. (2024, May 9). 3 Ways AI is Transforming Small Businesses. Retrieved from https://bipartisanpolicy.org/blog/3-ways-ai-is-transforming-small-businesses/

Bipartisan Policy Center. (2024, April 29). Small Businesses Matter: Navigating the AI Frontier. Retrieved from https://bipartisanpolicy.org/report/small-businesses-matter-navigating-the-ai-frontier/

Moving Forward Small Business. (2024, May 18). Essential AI Governance Framework for Small Businesses. Retrieved from https://www.movingforwardsmallbusiness.com/essential-ai-governance-framework-for-small-businesses/

US Chamber of Commerce. (2024, August 28). A Small Business Guide to AI. Retrieved from https://www.uschamber.com/co/run/technology/small-business-ai-guide

PriceWeber. (2024, August 22). AI Implementation for Small Businesses. Retrieved from https://priceweber.com/blog/ai-implementation-small-business/

Small Business Entrepreneurship Council (SBEC). (2024). Survey on AI Usage in Small Businesses. Retrieved from https://sbecouncil.org

CHAPTER 10: AI IN CLIENT ADVISORY SERVICES (CAS)

Introduction: The Role of AI in Enhancing Client Advisory Services

Imagine a client meeting where, instead of simply reviewing last quarter's financials, you present your client with precise, data-driven insights about their upcoming cash flow, potential challenges, and new opportunities—all thanks to AI-powered analysis. Just like a seasoned pilot relying on advanced instruments to navigate through changing skies, accounting firms today use AI as a co-pilot, helping them see far beyond the traditional numbers. This shift is transforming Client Advisory Services (CAS), enabling firms to go from reactive compliance work to proactive, strategic consulting that shapes the future of their clients' businesses.

In recent years, Client Advisory Services (CAS) have emerged as a critical growth area for accounting firms. By shifting from compliance-focused tasks to value-added advisory services, firms can offer strategic insights that help clients optimize their financial performance and make informed decisions. The integration of Artificial Intelligence (AI) into CAS has further transformed this area, allowing accountants to deliver deeper, more personalized insights with greater efficiency. AI-powered tools enable firms to automate data analysis, generate predictive forecasts, and deliver real-time advice, helping clients make better financial decisions in an increasingly complex economic environment.

Core Concepts

To understand how AI can transform Client Advisory Services, it's important to explore several core concepts that demonstrate AI's capabilities in enhancing CAS. These concepts provide insights into how AI empowers accountants to provide more value to their clients.

1. How AI is Transforming Client Advisory Services

AI has transformed CAS by taking over repetitive tasks, delivering insights that were previously unattainable through manual processes. With AI, accountants can focus on strategic decision-making while letting AI-driven systems handle the heavy lifting of data analysis and report generation. Firms can now deliver more personalized and proactive advisory services to their clients. For instance, a mid-sized firm in Ohio implemented AI-driven financial forecasting tools, which enabled them to offer tailored cash flow strategies to small business clients. This level of personalization improved client satisfaction and retention significantly.

2. AI for Financial Data Analysis

AI-powered systems can quickly analyze client financial data—including cash flow, revenues, and expenses—offering actionable insights. For example, a small accounting firm in California implemented an AI-based financial analysis tool, which helped them identify cash flow issues for a client before they became major problems. By addressing these issues proactively, the firm was able to significantly improve the client's financial stability and build a stronger advisory relationship. This enables firms to identify potential risks, opportunities, and areas for improvement in real time.

Real-World Example:

PwC has implemented AI-driven tools to analyze client financial data and provide tailored insights. These tools help accountants proactively identify risks and opportunities, optimizing clients' financial strategies and improving profitability. For example, PwC utilized AI to predict cash flow shortfalls for a retail client, enabling proactive measures that avoided significant financial issues. Smaller firms also benefit from these advancements by being able to offer services that were once reserved for larger competitors.

Another example is KPMG's implementation of Clara, an AI-powered audit and advisory platform. KPMG Clara has allowed the firm to continuously analyze client data, flagging potential compliance risks and providing real-time advisory opportunities. This has helped KPMG's clients stay ahead of regulatory changes and adapt quickly to shifting market conditions.

At the smaller firm level, Smith & Howard, an Atlanta-based accounting firm, implemented Xero's AI-powered solutions to automate bookkeeping and provide real-time financial insights to small business clients. By leveraging Xero's capabilities, Smith & Howard was able to provide strategic advisory services, which resulted in improved client satisfaction and increased demand for their services.

Personalized Financial Forecasting with AI

One of the most significant benefits of AI in CAS is the ability to generate personalized financial forecasts based on both historical data and real-time inputs. AI-powered predictive models provide firms with insights into potential financial trends and future risks, enabling accountants to offer forward-looking advice to clients.

AI-Driven Financial Forecasting

Using predictive analytics, AI tools can anticipate cash flow shortages, forecast revenue growth, and identify opportunities for investment. This level of insight allows firms to offer clients more precise and valuable advice, helping them navigate potential financial challenges.

Real-World Example:

Wolters Kluwer's CCH Axcess™ iQ is a powerful AI tool that offers predictive insights into a client's financial data. By generating real-time alerts, CCH Axcess™ iQ helps accountants guide their clients through potential financial risks and opportunities before they escalate. According to Peter Wesch, a partner at a mid-sized accounting firm, 'CCH Axcess iQ not only helped us proactively identify legislative changes impacting our clients but also allowed us to deliver higher-value advisory services, which significantly strengthened our client relationships.'

Additionally, Mazars, an international audit, tax, and advisory firm, has leveraged AI tools to predict tax liabilities and provide early advisory suggestions to their clients. By using AI to generate automated reports and forecasts, Mazars was able to save considerable time and deliver timely, accurate advice, leading to increased client retention and satisfaction.'

3. AI-Enhanced Financial Strategy and Planning

AI goes beyond basic data analysis; it also helps firms develop long-term financial strategies by automating performance analysis and market forecasting. AI enables accountants to offer comprehensive data-driven strategic recommendations that help clients grow their businesses and manage risks.

AI for Scenario Planning

AI tools simulate various financial scenarios based on market conditions, allowing firms to advise clients on strategies for growth, risk management, and investment.

Real-World Example:

IBM Watson is frequently used by firms to analyze market trends and client performance, helping accountants provide strategic financial recommendations. For instance, a mid-sized firm used IBM Watson to forecast market conditions for a manufacturing client, allowing them to strategically plan inventory purchases and manage cash flow more effectively. By using AI-generated insights, firms can offer tailored financial plans that address each client's unique situation.

Another example is Deloitte's use of CortexAI for strategic financial analysis. CortexAI helps firms provide deep insights into client financial performance, offering scenario-based planning and strategic guidance. This has enabled Deloitte to deliver more comprehensive strategic recommendations to its clients, particularly in industries facing high volatility, such as energy and retail.

AI Scalability for Firms of All Sizes

AI presents unique opportunities and challenges depending on the firm's size. Here is a deeper dive into how scalability and AI adoption differ for small, mid-sized, and large firms.

- **Small Firms**:

    o **Challenges**: Small firms often face budget constraints and lack dedicated IT support for implementing AI solutions. The initial cost of tools, ongoing maintenance, and skill gaps are significant barriers.

    o **Strategies**: Leveraging low-cost AI tools such as QuickBooks Intuit Assist, Zoho Books, and Botkeeper can help small firms start their AI journey. These tools focus on automating routine tasks like bookkeeping, allowing accountants to focus on higher-value client interactions. Collaboration with tech vendors for flexible pricing and using cloud-based AI platforms can also lower costs.

- **Mid-Sized Firms:**

    o **Challenges**: Mid-sized firms need to scale their services while maintaining quality. They often require more advanced AI tools to analyze larger datasets and handle increased client demands, but budget considerations remain important.

    o **Strategies**: Mid-sized firms can benefit from AI tools like Xero and IBM Watson to perform predictive analysis and scenario planning. Implementing scalable AI platforms that allow gradual enhancement of capabilities helps mid-sized firms manage their growth effectively. Firms like Mazars have demonstrated the effectiveness of using AI to enhance tax liability forecasting, saving considerable time while delivering high-value advisory services.

- **Large Firms/Multinationals:**

    o **Challenges**: Large firms deal with complex datasets, global regulatory compliance, and managing multi-national client portfolios. Implementing AI across different jurisdictions while adhering to diverse regulatory frameworks can be a major challenge.

    o **Strategies**: Large firms should look into robust AI platforms like KPMG's Clara or Deloitte's CortexAI, which are designed to handle global data and offer real-time advisory across multiple regions. AI tools that provide cross-border tax compliance support and real-time alerts for regulatory changes are crucial for managing multi-national operations. For instance, KPMG Clara's ability to flag compliance risks helps multinational clients stay ahead of global regulatory requirements.

Firm Size	Challenges	AI Strategies
Small Firms	Budget constraints, lack of IT support, skill gaps	Leverage low-cost AI tools like QuickBooks Intuit Assist, Zoho Books, Botkeeper; Collaborate with tech vendors for pricing flexibility
Mid-Sized Firms	Scaling services while maintaining quality, budget considerations	Use tools like Xero and IBM Watson for predictive analysis; Implement scalable AI platforms that allow gradual enhancements
Large Firms	Complex datasets, global regulatory compliance, multi-national client portfolios	Adopt robust AI platforms like KPMG Clara, Deloitte CortexAI; Implement tools for cross-border compliance and real-time alerts for regulatory changes

Figure 14 Tailored AI approaches for firms of different sizes: Overcoming unique challenges and leveraging targeted strategies for successful AI integration.

The table above illustrates the variety of challenges faced by firms of different sizes and the various AI Strategies for each.

4. Automating Routine Tasks to Enhance Client Relationships

Routine tasks such as budgeting, cash flow analysis, and performance reporting can now be automated using AI, freeing accountants to focus on building stronger client relationships. This increased efficiency allows firms to deliver personalized advice without being bogged down by time-consuming manual work. For example, a small accounting firm in Texas adopted Botkeeper to automate data entry and bookkeeping tasks. This automation freed up significant time for the accountants, allowing them to focus on providing personalized financial advisory services to their clients, ultimately strengthening client relationships and improving overall satisfaction.

AI in Client Communications

AI-driven communication tools automatically generate reports and summaries, allowing firms to keep clients updated on their financial status more frequently and accurately. This proactive approach fosters more meaningful client interactions and improves overall satisfaction.

Real-World Example:

Botkeeper is an AI-powered tool that automates routine bookkeeping tasks such as data entry and reconciliation. This has allowed firms to scale their CAS offerings efficiently while still providing personalized services to clients. For example, a small accounting firm in Texas adopted Botkeeper to automate their bookkeeping processes, which freed up more than 15 hours per week. This time saving enabled the firm to focus on delivering strategic tax planning services to clients, ultimately enhancing client satisfaction.

Another example is Aprio, a national accounting network, using Botkeeper alongside their traditional services. By automating routine data processing tasks, Aprio was able to allocate more time for advisory roles, allowing accountants to offer clients deeper insights into their financial data, which improved client trust and engagement.

5. The Future of AI in Client Advisory Services

As AI technology continues to evolve, its role in CAS will expand even further. AI-driven virtual CFO platforms, hyper-accurate financial forecasts, and integrated advisory platforms are just a few of the innovations on the horizon.

AI-Driven Virtual CFOs

AI systems may soon evolve into virtual CFOs for small and medium-sized businesses, providing real-time financial insights, forecasts, and strategic advice without requiring full-time human oversight.

Predictive Capabilities

AI's predictive capabilities will become even more sophisticated, offering firms hyper-accurate forecasts that allow businesses to optimize their strategies for growth.

Fully Integrated Advisory Platforms

AI tools are expected to evolve into integrated platforms offering real-time insights, forecasts, and personalized financial advice all in one place. These platforms will automate much of the analysis and planning process, enabling firms to efficiently scale their CAS offerings.

Global Focus for Large Firms

For large firms, handling complex, multi-national operations presents unique challenges. AI has a pivotal role in managing these global operations, from ensuring compliance to managing tax planning across borders.

- **Cross-Border Compliance**: Tools like Deloitte's CortexAI can monitor regulatory requirements across different countries, ensuring that firms are always in compliance. AI-driven systems provide real-time updates on changes in regulations, which helps firms manage risks effectively.

- **Tax Planning Across Borders**: AI can analyze cross-border tax implications and suggest optimized tax strategies. For instance, IBM Watson has been used by multinational firms to create tax-efficient structures that comply with diverse regional regulations.

- **Managing Complex Client Portfolios**: KPMG Clara's real-time capabilities allow firms to manage complex portfolios more effectively, offering insights that help streamline processes and address risks in different regions before they escalate.

Timeline of AI Adoption in Client Advisory Services

To truly appreciate how AI has evolved in Client Advisory Services, imagine the journey as a series of key milestones—each one marking a step closer to a more integrated and sophisticated advisory environment. From chatbots that answered basic banking questions to AI-driven CRM systems revolutionizing how firms interact with clients, this timeline captures the essence of transformation within the accounting industry.

The adoption of AI in Client Advisory Services (CAS) has evolved significantly over the years, with key milestones highlighting how AI has become a vital tool for accountants to enhance advisory services. The timeline below captures the pivotal developments that have driven the growth of AI in CAS, showcasing the journey from initial chatbot experiments to sophisticated financial advisory platforms.

In 2016, Bank of America introduced Erica, an AI-powered chatbot, to help with basic banking tasks. This marked one of the earliest examples of AI being used to improve client interactions, demonstrating how AI could provide real-time assistance and enhance customer experience. It laid the groundwork for using AI in broader financial advisory services.

The following year, in 2017, JP Morgan Chase launched the COIN (Contract Intelligence) platform, which leveraged AI to analyze legal documents. This innovation improved efficiency dramatically, reportedly saving over 360,000 hours of work annually compared to manual document review, while also increasing accuracy in identifying critical legal clauses. This innovation showed the potential for AI to tackle complex tasks previously performed by skilled professionals, setting a precedent for AI's use in accounting and advisory services.

By 2023, 45% of firms were testing or implementing generative AI. The growing adoption of generative AI highlighted its expanding role in content creation, drafting client reports, and providing initial analysis—all of which enabled firms to save time and focus on higher-value advisory work. Real-world examples include firms using generative AI to create draft versions of client communications, reducing manual workload and speeding up service delivery.

In 2024, nearly 79% of enterprises were expected to use AI-based Customer Relationship Management (CRM) systems. This shift allowed accounting firms to manage client interactions more effectively by providing personalized experiences, anticipating client needs, and enhancing the overall advisory relationship. AI-based CRMs have become instrumental in improving client satisfaction and loyalty.

Looking forward, conversational AI is projected to grow by 54% by 2027. This anticipated growth reflects the increasing reliance on AI-driven chatbots and assistants to handle routine client queries, freeing up human advisors to focus on more strategic, personalized engagements. AI tools like ChatGPT have enabled firms to offer consistent, round-the-clock support to clients, further enhancing the value of their services.

By 2028, the AI in accounting market is expected to reach $16 billion, demonstrating the substantial growth and investment in AI technologies for accounting and advisory services. Firms of all sizes recognize the need to integrate AI to remain competitive and provide more in-depth and strategic advice to clients.

The following timeline summarizes the adoption of AI in Client Advisory Services:

Year	Development
2016	Bank of America creates a chatbot for banking tasks
2017	JP Morgan Chase launches COIN platform for legal document analysis
2023	45% of firms are testing or implementing generative AI
2024	79% of enterprises expected to use AI-based CRMs
2027	Projected 54% growth in conversational AI market

2028	AI in accounting market expected to reach $16 billion

Table 2 Timeline of AI Adoption in Client Advisory Services (CAS)

These milestones illustrate how AI adoption has progressed from simple automation to more integrated and sophisticated tools that empower accountants to offer enhanced advisory services. From early chatbots to predictive analytics and integrated CRM systems, AI is continuously reshaping the accounting landscape. Firms that embrace these technologies are better positioned to deliver timely, personalized, and data-driven advice to their clients, ensuring a higher level of service and satisfaction.

Challenges and Overcoming Barriers

While AI presents numerous benefits, the journey to integrating AI into Client Advisory Services is not without challenges. Firms of all sizes—small, mid-sized, and large—face several obstacles that must be navigated to successfully leverage AI technology.

1. Data Privacy and Security

AI-driven solutions require access to significant amounts of client data, raising concerns about privacy and security. Firms must ensure they comply with data protection regulations and implement robust encryption and cybersecurity measures. Transparency in data usage and obtaining client consent are crucial to fostering trust.

2. Resistance to Change

Introducing AI often requires changes in workflows, and this can lead to resistance from staff who are used to traditional methods.

Overcoming this resistance involves providing adequate training and demonstrating how AI can reduce workloads, increase productivity, and enhance the quality of advisory services. Engaging employees early and maintaining clear communication are key strategies to reduce resistance.

3. Cost Considerations

While AI tools are becoming more affordable, the initial investment and ongoing costs may still be significant for some firms. To find cost-effective options, smaller firms can explore free or low-cost AI tools designed for small businesses, leverage trial versions, or consider tools that offer tiered pricing based on usage. Firms must conduct a cost-benefit analysis to ensure they are investing in the right AI tools that align with their strategic goals. Prioritizing high-impact areas for initial AI implementation can help firms realize value quickly and justify further investments.

Low-Cost AI Solutions for Client Advisory Services (CAS)

Smaller firms seeking cost-effective AI solutions for CAS can consider tools like QuickBooks Intuit Assist, FreshBooks, Zoho Books, and Fathom. These tools provide robust features at affordable rates, allowing firms to automate essential tasks without a large upfront investment. Additionally, platforms like ChatGPT and DALL·E 2 offer low-cost options for enhancing client communication and content creation, adding value to advisory services without significant cost burdens.

4. Skill Gaps

The adoption of AI requires accountants to acquire new skills, including data analysis, understanding AI outputs, and integrating AI tools into client advisory processes. Addressing this challenge involves providing upskilling opportunities for staff and considering partnerships with technology providers to bridge knowledge gaps. Firms that prioritize skill development will be better positioned to fully leverage AI capabilities.

5. Integration with Existing Systems

AI tools need to integrate seamlessly with the firm's existing software and infrastructure. Compatibility issues can hinder the effective use of AI, especially in larger firms with complex legacy systems. Working with vendors who understand the firm's systems and ensuring that AI tools can easily integrate with existing platforms is critical to overcoming this barrier.

Human-AI Collaboration

AI should not be viewed as a replacement for human expertise but rather as a powerful tool that enhances accountants' ability to serve their clients. The combination of AI-driven analysis and human judgment enables firms to deliver the best possible service. Accountants provide context, experience, and personalized client interaction—elements that AI cannot replicate. Successful firms will be those that harness the strengths of both AI and human advisors to create a collaborative approach that maximizes value for clients.

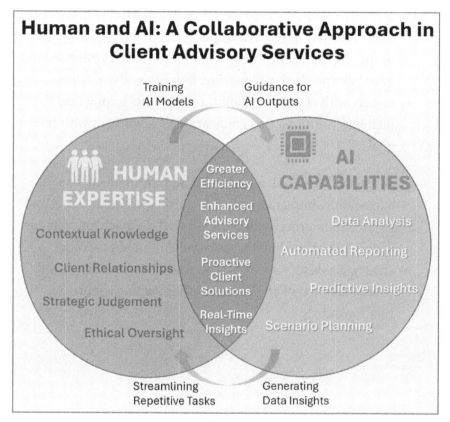

Figure 15 A Balanced Approach: Leveraging Human Expertise and AI Capabilities for Enhanced Client Advisory Services

Real-World Examples of Successful Human-AI Collaboration:

- **PwC** has integrated AI into its operations but emphasizes that human oversight is crucial for the success of AI initiatives. By using AI to handle complex data analysis and scenario modeling, PwC allows their accountants to focus on interpreting results and providing strategic recommendations tailored to each client's needs. This balance has enabled PwC to deliver highly personalized advisory services.

- **Deloitte** uses AI alongside human expertise in its CortexAI platform, which offers deep insights into client financial performance. While CortexAI handles the data analysis and generates predictive scenarios, Deloitte's advisors work closely with clients to adapt those insights to practical business solutions, ensuring strategic alignment with their goals.

- **Smith & Howard**, a mid-sized accounting firm, has successfully implemented AI to automate bookkeeping and routine data processing. This allowed their accountants to spend more time building relationships and providing strategic advisory services. The result has been improved client satisfaction and stronger, long-lasting client relationships.

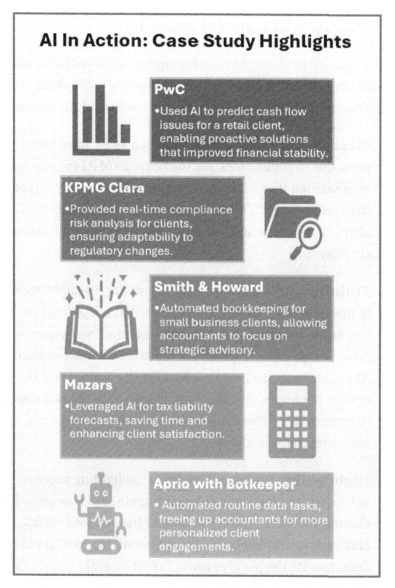

Figure 16 How Firms Leverage AI to Deliver Enhanced Client Advisory Services

Addressing Staff Concerns About AI:

Many firms face resistance to AI adoption from staff who worry about job security or struggle to adapt to new technologies. Addressing these concerns is critical to successful AI integration.

- **Clear Communication**: Firms such as EY have been proactive in communicating the purpose of AI to their staff, emphasizing that AI is a tool to enhance efficiency rather than replace jobs. This transparent approach helps to alleviate concerns and builds a sense of ownership among employees.

- **Training and Upskilling**: Firms are increasingly investing in upskilling initiatives to help their staff adapt to AI tools. For example, KPMG has launched an internal training program specifically aimed at educating their accountants on AI capabilities and how to work effectively alongside these new technologies. By empowering staff with the skills needed to leverage AI, firms can minimize resistance and build a more engaged workforce.

- **Highlighting Success Stories**: Highlighting success stories within the firm can help mitigate staff concerns. By sharing specific examples of how AI has reduced workloads and improved efficiency without eliminating jobs, firms can demonstrate the positive impact of AI on employees' roles. For example, Smith & Howard has shared internal case studies showing how automation has led to better work-life balance for their staff, as AI took over repetitive manual tasks.

Visual Summary: Key Benefits of AI in CAS

Figure 17 Visual Summary: Key Benefits of AI in Client Advisory Services

Actionable Insights

1. **Leverage AI for Proactive Advice**: Use AI tools like CCH Axcess™ iQ and Botkeeper to deliver proactive, real-time financial advice to clients based on predictive analytics. By leveraging AI's predictive capabilities, accountants can identify emerging trends, potential risks, and opportunities before they become critical. This allows firms to provide actionable guidance to clients, helping them make informed decisions ahead of time.

2. **Enhance Client Communication**: Implement AI-driven communication tools to improve the frequency and quality of client interactions. Automating routine reporting tasks allows accountants to focus on higher-value conversations with clients. AI-generated insights can help tailor client communications, making them more relevant and

personalized, ultimately leading to better client engagement and satisfaction. Tools like ChatGPT can generate draft emails, client reports, and even answer routine client queries, ensuring that clients receive timely responses without delays.

3. **Expand CAS Offerings with AI**: Use AI to expand your firm's advisory services, offering clients data-driven financial forecasts and strategic planning. With AI's capacity to analyze vast amounts of data and simulate different financial scenarios, firms can develop comprehensive financial strategies that align with their clients' business goals. Tools like IBM Watson and Fathom can provide in-depth analytics and visualization, helping accountants deliver value-added insights that support their clients' growth objectives.

Conclusion/Takeaways

The story of accounting firms using AI is much like a pilot using advanced navigation tools. With AI as a strategic partner, accountants are equipped to provide clients with real-time, predictive insights, enabling them to stay ahead of potential challenges and seize opportunities before they even appear on the horizon. Firms that embrace these advancements will continue to build stronger client relationships and remain leaders in the accounting profession as AI technology continues to evolve.

AI has already transformed Client Advisory Services, but the potential for future growth is vast. By automating data analysis, forecasting, and reporting, AI allows firms to deliver deeper, more personalized insights and build stronger client relationships. As AI technology continues to evolve, firms that embrace these advancements will be better positioned to lead the accounting profession into the future.

As we explore the transformative role of AI in client advisory services, it's clear that client communication is a critical element of delivering value. In the next chapter, we'll delve into how AI-driven tools are enhancing client communication and engagement, offering real-time insights and improving client relationships.

References

AssetMark. (2024, April 26). AI for Advisors: How To Scale Marketing and Reporting To Unlock Growth Potential. Retrieved from https://www.assetmark.com/blog/ai-for-advisors

Botkeeper. AI-Powered Bookkeeping. Retrieved from https://www.botkeeper.com

IBM. Watson for Financial Strategy. Retrieved from https://www.ibm.com/watson

PwC. AI-Driven Advisory Tools. Retrieved from https://www.pwc.com

The Fast Mode. How To Elevate Client Advisory Services Through AI. Retrieved from https://www.thefastmode.com

Thomson Reuters. (2024, August 7). The Future of Tax and Accounting: Embracing AI with Caution. Retrieved from https://www.thomsonreuters.com

Tipalti. (2024). 2024 Guide to AI in Accounting: Trends, Use Cases, and Tools. Retrieved from https://tipalti.com/ai-accounting-guide

Vention. (2024). AI Adoption Statistics 2024: All Figures & Facts to Know. Retrieved from https://vention.io/ai-adoption-2024

Wolters Kluwer. CCH Axcess™ iQ. Retrieved from https://www.wolterskluwer.com

Yahoo Finance. (2024, June 25). AI Adoption Gains Traction Among Financial Advisors, Highlights Opportunities for Enhanced Client Service and Efficiency: Horsesmouth Survey. Retrieved from https://finance.yahoo.com

CHAPTER 11: AI-DRIVEN CLIENT COMMUNICATION AND ENGAGEMENT

Introduction: The Role of AI in Client Communication

Understanding AI: A Brief Overview

Artificial Intelligence (AI) might seem like a complex, futuristic technology, but at its core, it's about making computers perform tasks that typically require human intelligence—like recognizing patterns, making predictions, or even holding simple conversations. Think of AI as a very smart assistant that can handle repetitive tasks, allowing humans to focus on what they do best.

In accounting, AI can mean anything from using chatbots to automate routine inquiries to deploying advanced algorithms that predict financial trends. For example, imagine AI as a calculator that not only solves equations but also learns from past results to provide better suggestions in the future. This chapter explores how AI is transforming client communication, and a quick introduction to key AI concepts will help set the stage for the tools and strategies discussed in the chapter.

Client communication is a cornerstone of accounting. It directly impacts client satisfaction, retention, and long-term engagement. In today's digital world, firms must adapt their interaction methods to meet rising client expectations for real-time updates, personalized advice, and proactive solutions. This chapter looks at how AI is transforming client communication, improving the quality of interactions while helping firms offer more valuable services.

Core Concepts

To better understand how AI is enhancing client communication in accounting, we will explore several key concepts that illustrate its practical benefits and its potential to foster stronger client relationships.

1. AI-Powered Client Communication Tools

AI automates many routine tasks like appointment scheduling, document requests, and deadline reminders. Tools like chatbots and virtual assistants manage basic client queries, freeing up human advisors to focus on complex, value-added work. AI also analyzes client data to deliver personalized communications tailored to each client's unique needs.

2. Affordable AI Solutions for Small Firms

For smaller firms with limited resources, AI adoption can still be practical and impactful. There are several budget-friendly or even free versions of AI tools available that help streamline communication without requiring significant investment. For example, firms can utilize free versions of chatbots such as Tawk.to or ManyChat to automate basic client inquiries at no cost. These tools provide simple integration and help small firms enhance efficiency without straining their budgets.

To provide more clarity on affordability, here are some specific pricing examples as of this writing (2024):

- **Tawk.to**: Offers a completely free version with basic features that cover essential chatbot needs for client communication. Additional premium features are available for $15 per month.

- **ManyChat**: Provides a free version for small-scale automation needs, with a Pro plan starting at $15 per month, which includes more advanced automation and analytics features.

The cost-benefit analysis for these tools indicates that, even with premium options, the return on investment can be significant. For instance, a small firm that spends $15 per month on ManyChat could save several hours of manual work each week, allowing accountants to focus on more value-added tasks and potentially increasing client satisfaction and retention.

3. Gradual AI Adoption: Starting Small

Small firms might face challenges when adopting AI, like the cost of implementation or the lack of in-house IT support, or even a general fear of the technology. One approach is to gradually integrate AI, starting with one tool that addresses a common pain point—such as a chatbot to handle FAQs. By initially focusing on one affordable solution, firms can slowly build up their AI capabilities as they become more comfortable with the technology.

Another way for small firms to ease into AI is by working with third-party vendors or outsourcing AI services. Many vendors offer consulting services to help firms identify the right AI tools for their needs, ensuring the solutions are both affordable and tailored to the firm's capabilities. Partnering with these vendors can make AI adoption less daunting and more feasible.

Checklist: Steps for Small Firms to Ease Into AI Adoption

- **Identify Key Pain Points**: Determine which tasks could benefit most from automation (e.g., client inquiries, appointment scheduling).

- **Start Small**: Choose one affordable AI tool to solve a specific problem your firm is facing, like using a chatbot for FAQs.

- **Pilot Test the Tool**: Run a pilot to evaluate how well the tool integrates with current workflows and assess initial benefits.

- **Work with Vendors**: Consider consulting with third-party vendors for guidance on tool selection and implementation.

- **Scale Gradually**: Once comfortable, expand AI capabilities incrementally—add tools for real-time insights, improved tax preparation or predictive analytics (AI tools that use historical data to predict future outcomes and assist accountants in making proactive decisions) based on your firm's needs.

This checklist provides a quick reference for busy readers, making the gradual AI adoption process more actionable.

4. Chatbots and Virtual Assistants in Practice

Consider a small accounting firm that implemented Drift as a chatbot. Initially, they faced challenges in responding to client inquiries in a timely manner, especially during tax season. By integrating Drift, they managed to automate over 60% of common client questions, significantly reducing the workload on their staff. As a result, they could dedicate more time to addressing specific client needs, ultimately boosting client satisfaction.

Client Outcome: Implementing Drift helped the firm meet client inquiries faster and with greater accuracy. Clients appreciated the timely responses, which led to an increase in client retention by nearly 20% during the busy tax season.

Testimonial Quote: "Integrating Drift into our client communication process was a game changer. We managed to automate over 60% of our routine inquiries, freeing up our staff to focus on deeper client issues. The proactive engagement made our clients feel more valued and supported." - *John Dowling, Managing Partner, Small Accounting Firm*

5. AI Email Assistants for Mid-Sized Firms

AI-driven email tools like x.ai help schedule appointments and follow up with clients automatically. Imagine a mid-sized firm struggling with maintaining consistent follow-ups after tax consultations. By adopting x.ai, they streamlined their appointment scheduling process, ensuring no client went unattended, thus enhancing overall client engagement. The automation reduced the administrative burden, allowing staff to focus on strategic advisory services.

Client Outcome: By automating follow-ups with x.ai, the firm reported a 25% increase in client satisfaction. Clients felt reassured by timely communications, and the firm experienced a reduction in missed appointments, ultimately improving efficiency and client loyalty.

Testimonial Quote: "Using x.ai to automate our client follow-ups transformed our workflow. Our clients received timely updates, and our advisors had more time to focus on delivering strategic insights rather than managing appointments. The improvement in client satisfaction was immediate." - *Jane Smith, Partner, Mid-Sized CPA Firm*

Real-World Success Stories

Example: Fathom's AI-enhanced financial reporting tool generates real-time reports, allowing clients to access up-to-date information and make informed decisions.

A mid-sized firm utilizing Fathom experienced a 40% reduction in the time spent generating client reports. The automation of data visualization allowed the firm's advisors to spend more time interpreting the data for clients, rather than preparing it, leading to a noticeable improvement in client advisory services.

Example: A large multinational firm adopted Oracle AI Compliance to handle complex cross-border tax regulations. By leveraging AI, the firm was able to reduce compliance errors by 25%, saving significant costs related to manual compliance checks. The AI system monitored regulatory changes across multiple jurisdictions, alerting advisors to take necessary actions in real time. This integration of AI not only reduced risks but also enabled the firm to provide timely and informed cross-border tax planning, enhancing their global advisory services.

Client Outcome: The use of Oracle AI Compliance allowed the firm to achieve a 30% increase in efficiency in handling cross-border issues. Clients appreciated the proactive approach to regulatory compliance, resulting in improved client trust and increased client retention in international markets.

Testimonial Quote: "Oracle AI Compliance helped us navigate the complexities of cross-border regulations effortlessly. We reduced compliance errors by 25%, and the real-time updates allowed us to focus on delivering more value to our international clients." - *Emily Johnson, Director of Compliance, Multinational Accounting Firm*

Real-Time Insights and Reporting

Today's clients expect timely and accurate financial insights. Imagine AI as a financial GPS, always recalculating and keeping clients on the right path. AI processes client data in real-time, offering instant access to financial reports and dashboards, similar to how a GPS recalculates a route when there is traffic ahead. By eliminating manual delays, AI boosts transparency and fosters trust.

How could real-time financial insights improve the services your firm offers? Are there specific areas where immediate access to data would enhance decision-making for your clients?

AI-enabled dashboards, such as those from Fathom and Microsoft Power BI, transform how clients receive financial updates. These dashboards present real-time data in easy-to-understand visuals, giving clients ongoing insight into their financial health. Firms can set up alerts for major financial changes, helping clients react quickly to challenges.

Beyond real-time insights, AI-driven tools enable dynamic forecasting, allowing firms to simulate various financial scenarios based on current data. These simulations help accountants advise clients on potential outcomes, empowering them to make more informed decisions.

Future of AI-Driven Client Communication

The future of AI-driven client communication will likely involve even more advanced tools that enhance the client experience. One major area of growth is virtual assistants powered by AI that can manage all aspects of client communication, from handling basic inquiries to generating complex reports. As AI becomes more sophisticated, these virtual assistants will be able to perform tasks that previously required human intervention, further streamlining the client communication process.

Predictive communication will also become more prevalent. AI systems will be able to analyze large volumes of client data to identify potential needs or challenges before they arise. For example, an AI system could notify an accountant when a client's cash flow is likely to decrease, enabling the firm to offer financial planning advice before the client faces any significant issues. This kind of proactive engagement will enhance the value that firms provide to their clients.

Moreover, AI will likely integrate more deeply with other technologies, such as blockchain and machine learning, to ensure greater data security and accuracy in communication. This will be particularly important as clients become more concerned about privacy and data protection. AI tools that incorporate secure data transmission and storage methods will help firms reassure their clients that their financial information is safe.

Firms that stay ahead of these AI advancements will be well-positioned to deliver cutting-edge client communication services. As AI continues to evolve, it will further empower accounting professionals to offer timely, personalized, and proactive advice, solidifying the firm's role as a trusted partner in their client's financial journey.

Best Practices for AI-Driven Client Communication

1. Transparency

Firms should inform clients about the role AI plays in communication and data analysis. This builds trust and ensures clients understand the value AI adds to their services, particularly in areas like tax planning and financial forecasting.

Transparency is key when introducing AI into client interactions. Firms should clearly communicate which parts of their services involve AI and how these technologies benefit clients. For instance, when using AI tools to create financial forecasts or manage tax planning, explain how AI is improving accuracy and efficiency. By being open about AI's role, firms can alleviate concerns clients might have regarding automation and show them that these tools are being used to enhance—not replace—human expertise. Additionally, clients should always have a point of contact if they wish to discuss or clarify AI-generated insights with a human advisor.

2. Customization

AI must be leveraged to personalize client interactions. Tailoring reports, communication, and advice based on individual client profiles and data ensures more relevant and impactful interactions.

AI-driven personalization helps firms provide a higher level of client service by using client data to customize financial reports, insights, and communications. Tools like Crystal Knows analyze a client's communication style and provide recommendations on how to tailor messages accordingly, ensuring more effective engagement. For example, AI can identify key metrics that are most relevant to a client's industry or business model and highlight these in the reports, making them more valuable and actionable.

Customization extends beyond just reports—it also involves understanding each client's unique financial goals and challenges. AI can analyze a client's past interactions and financial data to predict their preferences and offer tailored advice. This kind of deep personalization helps in building stronger client relationships and enhances the value of advisory services by addressing the specific needs of each client.

3. Human Oversight

While AI can handle routine tasks, human expertise is essential for reviewing AI-generated reports and insights. Accountants should ensure that the recommendations provided by AI are accurate and align with the firm's strategic goals.

AI excels at processing data quickly and recognizing patterns, but it lacks the nuanced understanding and contextual knowledge that human accountants bring to the table. Human oversight is crucial in validating AI-generated outputs, particularly in complex financial scenarios where judgment calls are necessary. Accountants must review AI-generated reports to ensure that the recommendations align with a client's specific circumstances and broader financial strategy.

For example, while an AI tool might flag a particular transaction as unusual based on historical data, a human advisor can assess the context—such as a one-time investment or an unexpected revenue boost—that the AI may not fully understand. Combining AI's efficiency with human insight ensures that clients receive accurate and thoughtful advice.

Accountants should also serve as the bridge between AI insights and clients, providing explanations and additional context that helps clients understand and trust the recommendations being made. This collaborative approach strengthens client relationships and helps position AI as a supportive tool rather than a replacement for human expertise.

4. Integration with Client Advisory Services (CAS)

Integrating AI-driven insights with CAS offerings allows firms to deliver more proactive and strategic advice. AI dashboards can highlight key advisory opportunities, such as tax savings or investment options, that human advisors can act on.

Client Advisory Services are all about providing tailored, high-value insights that help clients grow their businesses, and AI can significantly enhance this process. AI tools like IBM Planning Analytics can identify trends in client data that may not be immediately obvious, such as cash flow issues or underperforming revenue streams. By integrating these AI-generated insights into CAS offerings, firms can provide clients with proactive strategies for addressing potential problems before they escalate.

For example, an AI dashboard might indicate that a client's inventory turnover ratio is declining compared to previous periods. Human advisors can then step in to provide strategies to optimize inventory levels or renegotiate supplier terms, ensuring that the client remains on track financially. This level of insight transforms CAS from a reactive to a proactive service, delivering greater value to clients.

AI integration also helps firms scale their advisory services without a proportional increase in workload. By automating data collection and preliminary analysis, AI frees advisors to focus on interpreting data and offering strategic recommendations. This efficiency gain is particularly valuable for smaller firms looking to expand their CAS offerings without significantly increasing their staff.

Trends in AI-Driven Client Communication

1. Natural Language Processing (NLP)

NLP is increasingly used to facilitate natural, human-like conversations between AI systems and clients. AI-powered chatbots can respond to complex questions regarding tax filings, audits, or financial planning, delivering faster service without human intervention.

NLP technology has advanced significantly, enabling chatbots and virtual assistants to understand and respond to nuanced client queries. For example, tools like ChatGPT and Google's Dialogflow are being used by firms to automate client interactions with a conversational feel that mirrors human advisors. These chatbots can handle inquiries about tax deadlines, refund status, or even provide explanations of financial statements, freeing up human accountants to focus on more complex tasks. By facilitating round-the-clock support, NLP-driven AI helps improve client satisfaction and engagement.

2. AI-Enhanced Reporting and Dashboards

AI-powered dashboards and reporting systems are providing clients with real-time, data-driven insights into their financial performance. These systems offer greater transparency, allowing clients to monitor key metrics and receive regular updates without needing to wait for scheduled reports.

AI-enhanced dashboards, like those offered by Tableau and Fathom, not only present data but also provide context and insights that are easy for clients to understand. For example, an AI-enhanced dashboard might not just show a decrease in cash flow but also suggest potential causes and recommend corrective actions. This kind of actionable insight is invaluable to clients who rely on timely and accurate data to make strategic decisions. By making financial information more accessible and understandable, AI-enhanced dashboards build trust between the firm and the client, positioning the accountant as a proactive advisor rather than just a service provider.

3. Predictive Communication

With predictive capabilities, AI tools can anticipate when clients may need assistance, such as forecasting cash flow dips or tax deadlines. Predictive communication ensures that accountants can engage proactively, offering solutions before clients even realize they need them.

AI-driven predictive communication tools analyze historical and real-time data to identify potential challenges or opportunities that may affect clients. For instance, AI can monitor cash flow patterns and predict potential shortfalls, allowing accountants to proactively offer strategies to mitigate financial stress. This kind of proactive support demonstrates a deep understanding of the client's needs, fostering trust and loyalty.

AI-based predictive tools also help firms anticipate clients' questions during major financial events—such as tax season or regulatory changes—enabling them to prepare responses and outreach campaigns ahead of time. This preparedness enhances the client experience by providing timely, relevant information when it's needed most.

AI-Driven Communication and Client Satisfaction

AI-driven communication has a profound effect on client satisfaction. By offering real-time insights and responding quickly to inquiries, AI-powered tools can address one of the most common client complaints—delays in service. Automation also ensures consistent and reliable communication, which is crucial for maintaining trust, particularly when handling sensitive financial matters.

In addition, AI tools allow firms to provide more personalized services. By analyzing individual client data, AI can tailor recommendations, reports, and forecasts based on each client's unique financial situation. Clients value this level of customization, as it demonstrates that the firm is not just providing generic solutions but is genuinely focused on helping them achieve their specific goals.

AI also helps firms anticipate client needs, enabling proactive communication. For example, AI can monitor a client's financial performance and flag potential risks or opportunities, prompting advisors to reach out with tailored advice. This proactive approach not only enhances the client's experience but also strengthens the client-advisor relationship by demonstrating the firm's commitment to their long-term financial success.

Overall, clients are more likely to stay loyal to firms that leverage AI-driven communication, as these tools deliver faster responses, greater transparency, and more relevant insights. As AI technology continues to evolve, firms that integrate these tools into their communication strategy will see a significant boost in client satisfaction and retention.

Actionable Insights

1. **Start Small with AI Tools**: Firms, especially small and mid-sized, should begin their AI adoption journey with affordable, simple tools that address immediate needs, such as chatbots for routine inquiries. This approach ensures minimal disruption while building familiarity with AI's capabilities.

2. **Leverage Real-Time Data**: Use AI-driven dashboards to offer clients real-time financial insights. This allows firms to provide a higher level of service and strengthens the firm's role as a proactive advisor.

3. **Prioritize Customization**: AI can enhance client communication by delivering personalized interactions based on client data. Tools like Crystal Knows help firms analyze communication preferences, making client interactions more relevant and impactful.

4. **Focus on Ethical AI Use**: When implementing AI tools, consider ethical issues like data privacy and transparency. Firms must ensure AI usage aligns with compliance

standards and that clients understand the role AI plays in their services.

5. **Pilot Test and Scale**: Run pilot tests with selected AI tools to ensure they integrate smoothly and deliver desired benefits. Based on success, scale AI usage to cover more complex functions like predictive analytics for strategic advisory.

These actionable insights provide firms with a roadmap to navigate AI adoption effectively and maximize its impact on client communication.

Conclusion and Takeaways

AI has the potential to revolutionize client communication for accounting firms of all sizes. From automating routine tasks with chatbots to delivering real-time insights with advanced dashboards, AI tools can enhance efficiency, deepen client relationships, and create opportunities for proactive advisory services. The key is to start small, gradually integrating AI tools that align with your firm's needs and capabilities.

While the benefits of AI are clear, it is equally important to consider ethical practices, transparency, and compliance throughout the implementation process. By adopting a strategic approach to AI, firms can ensure they are not only leveraging technology to improve service quality but also building trust and maintaining high ethical standards with their clients.

After exploring how AI transforms client communication and engagement, we see the critical role of data-driven insights in fostering trust and delivering personalized experiences. Yet, the impact of AI extends far beyond client interactions. As accounting firms strive to provide strategic guidance, the ability to harness data analytics becomes essential to informed financial decision-making. In the following chapter, we'll examine how AI-powered data analytics equips accounting professionals with the insights needed to advise clients confidently, drive firm strategy, and make proactive, evidence-based financial decisions that align with evolving business goals.

References

Accenture. (2023). *Personalization Pulse Check*. Retrieved from https://www.accenture.com/us-en/insights/interactive/personalization-pulse-check

Allied Market Research. (2023). *Artificial Intelligence Market Outlook - 2030*. Retrieved from https://www.alliedmarketresearch.com/artificial-intelligence-market

Capgemini. (2023). *AI in Customer Experience*. Retrieved from https://www.capgemini.com/research/ai-in-customer-experience/

Gartner. (2023). *Gartner Predicts 70% of Customer Interactions Will Involve Emerging Technologies by 2025*. Retrieved from https://www.gartner.com/en/newsroom/press-releases/2023

Grand View Research. (2021). *Predictive Analytics Market Size & Share Report, 2021-2028*. Retrieved from https://www.grandviewresearch.com/industry-analysis/predictive-analytics-market

Juniper Research. (2023). *Conversational AI: Market Trends & Forecasts 2023-2027*. Retrieved from https://www.juniperresearch.com/researchstore

MIT Technology Review. (2023). *The AI Effect: How Artificial Intelligence is Impacting Customer Service*. Retrieved from https://www.technologyreview.com/2023/ai-effect-customer-service

PwC. (2023). *AI Predictions 2023*. Retrieved from https://www.pwc.com/gx/en/issues/technology/ai-predictions.html

Salesforce. (2023). *State of Marketing Report*. Retrieved from https://www.salesforce.com/resources/articles/state-of-marketing/

Servion Global Solutions. (2023). *AI will power 95% of customer interactions by 2025*. Retrieved from https://www.servion.com/ai-customer-interactions

SmartAsset. (2024). *How AI Is Changing the Financial Advisor Landscape*. Retrieved from https://smartasset.com/financial-advisor/ai-changing-financial-advisors

Thomson Reuters. (2024). *The future of tax and accounting: Embracing AI with caution*. Retrieved from https://www.thomsonreuters.com/en/resources.html

Tipalti. (2024). *2024 Guide to AI in Accounting: Trends, Use Cases and Tools*. Retrieved from https://tipalti.com/guide-ai-in-accounting/

Vention. (2024). *AI Adoption Statistics 2024: All Figures & Facts to Know*. Retrieved from https://www.vention.com/ai-adoption-statistics

Virtasant. (2024). *AI-Driven Customer Engagement: Strategies from Amazon, Nike, and Hilton*. Retrieved from https://www.virtasant.com/customer-engagement-strategies

Zendesk. (2024). *59 AI customer service statistics for 2024*. Retrieved from https://www.zendesk.com/blog/ai-customer-service-statistics/

CHAPTER 12: AI AND DATA ANALYTICS IN FINANCIAL DECISION-MAKING

Introduction: AI Empowering Data Analytics in Finance

Data analytics has long been an essential tool in accounting, helping businesses understand their financial performance and make informed decisions. The introduction of Artificial Intelligence (AI) has further empowered data analytics, allowing firms to process vast amounts of financial data, identify trends, and generate deeper insights. This chapter delves into how AI-powered data analytics tools are transforming financial decision-making, focusing on trend analysis, risk management, and resource optimization.

Core Concepts

1. AI-Driven Data Analytics for Financial Insights

AI-powered analytics tools can rapidly analyze massive amounts of financial data, providing firms with actionable insights to make smarter decisions. These tools help accountants spot trends, identify patterns, and predict future financial scenarios, ultimately improving financial performance and decision-making.

Pattern Recognition and Trend Analysis

AI tools are capable of detecting patterns in financial data, such as recurring expenses or revenue trends. By recognizing these patterns, businesses gain a deeper understanding of their financial health and can make proactive adjustments. For instance, AI-powered trend analysis helps firms identify cost-saving opportunities and potential growth areas before they become apparent to human analysts.

Real-World Example: Microsoft Power BI is a widely used business intelligence platform that integrates with accounting systems to offer real-time dashboards and visual reports. Power BI's AI capabilities allow firms to make data-driven financial decisions and monitor key performance indicators (KPIs) in real time.

Incorporating AI-driven data analytics can lead to significant improvements in efficiency. Studies show that 54% of executives say AI solutions have already increased productivity in their businesses, helping firms make data-backed decisions quickly and confidently.

Imagine a small accounting firm struggling to keep up with the increasing workload of analyzing client data. The introduction of AI analytics tools transformed their day-to-day operations. Instead of spending hours manually processing spreadsheets, the firm now relies on AI to highlight key trends and generate insights, enabling professionals to focus on advisory services that deliver value to their clients.

2. Predictive Analytics for Financial Forecasting

AI's predictive analytics capabilities enable firms to anticipate future financial performance based on historical data. Predictive models allow businesses to forecast revenue, detect cash flow issues, and identify potential risks, supporting proactive financial planning.

Forecasting Financial Performance

AI tools model different financial scenarios, helping businesses prepare for both best- and worst-case outcomes. This supports decisions regarding investments, budgeting, and risk management. Predictive analytics not only enables firms to identify risks but also allows them to take advantage of future opportunities. For instance, AI-driven predictive models can help firms estimate future revenue, improving planning and budgeting processes.

The global predictive analytics market is projected to reach $41.52 billion by 2028, growing at a CAGR of 24.5% from 2021 to 2028. This indicates the increasing importance of predictive capabilities in business strategies.

Real-World Example: CCH Axcess™ iQ uses AI-driven predictive analytics to provide real-time insights into potential financial risks and opportunities based on the client's tax return details. By analyzing return data and comparing it against new or pending legislation, iQ helps firms deliver more value to clients by proactively recommending actions to take to improve the client's tax situation.

Consider an accountant preparing for an important meeting with a client. In the past, they would have manually gathered data and extrapolated trends—a time-consuming and error-prone process. With CCH Axcess iQ, the firm can more quickly prepare for the client meeting and offer proactive recommendations to the client.

3. AI for Operational Optimization and Cost Reduction

AI tools help firms optimize operations by identifying inefficiencies and recommending strategies for improving financial processes. By detecting wasteful spending patterns or underperforming investments, for example, AI tools contribute to more effective resource allocation and cost reduction.

Cost Savings through Data Analytics

AI tools can analyze financial data, helping businesses cut costs by identifying inefficiencies. Over time, this leads to improved profitability and resource optimization. AI can reveal inefficiencies in spending, such as overlapping expenses, enabling firms to make data-driven changes to improve cash flow and profitability, as one example.

Real-World Example: IBM Watson uses AI-driven analytics to help firms optimize operations, offering actionable insights that enhance efficiency and reduce operational expenses. AI adoption is expected to automate routine tasks, freeing up as much as four hours per week for each professional in tax and accounting firms.

Picture an accounting firm that struggled with high operational costs due to inefficient processes. After adopting AI, the firm discovered overlapping software subscriptions and recurring vendor expenses that went unnoticed for months. By eliminating these inefficiencies, the firm significantly improved profitability, demonstrating how AI can identify and eliminate wasteful spending.

Best Practices for AI-Driven Financial Decision-Making

1. Leverage Predictive Analytics

Firms should utilize AI-powered predictive analytics tools to model various financial scenarios – for the firm and for its clients. These models help businesses anticipate risks, allowing them to make more informed, proactive decisions. In a survey, 61% of marketers identified AI as the most important aspect of their data strategy, underlining the critical role of predictive analytics in decision-making.

2. Incorporate AI for Resource Optimization

Use AI to detect inefficiencies and optimize resource allocation. By analyzing historical financial data, AI tools can suggest cost-saving measures that streamline operations and improve profitability. Firms using AI for customer insights and personalization have seen a 20% increase in customer satisfaction, which also indicates its value in optimizing services and resource allocation.

3. Ensure Human Oversight in AI Decision-Making

While AI can analyze vast datasets and generate insights, human review remains crucial. Firms should incorporate a mix of AI-driven insights and human expertise to ensure the accuracy and applicability of financial decisions. Human accountants can verify AI-generated outputs, providing the necessary contextual understanding that ensures decisions align with strategic goals.

A senior accountant at a mid-sized firm recalls a scenario where an AI tool flagged a transaction as potentially fraudulent. Upon review, the accountant realized it was an approved one-time vendor payment. This instance highlights the need for human oversight in AI-driven decision-making to avoid false positives and ensure nuanced understanding that as of today, can only be handled by humans.

4. Integrate AI with Client Advisory Services (CAS)

AI-driven insights should be integrated with CAS offerings to provide clients with real-time financial advice. AI-generated dashboards allow accountants to offer strategic advice, optimizing client performance and satisfaction. In the next 18 months, 83% of financial advisors believe AI will have a direct, measurable, and consistent impact on the client-advisor relationship, making it essential for firms to leverage these tools for enhanced client services.

REAL-WORLD EXAMPLES/CASE STUDIES

GreenTree Financial Case Study

GreenTree Financial, a mid-sized accounting firm, wanted to enhance its financial forecasting and decision-making processes using AI-driven data analytics. GreenTree struggled with inconsistent cash flow forecasting and difficulty identifying cost-saving opportunities. Their manual financial reporting processes were time-consuming and error-prone, leading to missed opportunities for operational efficiency.

So, what did they do? GreenTree implemented AI-powered analytics tools, including predictive models for cash flow management and real-time expense monitoring.

By using AI, GreenTree was able to improve cash flow forecasts by 25% and reduce operational costs by 15% within the first year. The firm now relies on AI-driven insights to offer more accurate financial advice to clients, increasing client satisfaction and retention.

One of GreenTree's accountants shared how their AI system flagged a seasonal dip in cash flow early enough to help a client secure a short-term loan with favorable terms. Without the AI's foresight, this client might have faced significant financial strain. Such success stories illustrate how AI empowers accountants to make timely, strategic interventions for clients.

The chart below shows the difference between using manual processes versus AI-driven processes for Forecast Accuracy and the amount of data that can be reviewed for risk detection.

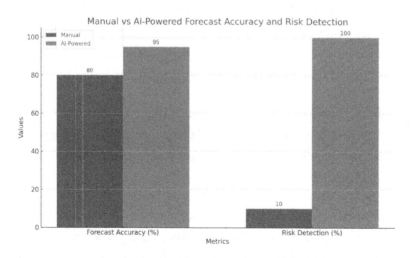

Figure 18 Manual and AI-Powered Forecast Accuracy and Percent of Data Reviewed for Risk Detection

Getting Started with AI in Financial Decision-Making

To help firms take the first steps in integrating AI, consider these simple, actionable steps:

1. **Assess Needs:** Start by identifying the areas where your firm could benefit most from AI. Are you struggling with manual financial analysis? Do you need more accurate forecasting?

2. **Choose a Tool:** Based on your needs, select an AI tool that aligns with your business objectives. Consider factors such as ease of integration with existing systems, cost, and scalability. Tools like Microsoft Power BI or IBM Watson can be great starting points.

3. **Train Your Team:** Provide training to your staff to ensure they understand how to use the AI tools effectively. This will also help alleviate resistance to change by demonstrating the value AI can bring to their daily workflows.

4. **Start Small:** Begin by implementing AI in one area, such as forecasting or operational optimization. Gradually expand its use as your team becomes comfortable and you begin to see the benefits.

5. **Monitor and Adjust:** Regularly review the AI's outputs and assess the impact on your firm's performance. Be open to adjustments based on feedback from both the AI system and your staff.

Actionable Insights

1. Adopt AI-Driven Predictive Models

Firms should adopt AI-driven models to improve cash flow forecasts and detect potential financial risks. Predictive analytics provides valuable insights that allow firms to anticipate issues before they arise, leading to proactive decision-making.

2. Use AI for Cost Reduction Strategies

AI tools can identify inefficiencies, helping firms reduce costs and optimize resources. Firms that adopt AI for cost management can improve profitability by detecting wasteful spending and suggesting areas for resource reallocation.

3. Enhance Client Advisory Services with AI

Firms should integrate AI-driven data analytics with their client advisory services to offer more personalized and actionable financial advice. By analyzing client data, AI helps firms tailor advice and improve client satisfaction. AI-driven insights can also help identify new opportunities for clients, such as potential investments or financial strategies that align with their business goals.

Conclusion/Takeaways

AI and data analytics have revolutionized financial decision-making, empowering firms to make smarter, data-driven choices. From predicting cash flow trends to optimizing operational costs, AI tools provide accountants with deeper insights and more accurate forecasts. Firms that integrate AI into their financial processes can expect improved profitability, better client advisory services, and enhanced operational efficiency. The key lies in balancing AI-driven insights with human expertise to make well-rounded, informed decisions that add value for your clients.

As we've explored, data analytics is reshaping financial decision-making by offering unprecedented insights, accuracy, and efficiency. The next horizon is to apply similar AI-driven rigor to another rapidly growing area of focus: Environmental, Social, and Governance (ESG) practices. Today, firms are not only responsible for financial performance but also for demonstrating accountability in these critical domains. Just as AI enhances our ability to parse financial data and make data-informed decisions, it can also play a transformative role in how organizations approach ESG. In the following chapter, we'll delve into how AI is helping firms navigate complex ESG requirements, automate reporting processes, and ultimately position themselves as socially responsible leaders in an increasingly transparent world.

References

Accenture. (2023). *Personalization pulse check*. Retrieved from https://www.accenture.com

Allied Market Research. (2023). *Artificial intelligence market outlook - 2030*. Retrieved from https://www.alliedmarketresearch.com/artificial-intelligence-market

Capgemini. (2023). *AI in customer experience*. Retrieved from https://www.capgemini.com/resources/ai-driven-customer-experience-transformation

Gartner. (2023). *Gartner predicts 70% of customer interactions will involve emerging technologies by 2025*. Retrieved from https://www.gartner.com/en/newsroom

Grand View Research. (2021). *Predictive analytics market size & share report, 2021-2028*. Retrieved from https://www.grandviewresearch.com/industry-analysis/predictive-analytics-market

IBM Watson for Operational Efficiency. *IBM Watson: AI-powered operational efficiency tool*. Retrieved from https://www.ibm.com/products/decision-optimization-for-watson-studio

Juniper Research. (2023). *Conversational AI: Market trends & forecasts 2023-2027*. Retrieved from https://www.juniperresearch.com/press/spend-over-conversational-commerce-to-near-135bn

Microsoft Power BI. *Power BI: Business intelligence tools for real-time data analysis*. Retrieved from https://powerbi.microsoft.com

PwC. (2023). *AI predictions 2023*. Retrieved from https://www.pwc.com/gx/en/issues/data-and-analytics/artificial-intelligence.html

Salesforce. (2023). State of marketing report. Retrieved from https://www.salesforce.com/resources/research-reports/state-of-marketing/

SmartAsset. (2024). *How AI is changing the financial advisor landscape*. Retrieved from https://www.smartasset.com

Thomson Reuters. (2024). *The future of tax and accounting: Embracing AI with caution.* Retrieved from https://tax.thomsonreuters.com

Tipalti. (2024). *2024 guide to AI in accounting: Trends, use cases and tools.* Retrieved from https://tipalti.com

Vention. (2024). *AI adoption statistics 2024: All figures & facts to know.* Retrieved from https://vention.io

Virtasant. (2024). *AI-driven customer engagement: Strategies from Amazon, Nike, and Hilton.* Retrieved from https://www.virtasant.com

Wolters Kluwer CCH Axcess™ iQ. *CCH Axcess™ iQ: AI-powered predictive analytics tool.* Retrieved from https://www.wolterskluwer.com

Zendesk. (2024). *59 AI customer service statistics for 2024.* Retrieved from https://www.zendesk.com/blog/ai-customer-service/

CHAPTER 13: AI FOR ENVIRONMENTAL, SOCIAL, AND GOVERNANCE (ESG) REPORTING

Introduction: AI Transforming ESG Reporting

As environmental, social, and governance (ESG) reporting becomes a critical concern for stakeholders, businesses, and regulators, companies are increasingly expected to provide transparent and accurate data regarding their sustainability efforts. However, the complex nature of ESG data collection and reporting poses significant challenges for firms. AI is playing a transformative role by automating these processes, improving data accuracy, and ensuring compliance with evolving regulations. This chapter explores how AI-driven tools are being used to streamline ESG reporting, enhance transparency, and offer real-time insights into corporate sustainability.

Core Concepts

1. The Growing Importance of ESG Reporting

ESG reporting is increasingly important for businesses to align with investor expectations and regulatory requirements. However, the complexity of gathering and analyzing ESG data, such as carbon emissions or labor practices, makes manual processes inefficient and prone to errors.

- **Demand for ESG Data**: The demand for ESG data is increasing due to regulatory pressure and stakeholder demands. Public companies face expanding requirements for ESG disclosures, impacting supply chains and smaller private companies. New regulations like the Corporate Sustainability Reporting Directive (CSRD) in Europe are driving the need for accurate ESG reporting.

- **Challenges in ESG Data Collection**: Companies face demands to track diverse metrics such as energy usage, employee diversity, and governance policies. AI-driven tools automate data collection and streamline the reporting process, reducing human error and improving accuracy.

Real-World Example: Wolters Kluwer's Enablon integrates AI to automate ESG data collection, allowing businesses to efficiently track their sustainability efforts and ensure compliance with evolving regulations. Enablon provides end-to-end solutions for ESG management, including data integration, automated reporting, predictive analytics, and risk assessment. It offers tools to identify potential risks and opportunities in sustainability initiatives, making it easier for companies to stay compliant and optimize their ESG performance.

Consider a large multinational company attempting to comply with the latest ESG standards. Before adopting AI, data collection required input from multiple departments, each with its own system and processes. With AI-driven solutions, the company automated data gathering and validation, cutting down the time spent on manual tasks and enhancing overall accuracy. This transformation allowed the firm to focus on improving its sustainability performance rather than just meeting regulatory requirements.

2. Automating ESG Data Collection and Reporting

AI-powered platforms automatically gather ESG data from various sources, such as supplier databases, environmental sensors, or internal reporting systems. These tools reduce the burden of manual data entry and ensure that reports are both timely and accurate.

- **AI Efficiency**: AI automates data collection and reporting tasks, reducing manual effort and improving accuracy. For instance, AI tools streamline workflows by automating data cleansing and survey response generation, enhancing efficiency.

- **Integration with Existing Systems**: AI platforms link to financial, supply chain, and environmental systems to collect necessary data, ensuring comprehensive ESG data coverage.

Real-World Example: IBM's AI for ESG Compliance uses AI to automate ESG metrics tracking and ensure compliance with global sustainability standards, continuously updating regulatory databases and alerting firms to changes in compliance requirements.

Table: Adoption of AI in ESG Reporting

Year	Development
2020	Initial integration of AI in basic ESG data collection
2023	Increased adoption due to regulatory pressures (e.g., CSRD)
2024	Widespread use of AI for real-time monitoring and predictive analytics

Table 3 Adoption of AI in ESG Reporting

3. Leveraging Predictive Analytics for ESG Trends

AI tools can use predictive analytics to forecast future ESG performance, allowing firms to anticipate sustainability challenges and proactively adjust their strategies. Predictive models also help companies align with long-term sustainability goals, such as net-zero carbon targets.

- **Predictive Capabilities**: AI's predictive analytics can forecast future ESG performance, helping organizations manage risks proactively. AI-driven tools automate benchmarking against industry standards, providing insights into relative performance.

For example, a company aiming for net-zero emissions by 2035 used AI-driven predictive analytics to model different pathways to achieve this goal. The AI system provided real-time insights into how various decisions, such as switching energy suppliers or investing in carbon offsets, would impact the company's progress.

Best Practices for AI-Driven ESG Reporting

1. Leverage Predictive Analytics for ESG Trends

AI tools can use predictive analytics to forecast future ESG performance, allowing firms to anticipate sustainability challenges and proactively adjust their strategies. Predictive models also help companies align with long-term sustainability goals, such as net-zero carbon targets.

2. Ensure Data Integrity with AI Validation

AI platforms should validate ESG data by comparing it to historical benchmarks or industry standards, ensuring accuracy and preventing greenwashing. AI enhances data accuracy by automating validation processes and detecting errors, providing a foundation for reliable ESG reporting.

A firm using AI validation discovered discrepancies between reported and actual energy consumption. The AI flagged these discrepancies, prompting a review that ultimately improved data accuracy and transparency, which, in turn, helped build trust with investors.

3. Automate Compliance Checks

AI-driven tools can automate compliance checks against standards such as the Global Reporting Initiative (GRI) and Task Force on Climate-related Financial Disclosures (TCFD). Firms should regularly update AI systems to keep pace with changing regulatory environments.

- **Adaptability**: Platforms like KEY ESG adapt to evolving regulations, ensuring compliance readiness. AI also enables real-time monitoring, offering insights and alerts to stay compliant with new guidelines.

4. Incorporate AI into Client Advisory Services (CAS)

Firms that offer ESG-related advisory services should leverage AI-driven insights to provide clients with actionable advice on improving sustainability practices. For example, AI-driven dashboards can highlight areas where clients can reduce emissions or improve governance practices.

A mid-sized consulting firm incorporated AI-driven ESG analytics into their advisory services. By using AI to generate tailored reports for each client, they were able to offer more targeted recommendations, helping clients improve their ESG performance and earn higher sustainability ratings.

REAL-WORLD EXAMPLES/CASE STUDIES

GreenTree Financial Case Study

Background: GreenTree Financial, a mid-sized accounting firm, sought to improve its ESG reporting processes to align with investor demands and regulatory requirements.

Challenge: GreenTree struggled with manual data collection for ESG metrics, which was time-consuming and prone to inaccuracies.

AI Solution: GreenTree implemented an AI-powered platform that automated ESG data collection, validated data against benchmarks, and ensured compliance with global standards such as the GRI and TCFD.

Outcome: With the AI tool in place, GreenTree reduced ESG reporting time by 40% and improved the accuracy of its sustainability reports. The firm was also able to provide clients with more transparent and verifiable ESG data, boosting client trust and satisfaction.

Additional Insight: One of GreenTree's clients, a manufacturing company, appreciated the firm's proactive use of AI in ESG reporting, which allowed the client to track their energy usage and make real-time adjustments. This level of transparency strengthened the client's relationship with GreenTree and led to additional consulting opportunities.

Actionable Insights

1. Use AI for Real-Time ESG Monitoring

Firms should adopt AI platforms to monitor ESG metrics in real-time, allowing them to track sustainability efforts continuously. This enables proactive adjustments to sustainability strategies based on real-time insights rather than waiting for periodic reviews.

- **Real-Time Monitoring**: AI provides real-time updates and insights into ESG performance, enabling swift responses to emerging issues.

2. Improve Transparency with AI Validation

Ensure that AI tools validate and cross-check ESG data to enhance transparency. Firms that provide accurate and reliable ESG reports are more likely to gain the trust of investors and regulators.

3. Automate ESG Compliance Reporting

Automating ESG compliance through AI can save time and reduce the risk of non-compliance penalties. Firms should ensure that their AI systems are equipped to automatically update compliance standards as regulations evolve.

Getting Started with AI for ESG Reporting

To help firms begin their journey in implementing AI for ESG reporting, here are practical steps to follow:

1. **Assess Needs and Set Objectives**: Determine the key ESG metrics your firm needs to track and the objectives for implementing AI in ESG reporting.

2. **Choose the Right Platform**: Research and select an AI-driven platform that fits your firm's requirements, such as Enablon, IBM AI for ESG Compliance, or KEY ESG.

3. **Data Collection Gap Analysis**: Evaluate existing data collection processes and identify gaps that AI can address, such as manual data entry or lack of integration between systems.

4. **Pilot Implementation**: Start with a small-scale implementation to test the chosen platform and its capabilities before expanding firm-wide.

5. **Staff Training and Buy-In**: Educate staff on how to use the AI tools and clearly communicate the benefits to gain buy-in from stakeholders.

Cost Considerations and ROI

Adopting AI for ESG reporting involves costs related to purchasing software, integrating it with existing systems, and training staff. However, the return on investment (ROI) can be substantial when considering the efficiency gains, reduced risk of non-compliance penalties, and enhanced ability to provide transparent ESG data.

- **Initial Costs**: Firms should be prepared for an initial investment that includes software licensing, integration fees, and possible infrastructure upgrades.

- **Efficiency Gains**: AI reduces the time required for data collection and reporting by automating repetitive tasks, leading to significant savings in labor costs.

- **Long-Term ROI**: Improved accuracy in ESG reporting and proactive compliance management can help firms avoid costly penalties and enhance their reputation, leading to better investor relations and potential new business opportunities.

Conclusion/Takeaways

AI is revolutionizing ESG reporting by automating data collection, enhancing transparency, and ensuring compliance with evolving regulations. As sustainability becomes a higher priority for businesses and regulators alike, AI-driven tools can help firms provide accurate, transparent, and timely ESG reports, enabling them to meet the expectations of stakeholders while improving overall sustainability performance.

As ESG reporting becomes more automated through AI tools, firms must also navigate the complexities of scaling AI across departments. In the next chapter, we will explore how mid-sized firms can successfully scale AI solutions to enhance operations, improve service offerings, and remain competitive.

References

Algorithma. (2024). *Advancing ESG reporting with AI solutions*. Retrieved from https://www.algorithma.se/our-latest-thinking/advancing-esg-reporting-with-ai-solutions.

Deloitte. (n.d.). *AI-powered ESG reporting tools*. Retrieved from https://www2.deloitte.com/us/en.html.

EcoSkills Academy. (2024). *How AI and ESG reporting technology shape sustainability*. Retrieved from https://ecoskills.academy/how-ai-and-esg-reporting-technology-shape-sustainability-from-2024-onwards/.

IBM. (n.d.). *AI for ESG compliance*. Retrieved from https://www.ibm.com/impact/2023-ibm-impact-report.

Journal of Accountancy. (2024). *Why sustainability information matters to CPAs*. Retrieved from: https://www.journalofaccountancy.com/issues/2024/jun/why-sustainability-information-matters-to-cpas.html

KEY ESG. (2024). *KEY ESG's use of AI: How we streamline ESG reporting*. Retrieved from https://www.keyesg.com/article/key-esgs-use-of-ai.

PwC. (2022, June 2). Responsible AI and ESG: The power of trusted collaborations. Retrieved from https://www.pwc.com/us/en/tech-effect/ai-analytics/the-power-of-pairing-responsible-ai-and-esg.html

Sweep. (2024). Using AI to simplify your ESG reporting disclosures. Retrieved from https://www.sweep.net/insights/using-ai-to-simplify-your-esg-reporting-disclosures.

WWT. (2023, November 28). Revolutionizing ESG reporting with AI: A critical move for today's businesses. Retrieved from https://www.wwt.com/article/revolutionizing-esg-reporting-with-ai-a-critical-move-for-todays-businesses.

Wolters Kluwer. (n.d.). Enablon ESG application. Retrieved from https://www.wolterskluwer.com/en/solutions/enablon

CHAPTER 14: SCALING AI SOLUTIONS IN MID-SIZED FIRMS

Introduction

As mid-sized accounting firms grow, so does the demand for efficient operations and enhanced client services. AI technologies offer a promising path forward by automating routine tasks, improving decision-making, and delivering personalized client services. However, successfully scaling AI across various departments presents unique challenges. This chapter explores how mid-sized firms can overcome these obstacles by effectively implementing AI, following best practices, and leveraging key tools to scale their operations.

Mid-sized firms face challenges distinct from those faced by smaller or larger counterparts. They must be agile enough to innovate while managing growing client expectations and operational complexities. AI can address these issues by enhancing productivity, improving accuracy, and enabling accountants to focus on higher-value tasks. Effectively scaling AI helps firms optimize workflows, reduce redundancies, and elevate client satisfaction. However, achieving successful AI integration requires understanding both the opportunities and the barriers that exist.

The growth of mid-sized accounting firms brings increased complexities, from meeting client expectations to managing regulatory compliance. AI helps balance these demands by streamlining operations, reducing errors, and enabling more strategic client interactions. By carefully selecting and implementing AI tools, mid-sized firms can make meaningful progress toward scalability without losing their unique value proposition. This chapter outlines the tools and practices that can make AI a transformative force in accounting.

Core Concepts

1. Industry Insights: AI Adoption in Mid-Sized Firms

Recent studies reveal that 71% of mid-tier managing partners expect their firms to invest in artificial intelligence (AI) over the next three years, while 38% of mid-tier firms have already made investments, with three-quarters of these being firms with more than 20 partners. These insights underscore the importance of selecting the right tools to ensure successful implementation and scaling across the organization. Additionally, these numbers reveal a growing recognition within the industry that AI is no longer a futuristic luxury but a necessity for sustaining competitive advantage. Firms that adopt AI early position themselves to offer superior client services and increased operational efficiency.

Moreover, 69% of mid-tier firms plan to invest more in virtual infrastructure over the next three years, indicating a trend toward enhanced technological capabilities that support AI adoption. The combination of AI and virtual infrastructure can provide mid-sized firms with the agility they need to respond quickly to market changes and deliver client services with precision and confidence. Embracing AI technologies not only meets current demands but also future-proofs firms against emerging challenges, ensuring they remain relevant and competitive in a rapidly evolving landscape.

The trend toward virtual infrastructure and cloud-based solutions is pivotal for firms needing to scale without the burden of heavy upfront technology investments. This evolution makes advanced AI tools accessible to more firms and enables seamless integration with existing systems. The flexibility offered by cloud-based AI tools, such as QuickBooks and Xero, allows mid-sized firms to enhance operational capabilities without incurring the prohibitive costs associated with traditional IT infrastructure.

2. Key AI Tools for Mid-Sized Firms

Selecting the right AI tools is critical for mid-sized firms to scale successfully. These tools should automate routine processes while providing meaningful insights that enhance both operational efficiency and client satisfaction. Below are some of the most effective AI tools to help mid-sized firms streamline their operations and expand their service offerings.

- **CCH Axcess™ iQ**: A predictive analytics tool designed to help firms anticipate client needs and streamline tax compliance. It offers real-time insights, helping firms manage client risks and optimize advisory services. By proactively identifying areas of potential risk and opportunity, CCH Axcess™ iQ empowers firms to provide more personalized client services, resulting in stronger client relationships and increased loyalty.

- **Xero**: An AI-powered accounting platform that automates financial reporting, tax filings, and reconciliations, improving operational efficiency while reducing manual errors. Xero's machine learning capabilities allow it to recognize patterns over time, making financial management tasks not only faster but also more accurate. The platform's user-friendly interface and real-time updates make it a valuable tool for mid-sized firms that need both flexibility and control over their financial processes.

- **IBM Watson for Accounting**: Provides advanced data analytics and machine learning capabilities to assist firms in identifying operational inefficiencies, uncovering cost-saving opportunities, and enhancing decision-making. IBM Watson's powerful natural language processing also helps firms analyze unstructured data, such as client emails or documents, offering actionable insights that would otherwise be time-consuming to gather manually. This tool is particularly useful in auditing, where it can sift through massive datasets quickly and accurately.

- **QuickBooks AI**: Offers small and mid-sized firms AI-driven tools for bookkeeping, invoice processing, and real-time financial management, allowing firms to scale without increasing staff workload. QuickBooks AI integrates seamlessly with other business applications, further simplifying workflow management and financial tracking. Its automated invoice processing speeds up billing cycles and minimizes human error, enabling firms to maintain consistent cash flow and financial accuracy.

Selecting the right AI tool depends on the firm's specific needs and long-term goals. Whether the focus is on improving tax compliance, financial forecasting, or client advisory services, integrating the right technology can significantly enhance operational performance and client satisfaction. Cost, ease of integration, and scalability are all crucial factors in ensuring that AI implementation delivers sustainable long-term benefits.

Best Practices for Scaling AI in Mid-Sized Firms

Scaling AI in a mid-sized firm requires more than just the right tools; it demands a strategic approach. Without a clear plan, AI implementation can lead to inefficiencies and resistance from staff. By adhering to best practices, firms can ensure a smoother transition and maximize the benefits of AI.

1. **Departmental Collaboration**: Collaboration between departments is crucial for scaling AI. Firms should create cross-functional teams to oversee AI integration, ensuring that each department's specific needs are addressed and aligned with the firm's goals. A cross-functional approach also helps mitigate siloed thinking, allowing insights from different areas to enhance the overall effectiveness of AI solutions. Collaboration fosters knowledge sharing, which helps identify new opportunities for AI utilization that may not have been evident initially.

2. **AI Governance and Transparency**: Establishing clear governance protocols is essential for ethical AI usage. Firms must be transparent about how AI is used, particularly when it comes to client data and decision-making processes, ensuring compliance with regulations like GDPR and CCPA. A well-defined governance framework includes setting guidelines for data handling, providing transparency reports to clients, and maintaining open communication about AI's role in decision-making. This approach builds trust and ensures that AI aligns with the firm's values and legal obligations. Governance protocols also help mitigate risks related to AI, such as biases in decision-making or errors in

data processing, by ensuring a structured approach to auditing and accountability.

3. **Phased Rollout**: Implement AI in stages, starting with back-office operations like payroll, tax filings, and financial reporting before expanding to client-facing services such as advisory and audit services. This approach allows firms to manage the transition effectively and address any issues early on. Phased rollouts make the process manageable, allowing firms to gather feedback from employees and clients and make necessary adjustments before full implementation. A staged introduction of AI also helps prevent major disruptions that could occur if multiple departments were to transition simultaneously without adequate preparation. By taking a phased approach, firms can ensure that employees feel comfortable with new technologies, thus minimizing resistance and maximizing efficiency.

4. **Continuous Training**: To maximize AI's potential, firms must invest in ongoing training for staff. Upskilling employees ensures they can effectively use AI tools and remain adaptable as new technologies emerge. Continuous training programs create a workforce that is not only capable of using AI but also confident in their ability to leverage its full potential. Training fosters a culture of innovation, encouraging staff to explore AI-driven solutions to existing problems, thus promoting overall growth within the firm. Firms should consider both formal and informal training sessions, such as workshops, webinars, and peer-to-peer learning opportunities, to keep their teams updated and engaged.

Following these best practices can mitigate the risks associated with AI deployment, reduce resistance to new technology, and improve overall firm performance. For example, 79% of mid-tier firms are planning to enhance their cloud-based software offerings over the next three years, highlighting the importance of scalable infrastructure. Scalable infrastructure provides the foundation for AI to operate effectively, ensuring that the technologies implemented today can grow alongside the firm's increasing needs.

A well-executed AI scaling plan that includes strategic phases, cross-functional collaboration, and continuous employee engagement creates an environment where AI is seen as an enabler rather than a threat. It encourages employees to embrace technology as a tool that empowers them to deliver better results, both operationally and in terms of client relationships.

3. Scaling AI Across Departments

AI can transform various departments within a mid-sized firm, from back-office operations to client advisory services. However, scaling AI across departments requires a strategic, phased approach to ensure that the firm maximizes the benefits without overwhelming staff or disrupting existing workflows.

- **Back-Office Automation**: Scaling AI should begin in areas like bookkeeping, tax compliance, and payroll, where repetitive tasks can be automated. Tools like Xero and QuickBooks provide real-time financial insights, reducing manual work and improving accuracy. Automating these processes allows employees to focus on more strategic tasks that require human judgment, such as analyzing financial reports or providing client recommendations. Back-office automation also ensures that tasks are completed consistently and with fewer errors, enhancing the overall quality of services provided to clients.

- **Client Advisory Services (CAS)**: After back-office automation, firms can leverage AI to enhance client services. Predictive analytics tools such as CCH Axcess™ iQ can identify opportunities for tax savings or investment strategies, allowing firms to offer more proactive advice to clients. By using AI to predict client needs, accountants can deliver tailored solutions that add value beyond standard compliance work, strengthening client relationships and positioning the firm as a trusted advisor. AI-driven insights enable firms to transition from a reactive to a proactive model of client management, addressing potential issues before they become significant problems.

- **Auditing and Fraud Detection**: AI tools like IBM Watson can be utilized in auditing processes, where machine learning algorithms analyze large datasets to detect anomalies, thereby reducing the risk of fraud and improving audit efficiency. AI can identify patterns that human auditors might miss, thus enhancing the quality of audits and providing greater assurance to clients. As fraud prevention becomes increasingly important, AI's ability to sift through massive amounts of data in real time can make a substantial difference in mitigating risks early on. This allows firms to offer a higher level of assurance, enhancing client trust and credibility.

A phased rollout of AI solutions across departments helps ensure that employees adapt comfortably and that AI is implemented where it will have the most immediate impact. As firms scale AI solutions, they should also continuously assess and refine their approach, ensuring each department sees tangible benefits, whether in efficiency, accuracy, or client satisfaction.

4. Trends for Mid-Sized Firms in AI

As AI technology evolves, mid-sized firms must stay up-to-date with emerging trends to maintain their competitive edge. From AI-driven decision support to cloud-based solutions, these trends are shaping the future of accounting for firms of all sizes.

- **AI-Driven Decision Support**: AI tools are increasingly being used for strategic decision-making, offering firms real-time data analysis to support forecasting, risk management, and financial planning. Predictive models enable firms to simulate different business scenarios and make informed decisions. For instance, AI-driven financial planning can identify potential cash flow risks, allowing firms to take proactive measures. This trend is reshaping decision-making processes, shifting them from reactive to proactive management.

- **Cloud-Based AI Solutions**: Cloud-based platforms offer scalability, cost-efficiency, and flexibility, making them an attractive option for mid-sized firms. AI tools like QuickBooks and Xero are integrating cloud technologies to provide real-time data access, further enhancing operational efficiency. 43% of mid-tier firms have invested in designing their own bespoke IT solutions over the past three years, showcasing a trend toward customized, cloud-based AI implementations (Predictive Analytics in...). The move toward cloud-based AI solutions reduces the need for on-premise hardware, lowering costs and simplifying maintenance, which is particularly beneficial for firms looking to scale their operations.

- **Robotic Process Automation (RPA)**: RPA tools are automating administrative tasks, such as document retrieval, tax filings, and reconciliations, reducing costs and allowing staff to focus on higher-value work. Adoption of RPA is expected to increase as firms look for ways to streamline workflows. By automating these mundane and repetitive tasks, firms can direct their workforce toward more complex, client-facing activities that require human expertise, thereby enhancing overall client service quality.

40% of firms have highlighted generative AI as one of their top three trends, showing that AI's influence is expanding beyond automation into content generation and advisory support (Predictive Analytics in...). Generative AI can be used to create draft reports, summaries, and even personalized client content, reducing the workload for accountants and allowing them to focus on higher-level strategic activities.

5. Future Outlook for Mid-Sized Firms and AI

AI adoption will continue to grow among mid-sized firms, particularly as tools become more affordable and accessible. The future will likely see deeper integration of AI into every aspect of the firm, from operational processes to client services. Firms that invest in AI will be better positioned to scale efficiently, deliver enhanced client value, and stay competitive.

By 2025, it is projected that 70% of organizations will have operationalized AI architectures, up from just 10% in 2020, underscoring a dramatic shift towards AI-driven operations (Predictive Analytics in...). For mid-sized firms, this means focusing on integrating AI into day-to-day operations to improve efficiency, profitability, and client satisfaction. AI's impact is not limited to automating tasks; it also enhances strategic decision-making, enabling firms to identify growth opportunities and mitigate risks more effectively.

The future points toward greater collaboration between AI and human accountants. As AI takes over routine tasks, accountants can concentrate on offering higher-value services, such as advisory and strategic planning. This evolution will require accountants to adapt and evolve, developing skills that complement AI, such as emotional intelligence, creative problem-solving, and deep client engagement.

Mid-sized firms that actively integrate AI across their functions will be better positioned to not only navigate the evolving landscape of accounting but also thrive in it. Staying ahead of the curve with the latest AI trends, investing in scalable technology, and ensuring continuous staff training are key components of long-term success.

REAL-WORLD EXAMPLES/CASE STUDIES

GreenTree Financial Case Study

- **Background**: GreenTree Financial, a mid-sized accounting firm, faced growing demands for tax compliance, auditing, and client advisory services. However, the firm's manual processes made it difficult to scale operations and deliver timely services to clients.

- **Challenge**: The firm needed to reduce the time spent on routine tasks such as tax filings and bookkeeping while improving the quality of client advisory services. These manual processes were not only time-consuming but also prone to errors, leading to potential compliance risks and client dissatisfaction.

- **AI Solution**: GreenTree adopted AI tools like CCH Axcess™ iQ for predictive analytics and Xero for automating tax compliance and financial reporting. By integrating these AI solutions, the firm automated mundane tasks and shifted focus to providing more strategic insights to clients. AI-driven analytics allowed GreenTree to better understand client needs and deliver tailored advice.

- **Outcome**: With AI-driven automation, the firm achieved a 25% increase in efficiency, a 40% reduction in tax preparation time, and improved client satisfaction by 35%. The firm also expanded its advisory services without increasing staff, leading to a 20% boost in revenue within a year (Predictive Analytics in...).

Actionable Insights

1. **Start with Back-Office Functions**: Begin by implementing AI in areas like bookkeeping and tax compliance. Automating routine tasks with tools like QuickBooks or Xero can significantly improve operational efficiency.

2. **Leverage AI for Client Advisory Services**: Use predictive analytics tools like CCH Axcess™ iQ to deliver proactive advice to clients. This will enhance client satisfaction and allow the firm to offer more personalized services.

3. **Develop an AI Governance Plan**: Ensure that the use of AI is governed by clear protocols. This includes setting guidelines on data privacy, transparency, and the ethical use of AI, especially in client-facing services.

4. **Invest in Staff Training**: Ongoing training is essential to ensure that staff can effectively use AI tools. This will also

foster a culture of innovation and adaptability within the firm, enabling it to stay ahead of technological changes.

Conclusion/Takeaways

Scaling AI solutions across mid-sized firms can lead to substantial improvements in efficiency, client satisfaction, and profitability. By implementing AI in stages, starting with back-office automation and gradually expanding into client-facing services, firms can manage the transition effectively. The key to success lies in ongoing staff training, governance, and continuous evaluation of AI tools.

As firms adopt AI across their operations, staffing and resource allocation become critical factors in driving success. In the next chapter, we will explore how AI can address staffing challenges in accounting firms, enhancing productivity and helping firms adapt to the evolving needs of the profession.

References

Arion Research. (n.d.). *Scaling up with AI: Strategies for small and medium businesses (SMBs)*. https://www.arionresearch.com/blog/scaling-up-with-ai-strategies-for-small-and-medium-businesses-smbs

Financial Cents. (n.d.). *The 10 best AI accounting software for firms in 2024.* https://financial-cents.com/resources/articles/best-ai-accounting-software/

IBM. (n.d.). *IBM Watson for accounting.* https://scribehow.com/library/ai-tools-for-accountants

Intuit. (n.d.). *QuickBooks AI tools for mid-sized firms.* https://www.arionresearch.com/blog/scaling-up-with-ai-strategies-for-small-and-medium-businesses-smbs

Ramp. (n.d.). *AI's impact on the future of accounting.* https://ramp.com/blog/ais-impact-on-the-future-of-accounting

Wolters Kluwer. (2024, May). *CCH Axcess™ iQ.* https://www.icaew.com/insights/viewpoints-on-the-news/2024/may-2024/evolution-of-midtier-firms-tech-investment-and-ai

Xero. (n.d.). *Xero AI-powered accounting software.* https://www.acecloudhosting.com/blog/best-ai-tools-for-accounting-professionals/

CHAPTER 15: AI TO ADDRESS STAFFING CHALLENGES IN ACCOUNTING

Introduction

The accounting industry is currently at a turning point. With experienced professionals retiring and fewer young graduates entering the field, firms are struggling to keep up with growing workloads using a shrinking workforce. This has put tremendous pressure on maintaining efficiency and meeting client expectations. Adding to this challenge are increasingly complex regulations and a greater demand for advisory services. AI is emerging as a potential solution by taking over repetitive tasks, allowing accountants to spend their time on more valuable work. In this chapter, we'll explore how AI can help firms tackle staffing issues, improve productivity, and support sustainable growth—without needing to drastically expand their teams.

How can your firm effectively adopt AI to address staffing gaps? Are you ready to leverage technology to enhance your team's capabilities? Let's dive in to discover practical ways to bridge these challenges.

AI's ability to address staffing issues isn't just about automation. It also amplifies what existing staff can do by freeing them from repetitive tasks and allowing them to focus on strategic, high-impact work. It's like having an extra set of hands that never gets tired, handling the heavy lifting so your talented staff can shine where they matter most. Firms wanting to scale their operations and deliver more value to clients can leverage AI to grow efficiently. This chapter dives into practical ways firms can use AI to overcome staffing challenges, boost productivity, and create sustainable growth opportunities.

Industry Data on the Talent Shortage

The shortage of talent in the accounting industry has become a major hurdle for firms. Let's look at some key statistics that paint a clear picture of the problem:

- **Decline in Accounting Graduates:** From 2010 to 2023, the number of accounting graduates dropped by 10%. This shrinking pool of new talent is putting pressure on firms to rethink their staffing strategies and find alternative ways to meet their needs.

- **Growing Demand for Advisory Services:** By 2025, the demand for advisory services is expected to grow by 20%. As clients look for more strategic financial advice, firms are finding it difficult to allocate resources, especially with fewer professionals to go around.

- **Difficulty in Hiring Senior Accountants:** Around 75% of firms say they struggle to hire senior accountants, leading to significant gaps in leadership. These roles are vital for building client relationships and providing valuable strategic insights.

- **Automation's Impact on Staffing:** Many firms have turned to AI to address these issues, with some reporting a 15% reduction in staffing needs while boosting productivity. This shows how AI can help fill the gap left by the talent shortage.

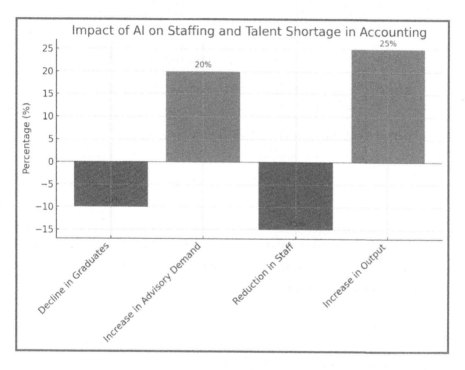

Figure 19 The Talent Shortage in Accounting: Illustrating the 10% Decline in Graduates, 20% Increase in Demand for Advisory Services, and How AI Implementation Led to a 15% Reduction in Staff While Increasing Output by 25%

These statistics and the chart above make it clear that traditional approaches are no longer enough. Firms need innovative solutions—like AI—to tackle staffing shortages while continuing to meet evolving client expectations.

These insights demonstrate how AI is transforming staffing models in accounting, addressing talent shortages while enhancing efficiency and creating new opportunities.

Timeline of AI Adoption in Accounting Staffing

Year	Development
2015	Initial use of AI for basic automation
2018	Introduction of advanced analytics tools
2020	Significant increase in demand for advisory services
2023	Widespread adoption of hybrid roles

Figure 20 Timeline of AI Adoption in Accounting

These milestones demonstrate how AI has gradually become an integral part of accounting, helping firms deal with staffing shortages while enhancing overall efficiency.

Core Concepts

AI as a Workforce Multiplier

AI acts like a tireless assistant. It handles data entry, reconciliation, and invoicing—tackling the repetitive tasks that used to bog down accountants, giving them more time to focus on high-value activities. Imagine having a colleague who never takes a sick day and never complains about mundane work—that's AI in action. This allows your talented people to shine in areas like client advisory and strategic planning, adding genuine value where it matters most.

Example: Platforms like Botkeeper use AI to automate data entry and reconciliation. Firms that use Botkeeper report reduced manual workloads and fewer staffing needs, enabling accountants to focus on more personalized client services. Sarah, an accountant at a mid-sized firm, described her experience: "At first, I was skeptical, but once I saw how much time it saved us, I was all in. It let me work on client strategy instead of just being stuck in spreadsheets all day."

Beyond Data Entry and Reconciliation

AI's capabilities go far beyond just automating the basics. Imagine having an extra brain for sophisticated tasks like financial analysis, audit preparation, and tax forecasting. AI tools don't just crunch numbers—they allow accountants to focus on providing insights, which is what clients value most. This shift gives accountants the freedom to dive into the more interesting and impactful parts of their jobs, adding depth to client relationships and making their work more meaningful.

Example: IBM Watson is being used in audit processes to identify anomalies in financial data, allowing auditors to focus on areas that require human insight, rather than sifting through endless data points. John, an auditor, recalled: "Using AI for initial audits was a game-changer. Instead of getting lost in data, I could use my expertise to dig into actual anomalies and provide real value."

AI as a Skill Gap Bridge

With experienced accountants retiring and fewer new professionals entering the field, many firms are dealing with significant skill gaps. AI tools can help less experienced accountants make informed decisions, providing insights and support that would typically require senior expertise. By guiding them through complex financial scenarios, AI empowers junior accountants to perform beyond their years, allowing firms to maintain high service quality despite staff shortages.

Example: Platforms like QuickBooks and Xero provide AI-driven insights that help junior accountants navigate complex financial situations, enabling them to make informed decisions that might have otherwise required a senior professional's guidance. Sarah, a junior accountant, shared: "I used to have to ask my manager for help every time a complex issue came up. Now, AI gives me the guidance I need to make confident decisions. It's like having a mentor by my side 24/7."

AI Leadership and the Rise of the Chief AI Officer (CAIO)

As AI becomes more embedded in accounting operations, dedicated leadership is essential to manage its integration effectively. The Chief AI Officer (CAIO) plays a key role in ensuring that AI is used in alignment with the firm's broader strategic goals. This position can be a game-changer, especially for firms facing talent shortages alongside the complexities of AI adoption.

A CAIO is responsible for driving AI initiatives that improve efficiency and enhance service delivery. They manage the integration of AI tools—from automating routine tasks to enhancing fraud detection and risk management—while ensuring that all AI systems adhere to ethical and regulatory standards.

Best Practices for Leveraging AI to Address Staffing Challenges

To effectively implement AI as a solution to staffing challenges, firms should follow certain best practices to maximize its impact and ensure a smooth transition:

Start with Automating Routine Tasks: AI should initially be deployed in areas where it can handle repetitive and time-consuming tasks, such as bookkeeping, reconciliations, and data entry. By focusing on these functions first, firms can quickly see the benefits of AI while minimizing disruption to their existing workflows. Starting with routine tasks also helps staff become comfortable with the new technology before expanding its use into more complex areas.

Invest in Continuous Staff Training: As AI technologies evolve, so must the skills of the workforce. Firms should invest in ongoing training programs to ensure their staff can work alongside AI tools effectively, using them to enhance client services and support decision-making processes. Continuous training also helps employees understand the value that AI brings, reducing resistance to adopting new technologies and fostering a culture of innovation.

Create AI Governance Protocols: Transparency and ethical use of AI are key to its successful implementation. Firms must establish clear AI governance to manage how AI systems handle client data, ensure compliance with regulations, and maintain accountability in financial reporting. Governance protocols provide a framework for ethical decision-making, ensuring that AI is used in a manner that aligns with both legal requirements and the firm's values.

Phase AI Implementation: Gradual deployment of AI allows firms to monitor the effects of automation and make adjustments as necessary. Starting with low-complexity tasks and progressively moving to more sophisticated functions ensures that firms can manage the transition effectively. This phased approach also allows firms to collect feedback from staff and clients, refine AI applications, and ensure they are meeting their intended objectives.

Balance Human Expertise with AI Insights: While AI can automate many tasks and provide valuable insights, human oversight remains essential for ensuring accuracy and making strategic decisions. Staff should be trained to interpret AI-driven insights and integrate them into client services, using AI as a tool to enhance rather than replace their expertise. By combining AI capabilities with human judgment, firms can offer a superior level of service to their clients.

REAL-WORLD EXAMPLES/CASE STUDIES

GreenTree Financial Case Study

Background: GreenTree Financial, a mid-sized accounting firm, faced significant challenges in meeting client demands due to a shortage of skilled staff. As the firm continued to grow, it became increasingly difficult to balance the workload without hiring additional employees, which would have strained their budget and reduced profitability.

Challenge: The primary challenge for GreenTree was to find a way to increase productivity and meet client expectations without adding more staff or compromising the quality of client services. The firm needed a scalable solution that could address workload imbalances while maintaining high service standards.

AI Solution: GreenTree adopted Botkeeper for automated bookkeeping and CCH Axcess™ iQ for predictive analytics in tax compliance and client advisory services. Botkeeper helped automate up to 60% of routine bookkeeping tasks, while CCH Axcess™ iQ provided predictive insights that enabled more proactive client advisory.

Outcome: With these AI tools in place, GreenTree was able to reduce tax preparation time by 30% and increase overall productivity by 25%. This efficiency allowed the firm to take on 20% more clients without expanding their workforce, resulting in increased profitability and improved client satisfaction. By leveraging AI, GreenTree not only addressed its staffing challenges but also positioned itself for sustainable growth.

Smith & Turner Accounting Case Study

Background: Smith & Turner is a small accounting firm that faced increasing difficulties managing workloads as their client base grew. With only a few staff members, they were at capacity, and hiring additional employees was not financially feasible.

Challenge: The firm needed a solution that would enable them to increase productivity without expanding their team. They were also looking for ways to reduce manual data entry and improve the quality of client interactions.

AI Solution: Smith & Turner implemented QuickBooks AI to automate routine bookkeeping and financial reporting tasks. They also used Vic.ai, an AI-powered automation tool for invoice processing, which significantly reduced the time spent on accounts payable.

Outcome: By automating up to 50% of their bookkeeping tasks, Smith & Turner increased their productivity by 20% and were able to take on 10 new clients without additional staffing. The adoption of AI allowed the firm's staff to focus more on advisory roles, enhancing client satisfaction and adding strategic value to their services.

Risk Management Considerations

AI adoption brings numerous opportunities, but it also comes with risks that must be carefully managed. Like any transformative technology, AI has its strengths and limitations, and recognizing these early is crucial for successful integration. Firms need to be proactive in addressing the inherent risks, from data privacy concerns to the challenges of over-reliance on automated systems. Implementing AI is much like incorporating a new team member; it must be monitored, guided, and understood to achieve its full potential without introducing unintended complications.

Data Security and Privacy: AI systems handle sensitive client information, which makes robust data security measures essential. Firms must ensure that data encryption, secure storage protocols, and compliance with privacy regulations like GDPR or CCPA are prioritized to maintain client trust and safeguard sensitive information. "It's like locking away your files but with digital fortresses," explained Lisa, an IT specialist. She emphasizes that keeping client trust is all about making sure AI is secure and ethically sound.

Over-Reliance on Automation: While AI can certainly boost efficiency, there's a risk in depending on it too much. Automated systems are powerful, but they can also make mistakes, especially if data inputs are flawed. Human oversight is essential, particularly in areas involving compliance and financial reporting, where even small errors can have significant consequences. Think of AI as your co-pilot—it's there to assist you, but you still need to keep your hands on the wheel.

Bias in AI Algorithms: AI systems are only as good as the data they are trained on. If biases are present in that data, the outputs can be flawed. Periodic audits of AI systems are necessary to ensure accuracy and fairness. This process is not just about technology—it's about maintaining the integrity of client services and making sure every output reflects a fair and ethical perspective. As one accountant put it, "The last thing we want is for a machine to make biased decisions—our clients deserve better."

Change Management: Introducing AI can stir anxiety among staff, particularly if they fear job displacement. To mitigate these fears, firms must develop a clear change management strategy that involves transparent communication, ongoing support, and reassurance about job roles. Resistance is often rooted in uncertainty, and the best antidote is inclusion—making staff part of the journey from the outset. "Once we saw how AI could help us, instead of replacing us, it changed everything," said Mark, an accountant at a small firm. "We felt like we were part of the future, not left behind."

Strategies for Staff and Client Buy-In

Successfully integrating AI into accounting operations is not solely a technical endeavor—it's a human one. The acceptance of AI by staff and clients will ultimately determine whether the technology thrives or falls short. For this reason, fostering buy-in across all levels of your firm is crucial. People must understand not only what AI can do but also how it can make their lives easier and work more fulfilling. Strategies must be proactive and considerate of the concerns and benefits from the perspectives of both employees and clients.

1. **Staff Engagement and Education**: Employees may worry that AI will replace them, making their jobs redundant. Training programs that focus on showing how AI assists, rather than replaces, staff are key. Offering examples of employees who have thrived alongside AI can shift perspectives. Involving staff in planning and deployment also fosters a sense of ownership, helping them feel that they are part of the solution. Sarah shared: "Once I realized AI wasn't here to replace me, but to help me get rid of the boring stuff, I was all in."

2. **Highlighting Benefits to Clients**: Clients may also have concerns. They might worry that automation will reduce the quality of service or lead to impersonal relationships. Firms should communicate clearly how AI helps provide faster, more accurate responses and improves financial insight. Real-world examples of client successes can provide reassurance and help shift attitudes toward AI positively. "When clients started seeing quicker turnaround times, they began to appreciate what AI could do for them," explained John, a partner at a mid-sized firm.

3. **Transparent Communication**: Both staff and clients value transparency. Firms should clearly explain why they are adopting AI, what specific tasks it will handle, and how this will ultimately benefit everyone involved. For employees, clarity reduces anxiety. For clients, it shows a forward-thinking approach to managing their finances.

4. **Incentives and Recognition**: Recognizing employees who embrace AI and effectively integrate it into their work can build positive momentum. Incentives, even if small, can be powerful motivators. Employees should be rewarded not only for productivity but also for adaptability, creativity, and using AI to provide enhanced client services.

5. **Personalized Training Paths**: Everyone learns differently, and this is particularly true when it comes to technology. Offering different training paths to accommodate various comfort levels with AI is critical. Some employees may need foundational training, while others are ready for more advanced AI applications. Providing support tailored to each person makes AI adoption smoother and ensures a confident, capable workforce.

Actionable Insights

Leverage AI for Routine Tasks: Firms should start by automating routine, repetitive tasks such as bookkeeping, data entry, and reconciliations. This will help free up valuable time for accountants to focus on more strategic, higher-value activities, such as providing client advisory services.

Implement AI in Phases: AI implementation should be gradual, starting with low-risk areas like bookkeeping and tax compliance. As employees become comfortable with the technology, AI can be expanded into more complex areas such as auditing and advisory services. This phased approach allows firms to adapt and refine their AI strategy based on real-world feedback.

Invest in Continuous Training: Upskilling staff to work alongside AI tools is essential. Firms should invest in continuous training to ensure that employees remain current with technological advancements and can effectively use AI to enhance productivity and client services. Providing regular training sessions, workshops, and access to online learning resources can help foster a culture of lifelong learning.

Establish AI Governance: To ensure the ethical and effective use of AI, firms must establish governance protocols that define how AI systems handle client data, manage decision-making processes, and maintain transparency. Regular audits of AI systems should be conducted to ensure compliance with ethical standards and regulations.

Long-Term Impacts of AI on Staffing Models

AI's growing role in accounting will have long-term implications for staffing models. Firms will need to transition from traditional roles to hybrid models where staff work alongside AI, and new roles will emerge that focus on managing AI technologies and data analytics.

Transitioning to Hybrid Roles

As AI takes over routine tasks, accountants will need to develop skills in areas such as data analysis and technology management. These hybrid roles will allow staff to provide more strategic value to clients while working closely with AI systems to ensure accurate financial reporting and advisory services.

New Roles in Technology and Data Analysis

The rise of AI will also create new roles focused on managing AI technologies, interpreting AI-driven insights, and ensuring the ethical use of AI in accounting. These roles will require accountants to be well-versed in both finance and technology, bridging the gap between these two critical areas.

AI-Driven Virtual CFOs

AI technologies will eventually lead to the rise of virtual CFOs, where AI systems handle financial planning, budgeting, and forecasting for firms. These AI-driven CFOs will allow firms to offer high-level strategic advice to clients without the need for additional human staff.

Talent Management with AI

AI tools are already being used to optimize staffing workflows and predict future staffing needs. By analyzing data on employee performance and workload distribution, firms can ensure they allocate resources efficiently and address skill gaps before they become problematic.

Integrated AI Advisory Platforms

AI will continue to integrate with advisory platforms, providing real-time, customized advice to clients. Firms that leverage these platforms will be able to offer high-quality advisory services with fewer staff, as AI takes on much of the data analysis and forecasting work.

Conclusion/Takeaways

AI provides accounting firms with the tools to address staffing shortages while maintaining high service quality. By automating routine tasks, firms can enhance productivity and focus on providing strategic value to clients. The impact was immediate— tasks that used to take hours are now completed in minutes, freeing up time for strategic planning. In the long term, AI will transform accounting roles, create hybrid positions that combine finance and technology skills, and allow firms to grow without adding excessive headcount. The key is to implement AI thoughtfully, ensure continuous staff training, and maintain clear governance. AI isn't just a solution for overcoming staffing challenges—it is a way to boost productivity and stay competitive in a rapidly changing industry.

As your firm considers adopting AI, what steps can you take to ensure a smooth transition? Have you thought about how to engage your team in this journey to make AI a valuable partner rather than a point of resistance? The next chapter will explore the transformative impact of cloud technology and how it supports remote work in accounting. Cloud technology not only allows for more flexible work environments but also integrates seamlessly with AI, creating opportunities for real-time collaboration and increased productivity. Let's move forward and discover how cloud and remote work can reshape accounting practices in Chapter 16: Cloud Technology and Remote Work in Accounting.

References

Ace Cloud Hosting. (n.d.). *AI tools for accounting professionals.* Retrieved from https://acecloudhosting.com.

Botkeeper. (n.d.). *AI-powered bookkeeping.* Retrieved from https://botkeeper.com.

IBM Watson. (n.d.). *IBM Watson for accounting.* Retrieved from https://ibm.com/watson.

McKinsey & Company. (n.d.). *The role of artificial intelligence in financial services.* Retrieved from https://mckinsey.com/ai-report.

QuickBooks. (n.d.). *QuickBooks AI tools.* Retrieved from https://quickbooks.com/ai-tools.

Ramp. (n.d.). *AI's impact on the future of accounting*. Retrieved from https://ramp.com/blog.

Thomson Reuters. (n.d.). *Leveraging AI to address staffing challenges in accounting*. Retrieved from https://thomsonreuters.com.

Vic.ai. (n.d.). *Vic.ai for invoice processing*. Retrieved from https://vic.ai.

Wolters Kluwer. (n.d.). *CCH Axcess™ iQ*. Retrieved from https://wolterskluwer.com/cch-axcess-iq.

CHAPTER 16: CLOUD TECHNOLOGY AND REMOTE WORK IN ACCOUNTING

Introduction

The accounting industry has undergone a significant transformation in response to the global shift toward remote work. The COVID-19 pandemic accelerated this change, prompting firms to adopt cloud technology to facilitate seamless collaboration and maintain productivity across dispersed teams. As firms continue to embrace flexible work models, the integration of cloud technology with Artificial Intelligence (AI) is playing a pivotal role in enabling accountants to access data securely, automate routine processes, and provide real-time insights to clients. One success story that illustrates this shift involves a mid-sized firm that, during the pandemic, transitioned to a cloud-based system and reported a 30% increase in productivity within just a few months. This chapter explores how AI-enhanced cloud platforms are helping accounting firms thrive in a remote work environment and highlights key trends shaping the future of accounting.

Core Concepts

To understand how cloud technology and AI are transforming accounting, it's essential to grasp the foundational concepts driving these innovations. Think of it like building a house—you need a solid understanding of the foundation before you can start adding the advanced features. In this section, we explore the role of cloud technology in supporting remote work and the various AI-powered tools that streamline workflow and enhance collaboration. By breaking down these core concepts, you'll gain a clearer understanding of how these technologies work together to improve efficiency and flexibility in accounting.

1. The Role of Cloud Technology in Supporting Remote Work in Accounting

Cloud technology has become essential for accounting firms because it allows teams to access financial data in real time from anywhere. With the rise of remote and hybrid work, cloud platforms are critical for keeping operations running smoothly and maintaining high-quality client service, no matter where team members are located.

2. Key Benefits of Cloud Technology:

- **24/7 Access to Financial Data:** Cloud-based platforms enable financial professionals to access client data anytime from any device. This accessibility is critical in hybrid or fully remote work environments, allowing teams to collaborate on tax returns, audits, and financial reports without delays. Imagine an accountant logging in late at night to quickly resolve a client query—cloud access makes this possible.

- **Scalability for Growing Firms:** Cloud technology scales easily, enabling firms to expand operations without investing in extensive IT infrastructure. Cloud solutions provide scalability, allowing companies to upgrade their plans as they expand. This means small firms can start with what they need and grow their technology footprint without major up-front costs.

- **Cost Savings and Sustainability:** EY reports that utilizing cloud technology can reduce IT operating costs by 20-40% and reduce the costs of both human labor and carbon footprints. Cloud-based software operates on a subscription-based model, often translating to significant cost savings. One accounting partner I spoke with, John, was initially skeptical about cloud technology. However, within months of switching to a cloud system, he saw his monthly IT expenses nearly halved, which came as a pleasant surprise. It also freed up resources, allowing the firm to improve client services in ways they hadn't imagined before.

Real-World Example:
QuickBooks Online allows teams to work together on financial reports, invoicing, and payroll management from different locations while ensuring data integrity and security. This flexibility has been instrumental for firms adopting hybrid work models. In fact, 90% of companies globally are using cloud computing to some extent, indicating its widespread adoption. Additionally, 95% of accounting practices in the UK have embraced cloud-based software to some degree, showcasing the industry's rapid shift toward cloud technology.

Cloud technology isn't just about convenience; it's about transforming the entire work culture of accounting. The ability to work anytime from anywhere has allowed many firms to hire talent outside of their immediate geographic areas, which wasn't as feasible before. This newfound flexibility has fundamentally altered how accounting firms recruit and retain talent—breaking down barriers that used to limit the potential of finding the right people for the job.

3. AI-Powered Tools for Streamlined Collaboration and Workflow Automation

AI is enhancing the power of cloud technology by automating repetitive tasks and improving collaboration among remote teams. Integrating AI with cloud platforms allows accountants to work more efficiently and focus on strategic decision-making.

- **Automated Data Processing:** AI can automatically extract and categorize data from receipts, invoices, and bank statements, eliminating the need for manual data entry. For example, Docyt uses AI to automate back-office and accounting tasks, which improves productivity by reducing time spent on data processing. Imagine an accountant who used to spend hours manually sorting receipts now being able to reallocate that time toward more meaningful client engagements—more time with clients, less time with data entry.

- **Workflow Automation:** AI tools built into cloud platforms can assign tasks, track progress, and send automated reminders for deadlines, enabling teams to stay organized without micromanagement. One firm owner I talked to shared how automated reminders transformed their team's efficiency, reducing missed tasks and improving overall accountability. It felt like having a diligent personal assistant who never missed a beat.

- **Enhanced Security:** Cloud platforms like Sage Intacct integrate AI-driven security features, which are crucial when dealing with sensitive financial data, including threat detection and end-to-end encryption. Data security is often one of the biggest concerns when moving to the cloud—it's not just about compliance; it's about earning your clients' trust every single day. By investing in strong encryption and

rigorous security audits, you're not just protecting data—
you're providing peace of mind to both your team and your
clients.

Example:
Botkeeper uses AI to automate bookkeeping, saving firms up to
20% on manual labor costs, while AI tools in Xero and CCH
Axcess™ streamline collaboration, improving efficiency across
remote teams. 75% of practices using Xero's cloud accounting
software for multiple tasks have seen an increase in profit over
the last year.

Best Practices for Cloud Technology and AI Integration

Integrating cloud technology and AI into your firm requires
more than just flipping a switch; it demands a thoughtful
approach and attention to detail. Picture it like preparing to run
a marathon—you don't just lace up your shoes and run. You need
to train, take smaller steps, and build your stamina gradually.
Below, we outline some of the best practices for successfully
implementing these technologies, focusing on practical steps you
can take to maximize the benefits while minimizing disruptions
to your day-to-day operations.

1. **Start with Low-Risk Tasks:** Begin by automating routine
    tasks like bookkeeping and data entry, which are less likely to
    disrupt critical operations. Gradually expand to more
    complex areas such as tax preparation and client advisory
    services. Think of it like dipping your toes into a pool before
    diving in—no need to make a splash until you're sure the
    water's the right temperature.

2. **Foster Collaboration Across Teams:** Cloud platforms
    provide centralized access to financial data, making it easier

for teams to collaborate in real time. Firms should establish strong communication channels and ensure teams across different departments can access necessary data. In a remote setting, casual office check-ins are missed, so having intentional virtual collaboration points becomes key.

3. **Ensure Data Security:** Data security is crucial, especially when dealing with sensitive client information. Adopting cloud platforms with built-in security features, such as end-to-end encryption, multi-factor authentication, and regular compliance audits, can safeguard client data. A firm partner I know mentioned that the decision to invest in strong data security helped alleviate clients' initial concerns about moving to the cloud, making them feel comfortable with this transition.

4. **Provide Ongoing Training:** Technology is only as effective as the people using it. Ensure that staff are trained to use cloud platforms and AI tools effectively as new features are introduced. Continuous learning and adaptation will ensure successful integration of cloud technology and AI into day-to-day operations. Change management strategies, including employee training and communication, are crucial for overcoming resistance and ensuring adoption goes smoothly.

5. **Ensure Data Compatibility:** Clean and normalize data to make it AI-ready. This step is critical to ensure that AI tools can effectively process and analyze the data without errors. Imagine trying to cook a big meal in a cluttered kitchen—it's far easier if everything is in its place before you start.

Getting Started Checklist

Now that you understand the core concepts and best practices for integrating cloud and AI technologies, it's time to take action. I know—it might feel overwhelming at first to transition to cloud-based systems. But start small, and you'll soon see the benefits. Below is a concise checklist to guide you through the initial steps needed to bring your firm into the digital age, ensuring you lay a solid foundation for long-term success.

1. **Assess Firm Readiness:** Evaluate your current processes and identify routine, manual tasks that could be automated.

2. **Choose Cloud Platforms:** Start with a cloud platform that meets your current needs but can scale as your firm grows (e.g., QuickBooks Online, Xero, or Sage Intacct).

3. **Select Low-Risk Tasks for Automation:** Begin by automating bookkeeping and data entry to gain confidence in the new technology.

4. **Invest in Security:** Ensure that any chosen cloud solution has robust security features like encryption and multi-factor authentication.

5. **Upskill Your Team:** Provide ongoing training for your staff to help them feel comfortable with new tools and processes.

6. **Implement Change Management:** Clearly communicate changes and benefits to your team to minimize resistance and ensure a smooth transition.

Actionable Insights

To truly leverage cloud technology and AI in accounting, it's not enough to simply adopt the tools—you need to integrate them thoughtfully into your overall strategy. This section provides key insights that will help you maximize the value of these technologies, drive productivity, and ultimately enhance client satisfaction.

1. **Adopt Cloud Platforms for Scalability:** If you're looking to scale your firm, prioritizing cloud-based platforms is a must. They not only offer the flexibility you need but also allow you to grow at your own pace without heavy upfront costs.

2. **Leverage AI for Task Automation:** Automating routine tasks with AI frees up staff to focus on advisory services, improving overall service quality and client satisfaction. AI tools like Botkeeper and Docyt provide efficient automation for repetitive tasks.

3. **Invest in Security Protocols:** Ensure that cloud platforms have robust security measures in place, including encryption and secure access protocols, to protect sensitive financial data. Remember, cloud providers invest heavily in cybersecurity so that you don't have to carry the burden alone.

4. **Upskill Staff in AI and Cloud Tools:** Ongoing training is critical to ensure that employees are proficient in both cloud platforms and AI-powered tools, maximizing their productivity. Training your team effectively ensures they can take full advantage of the technology you've invested in.

Future Trends in Cloud and AI for Accounting

As remote work becomes more entrenched in accounting, cloud technology and AI will continue to evolve, shaping the future of the profession. Here are some key trends to watch:

1. **Increased Integration of AI and Blockchain:** As AI continues to enhance real-time analytics, blockchain may be integrated into cloud platforms to create transparent, tamper-proof financial records. Imagine a world where every transaction is instantly verifiable—reducing audit workloads and increasing accuracy. This integration could be a game-changer for the industry, paving the way for new levels of transparency.

2. **AI-Driven Client Advisory Services:** AI will continue to evolve, providing more personalized insights into client financial performance. This will enable accountants to offer proactive advisory services that genuinely make a difference. With routine tasks out of the way, accountants can focus on helping clients achieve their financial goals—a shift that will ultimately improve relationships and satisfaction.

3. **Globalization of Remote Accounting Services:** Cloud technology is removing geographical barriers, enabling firms to serve clients globally while maintaining high-quality service delivery. This trend means you could have clients in entirely different time zones, bringing new opportunities and challenges. Imagine the new perspectives you could gain from working with a client in a completely different industry halfway across the world—cloud technology makes that possible.

The integration of AI and blockchain in cloud accounting software is expected to further revolutionize the industry. There's a growing focus on using AI for predictive analytics and forecasting in accounting, which will allow firms to provide more accurate financial insights and help clients make informed decisions. One accountant I spoke to shared how using AI to forecast cash flow allowed them to become more proactive in advising clients, resulting in better financial health for those businesses. It's stories like this that remind us why embracing these tools is essential.

Many accountants see cloud technology and AI as essential tools for improving efficiency and offering better services to clients. While AI and cloud technology won't replace accountants, they will significantly change the nature of accounting work—shifting the focus toward more strategic and advisory roles. Accountants who embrace these technologies are likely to be better positioned to add value to their clients and stay ahead of the competition.

Conclusion/Takeaways

The integration of AI and cloud technology is transforming the accounting profession, enabling firms to operate more efficiently in a remote work environment. By automating routine tasks and providing secure, scalable platforms for collaboration, cloud-based AI solutions are helping firms improve productivity, enhance client service, and scale operations. The future of cloud and AI in accounting promises even greater innovation, with tools like blockchain set to improve security and transparency.

I recall a conversation with another firm owner who said, "I never imagined I'd be advising a client while sitting on my back porch with my morning coffee." Cloud and AI technologies are more than just tools—they're enabling us to redefine how we work and find more balance while still delivering exceptional service. One thing is clear: embracing these technologies is no longer optional for firms that want to remain competitive. The most successful firms will be those that not only integrate AI and cloud technologies effectively but also continuously adapt to the changing landscape.

As we move into the next chapter, it's important to consider the ethical implications of these technologies—how do we maintain transparency, fairness, and accountability in AI use? We'll explore these critical questions next.

References

Ace Cloud Hosting. (2024). *Accounting trends overview.* Ace Cloud Hosting Blog. Retrieved from https://www.acecloudhosting.com/blog/accounting-trends/

ClientHub. (n.d.). *Leveraging cloud technology for remote accounting.* ClientHub Blog. Retrieved from https://clienthub.com/blog/cloud-accounting-remote/

Gridlex. (n.d.). *Cloud accounting for remote firms.* Gridlex. Retrieved from https://gridlex.com/cloud-accounting/

INAA. (2024). *Leveraging cloud technology for remote accounting.* INAA. Retrieved from https://www.inaa.org/cloud-accounting/

Intuit. (n.d.). *QuickBooks Online: All-in-one business solutions.* QuickBooks. Retrieved October 13, 2024, from https://quickbooks.intuit.com/online/

Sage Intacct. (n.d.). *Sage Intacct AI-driven security.* Sage. Retrieved from https://www.sageintacct.com/

SageNext. (2024). *Why AI and cloud accounting are the future.* SageNext Blog. Retrieved from https://www.sagenext.com/blog/ai-cloud-accounting/

Wolters Kluwer. (n.d.). *CCH Axcess™ iQ*. Wolters Kluwer. Retrieved from https://taxna.wolterskluwer.com/professional-tax-software/cch-axcess-iq

Xero Limited. (n.d.). *Xero cloud accounting*. Xero. Retrieved from https://www.xero.com/us/

CHAPTER 17: ETHICAL CONSIDERATIONS OF AI IN ACCOUNTING

Introduction

As Artificial Intelligence (AI) becomes an integral part of accounting, it introduces new ethical challenges alongside the benefits of automation, efficiency, and accuracy. AI's capabilities to manage financial data, automate processes, and generate real-time insights come with responsibilities. Accounting firms must navigate concerns related to data privacy, algorithmic bias, transparency, accountability, and the potential displacement of human professionals. The ethical implementation of AI is crucial for ensuring trust and maintaining the profession's integrity. This chapter outlines these ethical concerns and offers practical guidance for accounting firms seeking to implement AI responsibly, providing both real-world examples and actionable steps to address these issues.

Core Concepts

1. Data Privacy and Security Risks

AI in accounting relies on vast amounts of data, often including sensitive personal and financial information. This makes AI systems prime targets for cyberattacks and exposes firms to privacy risks if the data is misused or accessed without permission.

- **Compliance with Data Regulations**: Firms must ensure that their AI systems comply with regulations like the General Data Protection Regulation (GDPR) and the California Consumer Privacy Act (CCPA). These laws require firms to be transparent about how they use client data and to safeguard it. According to a recent survey, 78% of accounting firms reported concerns about meeting compliance requirements when using AI for client data. Non-compliance can lead to substantial fines and damage to a firm's reputation, making adherence to regulations a top priority.

- **Securing AI Systems**: AI tools should be equipped with strong encryption, access controls, and real-time monitoring to detect suspicious activities. Firms should also conduct regular penetration tests, which simulate cyberattacks to identify vulnerabilities and strengthen system defenses. The Ponemon Institute found that organizations with robust AI-driven cybersecurity measures are 60% less likely to experience a data breach. By investing in these security measures, firms can protect their clients' data and reduce the risk of cyberattacks.

- **Data Minimization**: Another essential practice is data minimization, which involves collecting only the data necessary for specific AI processes. This reduces the risk of sensitive information being compromised and ensures compliance with data protection regulations. For instance, firms that limit data collection to the minimum required for tax preparation or financial analysis can minimize potential exposure during a breach.

Real-World Example: IBM Watson for Data Security uses AI-driven cybersecurity to help accounting firms detect and respond to potential breaches in real time, ensuring data privacy and regulatory compliance. One mid-sized accounting firm that implemented IBM Watson reported a 40% reduction in security incidents within the first year of adoption, illustrating the effectiveness of AI-enhanced cybersecurity.

Data privacy and security are crucial for the ethical use of AI. Compliance with data regulations, securing AI systems, and minimizing data collection can help mitigate risks. Smaller firms can consider affordable solutions like managed security services or open-source tools to maintain data privacy effectively.

2. Bias in AI Algorithms

AI models are often trained on historical data, which can reflect existing societal biases. If not addressed, these biases can lead to unfair financial decisions and unequal treatment of clients.

- **Potential Ethical Concerns:** "An interesting question is what will financial AI resort to in order to increase profits? Possibly bilking customers or marketing useless products." This speculative insight highlights the importance of strong ethical considerations in the development and implementation of AI, beyond technical biases. Firms should prioritize inclusive data practices, ensuring that datasets used to train AI models reflect the diversity of their client base. By including data from different demographics, firms can reduce the risk of biased outcomes and provide fairer services to all clients.

- **Bias in Data Collection:** AI models may generate biased outcomes if trained on incomplete or skewed data sets. This issue is particularly concerning in areas like auditing and lending, where biased data can lead to discriminatory practices. A study by the World Economic Forum found that

64% of AI-driven financial services experienced issues with biased outcomes due to inadequate data diversity. Firms must be vigilant about the quality and diversity of the data used to train their AI models to avoid perpetuating existing biases.

- **Auditing AI Models**: Regular audits of AI systems are necessary to ensure that models are fair and unbiased. Firms should retrain their models with diverse datasets and monitor outcomes to detect and mitigate any discriminatory practices. In one example, a large accounting firm conducted quarterly audits of their AI systems, leading to a 30% reduction in biased decision-making. Audits should include both internal evaluations and external reviews to provide an unbiased assessment of AI performance.

- **Inclusive Data Practices**: Firms should prioritize inclusive data practices, ensuring that datasets used to train AI models reflect the diversity of their client base. By including data from different demographics, firms can reduce the risk of biased outcomes and provide fairer services to all clients.

Real-World Example: A financial institution using AI for credit scoring found that its models unfairly penalized minority-owned businesses due to biases in historical lending data. By auditing and adjusting its models, the institution improved the fairness of its decisions. This led to a 25% increase in loan approvals for minority-owned businesses, demonstrating the importance of addressing bias in AI systems.

Bias in AI can result in unfair treatment of clients if not addressed. Firms need to audit their models, use diverse datasets, and implement inclusive data practices to reduce bias.

Smaller firms can collaborate with external auditors to help ensure their AI systems are fair and unbiased.

3. Transparency in AI-Driven Decision-Making

Many AI algorithms function as "black boxes," meaning their decision-making processes are not easily explainable. This lack of transparency can raise accountability concerns, especially in high-stakes financial decisions.

- **Explainable AI**: Explainable AI refers to systems that provide clear, understandable reasons for decisions made by the algorithm, ensuring that clients and regulators can trust AI-generated outcomes. Firms should use explainable AI systems to build trust with their clients and demonstrate that their decision-making processes are fair and transparent. Explainable AI can also help firms comply with regulatory requirements, such as the EU's "right to explanation" under GDPR.

- **Accountability for AI Decisions**: Even when AI assists in decision-making, human professionals must retain ultimate accountability. It is essential to have a clear framework that defines responsibility for AI-driven outcomes. Research from Deloitte suggests that firms using explainable AI reported a 25% increase in client trust, as clients were better able to understand and accept AI-generated recommendations. Accountability frameworks should outline the roles of both AI and human professionals in decision-making, ensuring that there is always a human element involved in interpreting AI outputs.

- **Human Judgment and Skepticism**: As one professional put it, "AI cannot provide professional skepticism and judgment. That's why so many accountants who have been in the field for so many years are not scared." This underscores the indispensable role of human judgment and ethical oversight in accounting, even as AI becomes more prevalent. While AI assists in decision-making, human professionals must retain ultimate accountability. It is essential to have a clear framework that defines responsibility for AI-driven outcomes.

- **Client Education**: Firms should also focus on educating their clients about how AI-driven decisions are made. Providing clients with simple explanations and visualizations of AI processes can help demystify the technology and increase their comfort level with AI-generated outcomes.

- **Mid-Sized Firm Example:** A mid-sized accounting firm implemented an AI-based client collaboration tool to streamline communication and decision-making. By using explainable AI features, they were able to provide clear rationales for financial decisions during client meetings, which resulted in a 20% improvement in client satisfaction scores. This improved transparency and enhanced collaboration, fostering stronger client relationships.

- **Real-World Example:** FICO's credit scoring model uses explainable AI to provide "reason codes" that clarify how specific financial decisions, like credit scores, are determined. This approach has helped clients better understand the factors affecting their credit scores, leading to increased transparency and trust in the financial decision-making process.

Transparency is essential in AI-driven decision-making. Using explainable AI, establishing accountability frameworks, and educating clients can help build trust and compliance. Mid-sized firms, in particular, can benefit from improved client collaboration through the use of explainable AI tools.

4. The Impact of AI on Employment in Accounting

AI's ability to automate tasks traditionally performed by accountants raises concerns about job displacement. While AI can improve efficiency, it's critical to balance automation with the need for human expertise.

- **Redefining Roles in Accounting**: AI is freeing accountants from routine tasks, allowing them to take on more strategic, value-added roles such as client advisory services and financial analysis. A report from McKinsey estimated that 30% of accounting tasks could be automated, but this would also create opportunities for accountants to focus on more analytical and client-facing activities. Accountants who adapt to these changes can find themselves in more rewarding roles that emphasize strategic thinking and client interaction.

- **Balancing Automation and Expertise**: While AI can generate insights and automate decision-making, human oversight remains crucial. Accountants need to apply professional judgment, particularly in complex scenarios. A survey by EY found that 68% of clients still prefer a human professional to be involved in financial decision-making, even if AI is used to support the process. This preference underscores the importance of maintaining a balance between automation and human expertise.

- **Upskilling and Reskilling**: Firms should invest in upskilling and reskilling their employees to ensure they can work effectively alongside AI. Training programs that focus on data analysis, critical thinking, and client advisory skills can help accountants transition into roles that are less likely to be automated. According to a survey by the Association of Chartered Certified Accountants (ACCA), 72% of accountants believe that learning new skills is essential for staying relevant in an AI-driven workplace.

Real-World Example: Many firms using AI to automate compliance and bookkeeping have successfully transitioned staff into advisory roles, where human expertise remains essential. For example, a mid-sized firm that implemented AI for bookkeeping was able to reassign 40% of its staff to more strategic client advisory roles, leading to increased client satisfaction. This transition not only retained jobs but also enhanced the firm's service offerings, demonstrating that AI can complement rather than replace human professionals.

AI automation can enhance efficiency but raises concerns about job displacement. By focusing on upskilling, balancing automation with human oversight, and redefining roles, firms can ensure that AI complements rather than replaces accounting professionals.

5. Ethical Responsibility in AI Implementation

Firms must implement AI technologies ethically, ensuring that AI systems align with both professional standards and legal obligations. Developing clear policies for data usage, transparency, and accountability is essential to maintaining trust in AI systems.

Developing Ethical AI Guidelines

Firms should create comprehensive guidelines outlining the ethical use of AI, particularly around data privacy, fairness, and transparency. These guidelines should also include accountability frameworks that ensure human oversight of AI-generated decisions.

Ethical Risk	Description of the Risk	Solution/Best Practices
Data Privacy	Potential misuse or unauthorized access to sensitive client data.	Implement strong encryption, limit access, and ensure compliance with privacy laws (e.g., GDPR).
Bias	AI algorithms may unintentionally favor certain groups or outcomes.	Regularly audit AI models, ensure diverse data sets, and implement fairness checks.
Transparency	Lack of clarity on how AI models make decisions.	Maintain clear documentation of AI models and make explanations available to stakeholders.
Accountability	Difficulty in determining who is responsible for AI-driven decisions.	Establish clear guidelines on accountability and assign responsibility for AI outcomes.
Security	Vulnerabilities in AI systems could lead to security breaches.	Use robust security measures such as firewalls and continuous monitoring to protect AI systems.

Table 4 Ethical Risks and Solutions

Continuous Monitoring and Adaptation

AI systems evolve over time, and firms must regularly audit their AI tools to ensure ongoing compliance with ethical standards. This includes retraining AI models to address bias, updating security protocols, and ensuring transparency in decision-making processes.

Ethical considerations are a critical part of implementing AI at scale, especially for large firms with multi-departmental and global operations. With these complexities in mind, the next chapter will delve deeper into the strategies and challenges that large firms face when integrating AI systems across their organizations, offering insights on how to manage these implementations successfully.

Best Practices for Ethical AI Implementation

Ensure Transparency: Firms should implement explainable AI models and ensure that clients understand how decisions are made using AI. Providing clients with detailed yet comprehensible explanations helps build trust and mitigates concerns about the fairness of AI decisions.

Regular Audits: Regularly audit AI models for fairness, transparency, and accuracy to prevent bias and ensure compliance with ethical standards. Independent third-party audits can also provide an additional layer of credibility. Auditing should be an ongoing process, with periodic reviews to ensure that AI models continue to perform as intended.

Create Accountability Structures: Establish clear guidelines that define who is responsible for AI-driven decisions to ensure accountability. Accountability should be integrated into every phase of AI development and deployment, from data collection to model outputs. This includes assigning specific team members to oversee AI processes and ensuring that there is always a human responsible for interpreting AI-generated data.

Invest in Training and Adaptation: Staff should be trained to work alongside AI, and firms should maintain a balance between automation and human expertise. Upskilling initiatives can help employees transition into roles that require more strategic and analytical skills, ensuring that they continue to add value. Firms should also foster a culture of continuous learning, encouraging employees to stay updated on the latest AI advancements and ethical considerations.

Scalable AI Implementation for Mid-Sized Firms: For mid-sized firms looking to grow, implementing AI can help scale operations effectively. For example, a mid-sized firm adopted an AI-powered workflow automation system that enabled them to handle a 30% increase in client volume without additional hires. By leveraging scalable AI tools, these firms can grow efficiently while maintaining quality service.

Global Compliance Strategies for Large Firms: Large and multinational firms must consider global compliance challenges when implementing AI. These firms should establish centralized governance structures to oversee AI adoption across different jurisdictions, ensuring consistency in ethical standards and regulatory adherence. Leveraging AI tools capable of real-time compliance monitoring can help navigate complex, cross-border regulations more effectively.

Next Steps Checklist

- **Form an AI Ethics Committee**: Establish a group to oversee AI deployment and ensure adherence to ethical guidelines.

- **Conduct a Preliminary Audit**: Review current AI systems to identify potential biases and ensure fairness and transparency.

- **Start with Explainable AI**: Implement explainable AI models and prioritize transparency in decision-making processes.

- **Client Communication Plan**: Develop a plan for educating clients on AI use, including workshops, Q&A sessions, or informative materials.

Real-World Case Study: GreenTree Financial Background:

GreenTree Financial, a mid-sized accounting firm, adopted AI to automate tax preparation and client advisory services. However, they faced challenges in ensuring the transparency and accountability of their AI-driven decisions.

- **Challenges**: The firm initially struggled with explaining AI-generated recommendations to clients, leading to concerns over transparency and trust. Clients were hesitant to accept automated recommendations without a clear understanding of how they were generated.

- **AI Solution**: GreenTree adopted explainable AI models to clarify how decisions were made, allowing their accountants to better communicate the rationale behind financial forecasts and tax strategies. They also introduced regular client briefings to explain AI processes and address concerns. Additionally, the firm established an AI ethics committee to oversee the implementation and ensure that ethical guidelines were followed.

- **Outcome**: The firm improved client satisfaction by 15%, as clients felt more confident in AI-driven recommendations after understanding the decision-making process. Additionally, the firm saw a 20% reduction in the time required to generate client reports, thanks to the integration of explainable AI. The ethics committee also played a crucial role in maintaining client trust by ensuring that all AI-driven processes adhered to ethical standards.

Actionable Insights

1. **Adopt Explainable AI**: Use AI tools that provide clear, understandable insights into decision-making to improve client trust and accountability.

2. **Develop Ethical AI Guidelines**: Create and regularly review a set of ethical standards for AI use within the firm, focusing on transparency, fairness, and accountability.

3. **Audit AI Models Regularly**: Regular audits can help identify biases and ensure AI models meet ethical and regulatory standards.

4. **Balance AI with Human Oversight**: Emphasize human oversight in interpreting AI-generated data, especially in complex financial situations requiring nuanced judgment.

5. **Client Education**: Educate clients about AI processes and the value it brings to their financial services, through workshops or informational materials.

The Future of Ethical AI in Accounting

The future of AI in accounting will focus on improving transparency and accountability, particularly in light of global regulatory developments. As AI becomes more embedded in the profession, ethical considerations like privacy, fairness, and accountability will be even more critical. Firms must evolve their AI governance to implement robust frameworks for responsible AI use.

One emerging trend is the establishment of AI ethics committees within firms to oversee deployments and address ethical concerns. These committees can guide ethical best practices and ensure AI tools align with the firm's values and compliance obligations. Advancements in explainable AI are also expected to make AI-driven decisions more transparent, mitigating fairness and bias concerns.

Another significant development is the potential for regulatory bodies to introduce stricter guidelines for AI use in financial services. Firms that proactively establish ethical AI frameworks will be better positioned to adapt to new regulations and demonstrate their commitment to responsible AI use. The ethical application of AI will determine the trust clients place in their advisors, favoring firms that prioritize ethics, transparency, and accountability in their AI strategies.

The next chapter will explore how large firms can manage the complexity of AI implementation across multiple departments and jurisdictions, ensuring that implementation is both successful and ethically sound at scale. By addressing challenges like cross-departmental coordination and regulatory compliance, large firms can create a roadmap for responsible AI integration that enhances efficiency while maintaining public trust.

References

Association of Chartered Certified Accountants (ACCA). (n.d.). Survey. ACCA. https://www.accaglobal.com/.

Deloitte. (n.d.). Study on explainable AI. Deloitte. https://www.deloitte.com/.

FICO. (n.d.). Explainable AI in credit scoring. FICO. https://www.fico.com/.

IBM. (n.d.). Watson for data security. IBM Watson. https://www.ibm.com/watson.

McKinsey & Company. (n.d.). Report on automation in accounting. McKinsey & Company. https://www.mckinsey.com/.

Ponemon Institute. (n.d.). Cybersecurity and AI. Ponemon Institute. https://www.ponemon.org/.

PwC. (n.d.). AI-driven advisory services. PwC. https://www.pwc.com/.

World Economic Forum. (n.d.). Addressing bias in AI. World Economic Forum. https://www.weforum.org/.

The Automated Accountant

CHAPTER 18: MANAGING COMPLEX AI IMPLEMENTATIONS IN LARGE FIRMS

Introduction

Large firms face significant challenges when adopting AI technology due to their complex structures, multiple departments, and often international presence. Successfully implementing AI across such firms requires a strategic approach that addresses cross-departmental coordination, governance, compliance, and risk management. Additionally, large firms need to remain competitive by investing in tools that enhance productivity, automate routine processes, and provide valuable insights. The practical outcomes of AI implementation—such as cost reduction, increased productivity, and improved client satisfaction—are key drivers that make AI adoption an essential part of modern accounting. Highlighting these outcomes can help both senior executives and practitioners understand the clear business value AI brings.

As AI adoption continues to accelerate across the accounting sector, large firms face unique challenges. Have you ever wondered what makes AI implementation in a large firm so complex? Implementing AI in a large organization isn't just about choosing the right software—it's about navigating coordination across multiple departments, managing diverse data sets, and ensuring regulatory compliance. Think about how challenging it is to get different teams on the same page; now imagine doing that on a global scale! Large firms must also establish frameworks to integrate AI at scale while maintaining ethical standards and human oversight. This chapter examines best practices for managing complex AI implementations in large accounting firms, highlighting real-world challenges, strategies for successful execution, and tangible benefits such as reduced costs, greater efficiency, and enhanced client satisfaction.

Core Concepts

1. Phased Implementation of AI

When implementing AI in large firms, it is essential to adopt a phased approach, starting with smaller, lower-risk applications and gradually scaling AI to more complex tasks. This method allows firms to test the technology in specific areas, collect data on its effectiveness, and make necessary adjustments before rolling it out firm-wide.

A phased approach also helps the organization build confidence in the AI systems before tackling mission-critical tasks. Starting small allows the firm to learn from initial setbacks and refine its approach without jeopardizing large-scale operations. Think of it as starting with a few practice rounds before playing in the championship game—those early stages make all the difference.

- **Phases of Implementation**: Phased implementation typically involves the following stages:
  1. **Pilot Projects**: Start with small-scale pilot projects in non-critical areas such as payroll or data entry.

This stage allows the firm to identify and resolve potential issues early.

2. **Scaling Up**: Based on pilot results, gradually expand AI capabilities to more critical areas, such as compliance monitoring or fraud detection.

3. **Full-Scale Rollout**: Implement AI across departments while ensuring the infrastructure, training, and governance are robust enough to support full-scale adoption.

- **Metrics for Success**: Each phase should have specific key performance indicators (KPIs) such as cost reduction, time savings, error reduction, and increased productivity to measure the success of AI initiatives.

- **Example**: KPMG's Clara AI platform started with auditing processes. The phased rollout allowed KPMG to test AI in real-time audits, ensuring accuracy and compliance before expanding the platform to cover compliance monitoring and risk management. This phased approach not only improved audit quality but also allowed for smoother, firm-wide AI adoption.

2. Strategic Planning for AI Integration

Large firms often operate across multiple departments, each with its own workflows, data systems, and goals. Strategic planning is critical to align AI initiatives with the firm's overall business objectives and to ensure that AI tools are deployed where they can add the most value.

- **Assessing Business Needs**: Before implementing AI, firms must assess which areas can benefit the most from automation or data analysis. For example, areas like audit, fraud detection, tax preparation, and client advisory services can see significant benefits from AI integration. A comprehensive evaluation can help pinpoint pain points that AI can alleviate, such as reducing manual labor, enhancing decision-making capabilities, or improving data accuracy.

A large accounting firm, for instance, found that their tax preparation department was overwhelmed with repetitive data entry tasks. By evaluating the workload and inefficiencies, the firm realized that automating these tasks with AI could save hundreds of labor hours each year—time that accountants could then spend providing value-added advisory services.

- **AI Roadmap Development**: A clear roadmap that outlines the implementation phases, goals, and expected outcomes is crucial for successful AI adoption. The roadmap should include timelines, budgets, key performance indicators (KPIs), and milestones to track progress. Including all stakeholders in the planning stage ensures everyone has a clear understanding of how AI will impact their departments and the firm overall.

Real-World Example: A large accounting firm in Europe developed a detailed roadmap for AI integration over three years, beginning with automating data entry in the tax department, followed by using machine learning for predictive client insights. By phasing in AI adoption, the firm was able to achieve measurable milestones while minimizing disruptions to existing workflows.

3. Cross-Departmental Coordination

Large firms operate across numerous departments, and AI implementation must be aligned with the firm's overall objectives. The success of an AI initiative depends on effective collaboration between departments like tax, advisory services, auditing, and legal compliance. For example, aligning the goals of the finance and IT departments can ensure that AI solutions meet both operational and security needs.

Checklist: Cross-Departmental Coordination

- Establish cross-functional teams with representatives from all relevant departments.

- Schedule regular meetings to address challenges and maintain alignment.

- Use project management tools to track progress and improve transparency.

- Align department-specific goals with the overall AI initiative.

- Identify potential communication roadblocks and address them proactively.

Case Study: Thompson & Co.

Thompson & Co., a mid-sized firm, struggled initially with cross-departmental communication during their AI rollout. To overcome this, they created cross-functional teams involving representatives from finance, IT, and compliance. Weekly meetings helped align department-specific needs and address any roadblocks early. This structured communication approach ultimately smoothed their transition to using AI across audit and advisory services.

- **Creating Cross-Functional Teams**: Establishing cross-functional teams can help manage AI projects that affect multiple parts of the organization. Each department should have representation in the AI project team to provide insights, identify specific needs, and prevent siloed implementation. This structure facilitates communication and ensures that the AI initiative meets the broader needs of the firm.

One tax director at a large firm once mentioned, "The biggest win we had in AI was getting everyone on the same page early on. Our finance, compliance, and IT teams met weekly for the first three months of our AI rollout. That communication made all the difference when we started scaling."

- **Project Management Tools**: Using project management tools can help coordinate AI initiatives across departments, particularly in large firms. These tools provide transparency on project status, progress, and potential bottlenecks. Regular meetings and updates help ensure alignment, address challenges, and maintain momentum.

Real-World Example: At EY, their Helix AI platform spans multiple departments, using AI for fraud detection, compliance, and risk management. Cross-department collaboration has been key to ensuring the platform's successful integration across global operations.

4. AI Governance and Compliance

Large firms must develop robust governance frameworks to manage the ethical, legal, and compliance-related aspects of AI. AI systems handling sensitive client data must be carefully regulated to ensure compliance with global data privacy regulations like the General Data Protection Regulation (GDPR) in Europe and the Sarbanes-Oxley Act (SOX) in the United States.

- **Establishing an AI Ethics Committee**: Firms should establish an AI ethics committee to oversee implementations, review ethical concerns, and develop policies for responsible AI use. The committee should include members from different departments to provide a balanced perspective and ensure ethical considerations are integrated into all AI deployments.

An AI ethics committee could also serve as a bridge between technical and non-technical stakeholders, ensuring that complex AI topics are communicated in understandable terms to clients and internal teams.

- **Compliance Management**: Firms must comply with a range of regulations, such as GDPR, the California Consumer Privacy Act, and other financial regulations. Maintaining compliance at scale requires having dedicated compliance officers who understand how AI affects data privacy, client confidentiality, and the regulatory landscape. Regular compliance audits should be conducted to identify and address any gaps in adherence.

Real-World Example: KPMG's Trusted AI framework combines AI governance with human oversight to ensure transparency and accuracy in audits. By employing a human-in-the-loop approach, KPMG ensures that AI decisions meet professional standards.

Handling Large-Scale AI Adoption

Large-scale AI adoption in a firm can be a daunting process, requiring detailed planning, resource allocation, and a clear understanding of the organization's needs. Below is a step-by-step approach to handling large-scale AI adoption.

Checklist: Large-Scale AI Adoption

- ✓ Conduct an AI-readiness assessment. Are you truly ready to adopt AI, or are there still gaps in your infrastructure or team skills?

- ✓ Identify departments with the highest potential for AI automation.

- ✓ Define clear and measurable goals for the AI initiative.

- ✓ Invest in cloud-based or scalable AI infrastructure.

- ✓ Initiate pilot projects in key departments and gather feedback.

- ✓ Gradually expand AI capabilities while addressing any challenges.

Case Study: Baker & Sons

Baker & Sons, a small accounting firm, was initially hesitant about AI due to limited resources. They began with a simple AI readiness assessment to identify areas of inefficiency. The assessment showed that internal reporting was taking up significant time. By implementing a cloud-based AI tool for reporting, they saved over 200 hours annually, demonstrating that even small firms can benefit from strategic AI use.

1. Assessment and Planning

Before implementing AI, firms should conduct an AI-readiness assessment. This evaluation includes identifying the areas where AI can add the most value, determining which departments will benefit the most from AI automation, and defining clear, measurable goals for the AI initiative.

- **Best Practice**: Start with an AI pilot program in a non-critical area of the firm (e.g., payroll or internal reporting) to assess how AI integrates with existing processes and to identify any potential challenges before a full-scale implementation.

2. Building the Infrastructure

Implementing AI requires significant investments in infrastructure, especially cloud computing. Large firms should consider using cloud-based AI platforms that offer scalability, such as Microsoft Azure AI or AWS AI. These platforms provide the computational power necessary for AI to analyze large datasets and provide real-time insights across global operations.

- **Example**: EY leveraged the scalability of Microsoft Azure to build its Helix AI platform, which now supports AI-driven auditing and compliance functions globally.

3. Pilot and Gradual Rollout

Once the infrastructure is in place, firms should initiate pilot projects in key departments such as tax, auditing, or compliance.

Based on the results, firms can expand AI applications to other areas, focusing on continuous improvement and feedback from key stakeholders.

Gradual rollouts help identify challenges that might only surface during real-world usage—it's like test-driving a car before committing. You learn what needs tweaking before putting everyone behind the wheel.

4. Future Planning and AI Scalability

As AI systems evolve, firms must ensure that their technology infrastructure can scale accordingly. Large firms should consider adopting open platforms or flexible AI solutions that can integrate with other technologies as new needs arise. Additionally, they must continually reassess their AI strategies to align with emerging trends and regulatory developments.

- **Best Practice**: Invest in flexible, scalable platforms like Google AI that allow for future expansion without needing to overhaul the system completely.

Best Practices for Large-Scale AI Implementations

1. **Develop a Centralized AI Strategy**: Ensure that all AI projects align with the firm's overall strategy. A centralized approach prevents fragmented implementations that can lead to inefficiencies.

2. **Invest in Training Programs**: Large firms must invest in training programs that upskill employees to work alongside AI. Training should focus on both technical skills and ethical considerations.

One accounting professional once shared, "Our biggest fear with AI was losing the human touch. But when we invested in training our team—teaching them how to use AI for data analysis and advisory roles—we realized we could enhance our human skills instead of replacing them."

3. **Scalable AI Solutions**: Choose AI solutions that are designed to scale with the firm. Technologies that integrate well with existing systems and can grow as the firm's needs expand will be more effective in the long term.

4. **Regular Evaluation and Adaptation**: Implement a feedback loop to continuously evaluate AI initiatives. This involves measuring outcomes, gathering feedback from users, and making necessary adjustments to improve performance and alignment with the firm's goals.

Case Study: GlobalReach Accounting Firm

Background: GlobalReach, a large international accounting firm, sought to leverage AI to streamline audits and enhance predictive analytics in client advisory services. The scale of implementation presented challenges related to data integration, cross-departmental coordination, and maintaining ethical standards.

- **Challenges**: The firm faced significant obstacles in integrating data from its numerous offices worldwide, each using different systems. Additionally, coordinating AI adoption across various teams proved complex, and ensuring compliance with international data privacy laws was challenging.

The head of the IT department at GlobalReach shared, "We had offices in ten countries, each with different systems and standards. Getting everyone on board felt like herding cats. But having a structured data governance plan and dedicated project managers really made the difference."

- **AI Solution**: GlobalReach established an AI governance team that included members from IT, compliance, audit, and advisory services. The team developed a unified data framework that allowed for the standardization of data across offices. The firm also created regional AI ethics committees to ensure adherence to local regulations and address ethical concerns.

- **Outcome**: The firm successfully implemented AI across its audit and advisory services, reducing audit processing times by 35% and improving the accuracy of client financial forecasting by 20%. By establishing a structured governance model, GlobalReach ensured ethical AI implementation and compliance across all jurisdictions.

Actionable Insights

1. **Align AI Projects with Business Objectives**: AI initiatives should directly support the firm's strategic goals, whether that's improving client service, reducing operational costs, or enhancing data accuracy.

2. **Standardize Data Management**: Invest in a data governance framework to standardize and integrate data across the organization, ensuring that AI models receive high-quality inputs.

3. **Promote Cross-Departmental Collaboration**:
   Establish cross-functional teams for AI initiatives, with
   representation from all impacted departments to ensure
   diverse perspectives and address potential challenges early.

4. **Develop an AI Ethics Framework**: Create and maintain
   an AI ethics committee to oversee responsible AI
   deployment, ensuring transparency, fairness, and
   compliance.

5. **Invest in Training and Change Management**: Upskill
   employees and provide ongoing support to help them adapt
   to working with AI. This includes not only technical training
   but also fostering an understanding of AI's ethical and
   practical impacts on the firm.

Conclusion

Implementing AI in a large accounting firm requires strategic
planning, cross-departmental coordination, and a commitment
to ethical governance. By adopting a phased approach, building
the right infrastructure, and fostering collaboration between
teams, large firms can successfully integrate AI into their
operations. The benefits of AI—ranging from increased efficiency
to enhanced data insights—are within reach for firms that invest
in a thoughtful, systematic approach. As the next chapter will
explore, ensuring that AI initiatives are sustainable in the long
term requires aligning these implementations with the firm's
broader business objectives and fostering a culture of innovation
and adaptability.

With the complexities of large-scale AI implementations
covered, it's clear that managing such technology requires a
careful balance of strategy, resources, and foresight. Yet, as AI

becomes a core component of advanced firm infrastructure, another technology is emerging to further secure and streamline these implementations: blockchain. For accounting leaders, understanding how AI and blockchain can work together is essential for safeguarding data integrity, enhancing transparency, and reducing fraud. In the next chapter, we'll explore the fundamentals of blockchain, its unique synergies with AI, and how this powerful combination can reshape the future of secure accounting practices.

References

EY. (n.d.). EY Helix AI.
https://www.ey.com/en_gl/assurance/ey-helix.

Google. (n.d.). Google AI platform.
https://cloud.google.com/products/ai.

IBM. (n.d.). Watson for NLP in compliance.
https://www.ibm.com/watson.

KPMG. (n.d.). Clara AI.
https://home.kpmg/xx/en/home/services/clara.html.

Microsoft. (n.d.). Azure AI. https://azure.microsoft.com/en-us/services/cognitive-services/.

CHAPTER 19: AI AND BLOCKCHAIN – A GUIDE FOR ACCOUNTING LEADERS

Introduction

As the accounting profession evolves, the convergence of AI and blockchain is creating revolutionary changes in how financial transactions are recorded, analyzed, and audited. AI is transforming accounting by automating repetitive tasks and enhancing decision-making, while blockchain adds layers of security, transparency, and immutability. Together, these technologies provide firms with the tools they need to improve compliance, reduce fraud, and increase operational efficiency. In this chapter, we explore how firms of all sizes can leverage AI and blockchain using real-world examples, practical insights, and actionable strategies for implementation.

Core Concepts

1. Blockchain's Role in Securing Financial Transactions: Blockchain works like a digital notebook shared among many people. Each page (or block) is locked once it's filled, and no one can change it without everyone noticing. This makes blockchain a secure way to record financial transactions, ensuring transparency and minimizing the risk of tampering. This provides a secure foundation for audits, transaction reconciliation, and compliance reporting—particularly crucial in highly regulated environments.

Blockchain is revolutionizing financial transaction security by providing enhanced transparency and reducing fraud. A striking 90% of accountants believe that blockchain will significantly impact their business in the future.

Due to its decentralized nature, blockchain records are nearly tamper-proof. Each block is like a locked box with a unique key. It also refers to the previous block's key, creating a chain that is very hard to break or alter without everyone knowing. This feature makes unauthorized changes nearly impossible. This feature is vital in accounting, where the integrity of financial records is paramount.

Example: EY's blockchain-enabled platform allows auditors and clients to view tamper-proof transaction records in real time, significantly reducing audit effort. The platform's transparency has led to a reported 40% reduction in time spent on verification activities.

Additionally, JPMorgan is rolling out a blockchain network to facilitate customer transactions, showcasing the potential of blockchain technology in large-scale financial operations. Citigroup has also made significant investments in blockchain projects, which are expected to yield returns by 2024.

Flowchart of AI and Blockchain Integration

Below is a suggested flowchart summarizing the integration process of AI and blockchain in accounting firms:

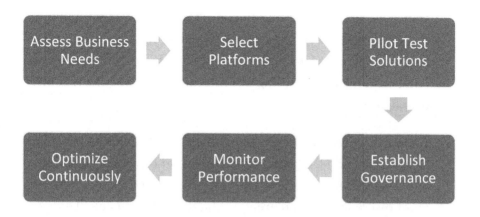

Figure 21 Flowchart of Integration Process

This flowchart helps firms visualize the key stages in adopting AI and blockchain technologies.

2. AI's Role in Enhancing Decision-Making:

"AI will augment us but not replace. [...] It's allowed us to provide more service, get better results and have more complex regs that we follow. And, there are more accountants now than ever. Same thing will happen with AI. Until computers can use judgement and be creative, we'll all still have plenty of jobs," reported one user on Reddit.

AI is transforming decision-making in accounting by analyzing massive datasets and providing actionable insights. Approximately 79% of corporate strategists believe that AI, automation, and analytics will drive business success in the next two years. AI has been shown to save 16% of the total cost of finance functions, significantly improving overall efficiency.

Scenario: Imagine auditors dealing with tens of thousands of transactions from multiple clients. Traditionally, identifying inconsistencies or red flags would be labor-intensive and prone to human error. AI algorithms, trained on historical transaction data, can now instantly flag irregularities, reducing the risk of oversight.

Example: PwC's Aura platform integrates AI and blockchain to streamline audits, improving accuracy and reducing time. Since adopting this solution, PwC has reported a 30% reduction in audit discrepancies and greater reliability in audit conclusions. Moreover, AI has allowed auditors to focus more on strategic areas rather than mundane data entry tasks.

Real-World Use Case: Enova uses AI and machine learning in its lending platform to provide advanced financial analytics and credit assessments. Similarly, DataRobot helps financial institutions build accurate predictive models for issues like fraudulent credit card transactions and digital wealth management.

3. Smart Contracts for Financial Transactions:

"I've cut outside lawyers, tax accountant, and consultant fees in half. Not to mention my internal staff is better at doing almost everything. ...And that's in a single year - a single yr where half the yr it was useless and people didn't know how to use it at all."

Smart contracts promise to automate complex multi-party financial transactions. For example, a smart contract can automate the release of payment only after specific conditions, like delivery of goods or services, are met. This not only streamlines operations but also reduces disputes.

Smart contracts minimize errors by reducing manual input and automating payment processes. Their adoption began as early as 2016, marking a milestone in financial technology. Firms using smart contracts for vendor payments have seen administrative costs drop by approximately 25%.

Example: Large firms can use smart contracts to automatically execute payments after verifying invoices with AI-driven analysis, creating a clear audit trail and boosting efficiency.

4. AI-Driven Predictive Analytics with Blockchain Data:

"Up until beginning of this year, both compute and API tokens were prohibitively expensive to use for 'everyday' purposes. [...] So really soon, lot of finance platforms will integrate gen AI capabilities... You'll be able to generate state of art board decks and presentation from FP&A platforms directly... Automate financial statement notes..." (Reddit).

AI's ability to analyze blockchain data provides a powerful tool for predictive analytics. Machine learning, which is like teaching a computer to recognize patterns based on past examples, helps improve the accuracy of financial analysis and reporting. Predictive analytics are also useful for analyzing financial data and providing insights into future trends, enabling firms to make informed decisions.

Example: EY uses AI-driven predictive analytics on its blockchain platform to help firms manage risks and forecast trends. A recent study showed that firms using this approach experienced a 15% reduction in unexpected cash flow issues. Companies like Futrli use machine learning to identify patterns, empowering firms to make better decisions regarding risks and opportunities, ultimately enhancing financial planning and fraud detection.

Real-World Examples

"I lead corporate operations and finance at an AI startup, and have personally initiated and led ChatGPT rollout to all employees [...] in the next 12 months, you'll see more changes to the accounting profession than the past 10 years combined."

Case Study: Small Firm Adopts Blockchain for Expense Tracking

- **Background**: A small accounting firm with limited resources needed an affordable solution to streamline expense tracking and improve accuracy.

- **Challenge**: Manual tracking of expenses was prone to errors, consuming valuable time that could have been spent on client service.

- **Solution**: The firm adopted a blockchain-based expense tracking tool offered through a SaaS model. The tool provided transparency and immutability without requiring significant upfront investment.

- **Outcome**: The firm saw a 25% reduction in time spent on expense management and improved accuracy, which allowed them to allocate more time to client advisory services.

Case Study: Mid-Sized Firm Uses AI to Enhance Client Collaboration

- **Background**: A mid-sized accounting firm sought to improve client collaboration and enhance communication, as they were facing issues with data sharing and delayed responses.

- **Challenge**: The firm needed a solution that could help automate client communication while still providing a personal touch.

- **Solution**: The firm integrated an AI-driven chatbot system that was customized for their client needs. This allowed clients to receive quick answers to common questions and facilitated the exchange of documents through a secure portal.

- **Outcome**: Client satisfaction increased by 30%, and the firm reduced the time spent on routine client queries by 40%. This enabled staff to focus more on complex client needs and personalized service.

Case Study: PwC's AI and Blockchain Solutions for Auditing

- **Background**: PwC sought a more efficient and transparent way to manage audits, as traditional processes were time-consuming and error-prone.

- **Challenge**: Modernize the audit process to reduce manual effort and enhance transparency.

- **Solution**: PwC's Aura platform integrates AI for automating data analysis and blockchain for immutable transaction verification.

- **Outcome**: PwC achieved a 35% reduction in audit times, 20% fewer errors, and increased client satisfaction.

To illustrate further, consider this: Before implementing Aura, auditors spent approximately 60% of their time on manual data entry and verification. Now, with AI and blockchain, that figure has dropped to just 25%, allowing auditors to focus on strategic analysis and client interaction. Moreover, PwC developed a blockchain-based platform called "Halo" for auditing cryptocurrency transactions, ensuring transparency and trust in the emerging digital asset space.

Best Practices for Blockchain and AI Integration

- **Considerations for Small Firms**: When integrating AI and blockchain, small firms should start small. Here are practical, actionable steps small firms can take today to start integrating AI without significant investment:

    1. **Identify Pain Points**: Start by identifying repetitive tasks that take up a lot of time, such as data entry or transaction reconciliation.

    2. **Utilize Free or Low-Cost Tools**: Leverage SaaS platforms that offer AI-based tools for free or at a low cost, such as QuickBooks for automated bookkeeping or Xero for transaction matching.

    3. **Partner with Vendors**: Seek partnerships with AI vendors offering affordable solutions that are scalable over time. Look for platforms that allow you to start small and upgrade as needed.

    4. **Pilot Basic AI Solutions**: Implement simple AI tools like chatbots for client communication or AI-driven analytics for basic financial reporting. This allows you to gain experience before committing to larger investments.

5. **Training and Familiarization**: Invest in basic training for staff to familiarize them with AI tools. Understanding the benefits of automation will help in reducing resistance and building comfort with new technologies.

These steps provide a cost-effective way for small firms to begin integrating AI, ensuring that they do not face overwhelming upfront costs and can gradually scale their capabilities.

- **Selecting the Right Platforms**: Successful AI and blockchain integration depends on choosing the appropriate platform based on scalability, security, and cost.

Platform Examples:

  o **IBM Blockchain**: A robust blockchain solution designed for enterprises, offering high scalability and seamless integration with IBM Watson for AI-driven insights. It is ideal for firms looking for advanced fraud detection and high-quality data security measures.

  o **Microsoft Azure Blockchain**: Provides a cloud-based blockchain service that integrates with Microsoft's AI solutions, suitable for firms interested in combining blockchain with their existing Azure infrastructure for enhanced analytics and process automation.

  o **Hyperledger Fabric**: An open-source blockchain platform tailored for enterprise use, suitable for mid-sized firms looking for a highly customizable blockchain framework.

Action Step	Description
Integrate Blockchain to Secure Transactions	Pilot blockchain for transparency and efficiency.
Utilize AI to Enhance Decision-Making	Train staff on AI tools to identify risks and patterns.
Adopt Smart Contracts for Automation	Use smart contracts for vendor payments to reduce errors.

Table 5 Key Action Steps

The above table provides a quick reference for the actionable insights discussed, making it easier for readers to understand and implement these steps.

Actionable Insights

Addressing Staff Resistance and Fostering Innovation

When implementing AI and blockchain technologies, one of the key human factors firms must address is staff resistance. Employees may be wary of new systems that seem to threaten their roles or require a shift in established workflows. To foster an innovation-friendly environment, firms should consider the following steps:

1. Develop Training Programs: Provide comprehensive training sessions that emphasize how AI and blockchain can make daily tasks easier and more efficient. Highlighting specific use cases where technology has led to positive outcomes will help staff understand the value.

2. Involve Employees Early: Engaging staff in the planning and implementation phases helps them feel invested in the success of the technology. Employee feedback can be invaluable in refining deployment strategies and identifying potential pitfalls before they become issues.

3. Showcase Success Stories: Sharing testimonials and case studies from within the industry can help alleviate fears. For example, "I've cut external consultant fees in half thanks to AI tools, and our internal staff is now more efficient," shared a firm partner who recently led a successful AI integration.

4. Create an Innovation Culture: Encourage open discussions about the role of new technologies in shaping the future of the firm. Establishing an innovation committee or hosting regular brainstorming sessions can help staff see themselves as part of the digital transformation journey.

These strategies not only reduce resistance but also encourage employees to take an active role in adopting and leveraging new technologies.

The Future of AI and Blockchain in Accounting

Using AI for Global Compliance in Cross-Border Operations

Large accounting firms face unique challenges when managing multi-national portfolios, including navigating different regulatory environments and ensuring compliance across borders. AI can be instrumental in this regard by analyzing regulatory requirements in real-time, automating compliance processes, and predicting changes that could impact global operations.

- **Automated Compliance Monitoring**: AI tools can continuously monitor global regulatory changes and ensure that firms adapt their processes accordingly. For example,

AI-driven compliance platforms can automatically adjust financial reporting practices in response to new tax laws in different countries.

- **Cross-Border Tax Planning**: AI's predictive capabilities enable firms to model tax scenarios across multiple jurisdictions. This helps firms optimize their tax strategies while ensuring they meet local regulatory requirements.

- **Standardized Reporting with Blockchain**: Blockchain ensures that all transactions are logged in a standardized format across all jurisdictions, providing transparency and easing regulatory reporting. Combined with AI, firms can quickly generate compliance reports tailored to specific regions, reducing the administrative burden on staff.

Example: A large multinational accounting firm used an AI platform to stay updated with regulatory changes across 15 different countries. This proactive approach helped the firm avoid compliance issues and saved an estimated 20% in potential penalties and fees by automating the update of internal compliance processes.

Future Opportunities for Small and Mid-Sized Firms: Small firms will have opportunities to adopt scalable solutions as technology becomes more affordable. For mid-sized firms, the ability to integrate client collaboration tools with AI-driven insights will help scale services efficiently. Large firms will continue to benefit from advanced AI systems that can handle cross-border compliance and complex financial data.

3-Year Growth Roadmap for Mid-Sized Firms

To help mid-sized firms plan their journey towards AI and blockchain adoption, a structured growth roadmap is provided:

- **Year 1: Foundation Phase**

  o **Assessment**: Identify pain points and assess which processes are the most suitable for automation or blockchain integration.

  o **Platform Selection**: Choose scalable, cost-effective platforms that fit the firm's needs.

  o **Initial Implementation**: Start small by implementing AI-driven automation for repetitive tasks, like transaction reconciliation and basic data analysis.

- **Year 2: Expansion Phase**

  o **Pilot Advanced Solutions**: Run pilot programs for blockchain in expense tracking and smart contracts for client/vendor transactions.

  o **Client Engagement Tools**: Introduce AI-based client portals and chatbots to enhance communication and provide quick solutions.

  o **Staff Training**: Expand training initiatives to cover more advanced AI functionalities, empowering staff to use new tools effectively.

- **Year 3: Optimization Phase**

  o **Full Integration**: Implement blockchain solutions for audit trails and compliance reporting.

  o **Advanced AI Adoption**: Integrate predictive analytics into financial planning and forecasting.

o **Continuous Improvement**: Establish an ongoing review mechanism for AI and blockchain processes, ensuring continuous optimization and addressing any emerging challenges.

Conclusion

AI and blockchain are fundamentally transforming the accounting landscape, offering unprecedented opportunities for improving efficiency, security, and decision-making capabilities. By understanding the core concepts, adopting best practices, and following actionable insights, accounting firms can leverage these technologies to their advantage, regardless of their size.

The journey toward AI and blockchain integration begins with small, practical steps—whether it's piloting an AI tool to streamline workflows or implementing blockchain to secure transactions. Firms that are proactive in embracing these technologies will position themselves at the forefront of the digital transformation of accounting.

References

Reddit. (n.d.). Looking for feedback on a crypto accounting [Online forum post]. Reddit. https://www.reddit.com/r/Accounting/comments/wqfq5 8/looking_for_feedback_on_a_crypto_accounting/

Reddit. (n.d.). AMA: I'm a CPA working in a Big 4 indirect tax [Online forum post]. Reddit. https://www.reddit.com/r/Accounting/comments/e1klm g/ama_im_a_cpa_working_in_a_big_4_indirect_tax/

Reddit. (n.d.). Hot take: AI will never be a threat to accountants [Online forum post]. Reddit. https://www.reddit.com/r/Accounting/comments/1at5z y1/hot_take_ai_will_never_be_a_threat_to_accountant s/

Reddit. (n.d.). You guys are underestimating the impact AI will have [Online forum post]. Reddit. https://www.reddit.com/r/Accounting/comments/1f505 nw/you_guys_are_underestimating_the_impact_ai_wil l/

Reddit. (n.d.). Don't worry, we won't be replaced with AI [Online forum post]. Reddit. https://www.reddit.com/r/Accounting/comments/1cuk5 vq/dont_worry_we_wont_be_replaced_with_ai/

Reddit. (n.d.). AI won't take our jobs, but outsource will [Online forum post]. Reddit. https://www.reddit.com/r/Accounting/comments/134zr dg/ai_wont_take_our_jobs_but_outsource_will/

Reddit. (n.d.). AI is coming for us all [Online forum post]. Reddit. https://www.reddit.com/r/Layoffs/comments/1ablxpx/a i_is_coming_for_us_all/

Reddit. (n.d.). Blockchain and the accounting profession [Online forum post]. Reddit. https://www.reddit.com/r/Accounting/comments/72dgd 2/blockchain_and_the_accounting_profession/

The Automated Accountant

CHAPTER 20: FUTURE-PROOFING ACCOUNTING: STRATEGIES FOR NAVIGATING AI TRANSFORMATION

Introduction

As Artificial Intelligence (AI) continues to reshape the accounting profession, how can firms of all sizes develop effective strategies for implementing these powerful tools? While AI holds the promise of automating routine tasks, improving decision-making, and enhancing client service, a successful implementation requires careful planning, assessing firm readiness, selecting appropriate tools, and managing workforce changes. In this chapter, we will explore a strategic framework for integrating AI into accounting firms—from readiness assessments to risk management—ensuring firms maximize benefits while minimizing disruption.

AI can revolutionize how accounting firms function, offering growth opportunities, greater efficiency, and improved client services. However, successful AI implementation is complex and demands a thorough understanding of a firm's unique capabilities, goals, and challenges. Firms must look beyond the initial allure of AI—what does it take to truly harness its power? Comprehensive assessments, detailed planning, and ongoing evaluation are key to success. This chapter delves into the core concepts that will guide accounting firms through the successful integration of AI, providing actionable insights and real-world examples to illustrate the journey.

Core Concepts

1. Assessing Firm Readiness and Identifying Problems

Before adopting AI, have you assessed whether your firm is ready? Identifying specific challenges that AI is meant to address is a crucial first step. A successful AI strategy starts with understanding key pain points and aligning AI solutions with the firm's goals.

Readiness Assessment: Firms need to evaluate their existing technological infrastructure, staff skills, and willingness to embrace AI-driven workflows. This includes reviewing hardware, software, and security protocols to ensure the firm can support AI tools. According to a 2023 survey by the Association of International Certified Professional Accountants (AICPA), 48% of finance and accounting professionals believe their organizations are not adequately prepared for AI implementation. To help firms assess readiness, the AI Readiness Assessment Tool developed by the AICPA is a useful resource, evaluating factors such as data quality, technology infrastructure, and staff skills.

Firms also need to consider whether their workforce is ready to embrace new technology. How employees feel about AI can greatly influence its adoption. For example, when Sunshine Accounting introduced AI tools, they focused on building enthusiasm through workshops and open discussions, which helped ease the transition and led to greater acceptance. By fostering a culture that embraces innovation and emphasizes the benefits of AI, firms can improve their readiness for implementation. Leadership must play a pivotal role in promoting an open mindset toward AI and addressing any concerns that employees may have about job displacement or changing roles.

Identifying Problems: Pinpoint the problems AI can solve. Are manual tasks overwhelming staff? Is there a need for advanced analytics to improve advisory services? Understanding where AI can make the most impact will drive its successful adoption. Identifying specific use cases where AI can add value is crucial. For example, AI can streamline repetitive tasks like data entry, enabling accountants to concentrate on more strategic activities such as financial analysis and client consultation. Alternatively, AI can assist in reconciling accounts or generating routine financial reports, further freeing up time for higher-level work.

Real-World Example: In 2022, PwC implemented an AI-powered tool called "Cash.ai" to automate cash flow forecasting for its clients. This tool reduced the time spent on cash flow analysis by 30% and improved forecast accuracy by 25%. PwC's experience underscores the importance of conducting a readiness assessment before integrating AI into workflows. By identifying gaps in their technology and workforce capabilities, PwC was able to implement AI successfully, enhancing both efficiency and accuracy.

The table on the following page reviews various aspects of accounting and compares Traditional accounting methods to AI-Enhanced accounting methods.

Aspect	Traditional Accounting	AI-Enhanced Accounting
Data Entry	Manual, slow, prone to errors	Automated with AI-driven data capture (OCR)
Reconciliation	Manual matching of transactions	Automated with Robotic Process Automation (RPA)
Financial Reporting	Manual compilation and analysis	AI generates real-time, dynamic reports
Compliance	Manual tracking of regulation changes	AI monitors compliance in real time and updates systems
Advisory Services	Limited by time spent on transactional tasks	AI frees accountants to focus on strategic advisory
Accuracy	Prone to human errors	AI reduces errors with automated processes
Cost Efficiency	High labor costs	Lower operational costs due to automation
Scalability	Challenging with limited human resources	Scalable with AI handling increasing data and tasks

Table 6 Traditional vs. AI-Enhanced Accounting

2. Selecting the Right AI Tools

Choosing the right AI tools requires careful evaluation of the firm's long-term goals and specific needs. With various AI applications available for different accounting functions—from tax compliance to predictive analytics—selecting the right tools can ensure a smoother implementation.

Evaluate AI Vendors: When evaluating AI vendors, firms should consider factors such as vendor reputation, industry specialization, and customer support. For instance, one mid-

sized firm chose an AI vendor based solely on cost, only to face
significant integration issues that delayed their project by several
months. This experience highlighted the importance of not
overlooking vendor track records and customer support
capabilities. According to a 2022 Deloitte survey, 47% of
organizations struggle with integrating AI into their existing
processes, highlighting the importance of vendor support during
and after implementation. The vendor's ability to provide
training, ongoing technical assistance, and regular software
updates can significantly affect the success of AI adoption.

Scalability: Choose AI solutions that can grow with your firm.
Cloud-based AI platforms, such as IBM Watson and Microsoft
Azure, offer scalable solutions that can adapt to increasing data
volumes and user needs.

Scalability is essential, especially for growing firms that plan to
expand their AI initiatives over time. The ability to handle larger
datasets and integrate new features is crucial for long-term
success.

Pilot Programs: Implement pilot programs to test AI solutions
before full-scale adoption. For instance, KPMG conducted a six-
month pilot of an AI-powered audit tool in 2021, which led to a
15% reduction in audit hours. A checklist to help firms evaluate
pilot program readiness—including resources required,
timelines, and metrics for success—would further assist in
making these initial trials effective and manageable for all firm
sizes. Including data visualizations that show the progress and
results of pilot programs can provide firms with a clearer
understanding of the value and potential challenges involved.
Pilot programs help identify challenges early on and provide
valuable insights into AI effectiveness. By running pilot
programs, firms can gather data on how well AI tools integrate

with existing systems, measure improvements in efficiency, and make informed decisions about broader implementation.

Examples of AI Platforms: Several AI platforms are transforming accounting. Xero provides AI-powered bank reconciliation, Sage Intacct offers financial management with AI-driven insights, UiPath specializes in Robotic Process Automation (RPA) for accounting tasks, and MindBridge focuses on AI-powered audit and risk assessment. To appeal to a broader audience, let's consider scalable examples across different firm sizes. Small firms, for instance, could use Xero for AI-powered bank reconciliation, which is budget-friendly and easy to implement. Mid-sized firms might benefit from Sage Intacct for comprehensive financial management with AI-driven insights, supporting both growth and operational scalability. Large multinational firms, on the other hand, can utilize IBM Watson for sophisticated AI needs, including predictive analytics and cross-border compliance.

Steps for Selection:

1. Define specific accounting problems to solve.

2. Research available AI solutions.

3. Evaluate vendor capabilities and track records.

4. Conduct pilot programs.

5. Assess scalability and integration potential.

6. Consider total cost of ownership.

7. Make a decision based on ROI and strategic fit.

Selecting AI tools is not just about functionality; it is about finding solutions that align with the firm's vision and can deliver measurable value. Firms should involve key stakeholders in the selection process, including IT specialists, accountants, and decision-makers, to ensure the chosen tools meet diverse needs.

3. Preparing the Workforce for AI

Implementing AI is more than just introducing new technology— how can you prepare your workforce and adapt your firm's culture to ensure success? Staff must understand how AI will change their roles and enhance their productivity.

Training and Upskilling: Firms should invest in comprehensive training programs to ensure employees are ready to work with AI tools. Upskilling refers to the process of teaching employees new skills, particularly those needed to effectively use and manage AI technologies. Training should be tailored to different roles within the firm. This ensures that both technical and non-technical staff understand how AI fits into their daily tasks. For example, a successful training program at Abacas Accounting included hands-on workshops that helped both IT staff and accountants see the practical benefits of AI, making the transition smoother. Providing hands-on experience and practical training sessions can help employees become comfortable with new AI-driven processes.

Communication: Clearly communicate the benefits of AI to reduce resistance and fear of job displacement. For example, when Smith & Jones Accounting introduced AI-driven automation, they held town hall meetings and one-on-one sessions with employees to discuss how AI would enhance, not replace, their roles. This transparent approach helped ease concerns and improved overall acceptance of the new technology. Effective communication is critical to fostering a positive attitude toward AI adoption. Employees must see AI as a tool that will enhance their capabilities, not replace them. Leaders should emphasize how AI can reduce mundane tasks and provide more opportunities for strategic, value-added activities.

Creating AI Champions: Identify tech-savvy employees to lead AI adoption efforts, demonstrating the value of AI tools to their colleagues. AI champions can act as mentors, helping their peers navigate new technologies and promoting a culture of innovation. These champions are instrumental in building enthusiasm for AI and addressing concerns that may arise during the transition.

Real-World Example: Deloitte adopted a proactive communication strategy and positioned AI as a tool to complement human expertise. This helped overcome employee concerns and led to widespread adoption. Deloitte also identified early adopters within their workforce to serve as AI champions, which facilitated smoother transitions and increased overall acceptance of AI tools.

4. Handling Large-Scale AI Adoption

For large firms, how can AI adoption be handled strategically? It all starts with a clear plan and future-proofing for scalability.

Start Small: Start with a pilot in a specific department to see how well AI works before expanding. Each firm's needs are unique, so use these small-scale trials to gather data and refine strategies. Start small, but think big—pilot projects let you see AI's benefits firsthand, providing proof of concept and confidence to scale up.

Evaluate Progress: Measure how AI is working by tracking metrics like time savings and error reduction, and get employee feedback. Adjust as needed. Regular reviews ensure AI stays on track and any issues are quickly addressed. It's all about keeping the technology working well and getting real value from it.

Plan for Future Growth: Think ahead and make sure AI tools can scale as your firm grows. Technology will change, so be prepared to keep your systems up to date. Future-proofing means choosing flexible platforms and making regular updates to stay ahead.

Real-World Example: PwC regularly reviews how well their AI-driven audit solutions perform by checking metrics and getting staff input. This process helps PwC keep its AI up to date and effective, showing how staying agile with technology can lead to better outcomes.

5. Establishing Robust Governance Frameworks

A strong governance framework is key to managing AI tools, especially in large firms where data security, compliance, and ethical considerations are vital. Governance frameworks, in the context of AI, refer to the systems and processes put in place to ensure responsible use, fairness, transparency, and accountability of AI tools. These frameworks help firms manage the risks associated with AI and ensure that AI models are used ethically and in compliance with regulations. For example, one firm faced severe reputational damage due to inadequate oversight of their AI implementation, which led to biased decision-making. This highlights the importance of establishing thorough governance processes from the start.

Examples of Governance: The AICPA and CIMA have developed an AI ethics framework for accountants, which includes principles such as fairness, transparency, and accountability. Firms like EY have adopted governance frameworks that include dedicated AI oversight committees and comprehensive data privacy policies. Establishing governance frameworks ensures that AI tools are used responsibly and that their outputs are consistent with regulatory standards.

IRS and Government Guidelines: The IRS has published guidelines on the use of AI in tax compliance, emphasizing the importance of human oversight and explainable AI models. Explainable AI refers to AI systems designed in a way that their operations can be easily understood by humans, ensuring transparency and accountability in their outputs. Firms must adhere to these guidelines to ensure compliance and ethical use of AI in their operations. Governance frameworks should also address issues such as data quality, algorithmic bias, and accountability.

A robust governance framework includes clear policies for data handling, transparency, and ensuring that AI models are explainable and fair. Firms should also establish oversight bodies responsible for monitoring AI applications and ensuring they meet ethical and legal standards.

6. Continuous Monitoring and Optimization

AI is not a one-time solution—it requires continuous evaluation and optimization to ensure it remains effective.

What to Monitor: Firms should track key performance indicators (KPIs) such as accuracy of AI-generated outputs, time and cost savings, user adoption rates, data quality, and compliance with regulatory requirements. Monitoring these metrics helps identify areas where AI is performing well and where improvements are needed. Consistent evaluation is essential to maintain the value AI brings to the firm.

Optimization: Regularly updating AI models with new data and retraining them can significantly improve performance. For example, a mid-sized accounting firm saw a 20% improvement in processing accuracy after updating their AI models quarterly, demonstrating the value of continuous model optimization. For example, EY's AI-powered lease accounting tool improved its accuracy from 85% to 95% over a year through continuous learning. Optimization also involves adapting AI tools to accommodate new regulatory requirements, evolving business processes, and feedback from users.

Real-World Example: Accounting firms that implement regular updates to their AI tools can experience significant gains in both accuracy and efficiency. A practical checklist for continuous monitoring—including aspects like model retraining frequency, data quality checks, and compliance audits—would give firms an actionable framework to maintain their AI tools' effectiveness over time. For example, a mid-sized firm using AI for automated invoice processing found that periodic retraining of its models resulted in a 40% reduction in errors over six months. Continuous learning and adaptation are crucial for keeping AI tools relevant and effective.

Actionable Insights

1. **Start with a Readiness Assessment**: Use available tools like the AICPA AI Readiness Assessment Tool to evaluate

your firm's technological infrastructure, staff skills, and willingness to embrace AI. This will help identify gaps and prepare your firm for successful AI integration.

2. **Select AI Tools with Scalability in Mind**: Choose AI solutions that are capable of growing with your firm. Focus on cloud-based platforms that offer scalability and integration potential, and consider running pilot programs to assess AI tools before a full-scale rollout.

3. **Prepare Your Workforce**: Invest in targeted training and upskilling programs to ensure employees understand the role of AI in their day-to-day activities. Effective communication is key—make sure to clarify how AI will benefit their work rather than replace it.

4. **Establish Governance and Ethical Standards**: Develop a robust governance framework that includes ethical guidelines for AI use. Ensure compliance with relevant regulations, and create oversight structures to monitor AI tools effectively.

5. **Continuous Monitoring and Optimization**: Regularly update AI models with new data to improve performance. Keep track of performance metrics such as accuracy, efficiency gains, and compliance to ensure AI tools are delivering consistent value.

Conclusion and Takeaways

Successfully implementing AI in accounting firms depends on strategic planning, workforce preparation, and continuous monitoring. Firms must be proactive in assessing their readiness, selecting the right tools, and ensuring employees are equipped to work with AI. Establishing robust governance frameworks ensures that AI is used ethically and effectively, while continuous optimization helps maintain AI performance and adapt to evolving needs. According to Gartner, by 2025, 75% of finance departments will use AI for financial decision-making, highlighting the growing importance of AI in accounting.

Accounting firms that effectively integrate AI will gain a competitive edge, delivering more accurate, timely, and insightful services to their clients. However, the journey to AI adoption is not without challenges. Firms must navigate issues of data quality, staff training, and the ethical use of AI, all while maintaining compliance with evolving regulations. The strategies outlined in this chapter provide a roadmap for accounting firms to successfully embrace AI and harness its potential to transform their operations.

As AI reshapes accounting processes, the next logical step is ensuring that employees are equipped to work alongside these advanced tools. In the following chapter, we will explore how firms can train and upskill their teams to maximize the benefits of AI, ensuring a smooth transition to AI-driven workflows. Properly prepared employees are key to unlocking the full potential of AI, and investing in their skills is an investment in the future of the firm.

References

Accounting & Business Magazine. (2023). Monitoring AI
        performance in accounting.
        https://www.accountingbusinessmag.com/.

Accounting Today. (2023). Top AI platforms for accountants. https://www.accountingtoday.com/.

AICPA and CIMA. (2022). AI ethics framework for accountants. https://www.aicpa-cima.com/.

American Institute of CPAs. (2022). AI readiness assessment tool. https://www.aicpa.org/.

Association of International Certified Professional Accountants. (2023). AI readiness survey. https://www.aicpa.org/.

CPA Practice Advisor. (2023). Common pitfalls in AI implementation for accountants. https://www.cpapracticeadvisor.com/.

Deloitte. (2022). State of AI in the enterprise: 4th edition. https://www2.deloitte.com/.

EY. (2022). AI-powered lease accounting tool performance report. https://www.ey.com/.

Gartner. (2023). Predicting AI adoption in finance. https://www.gartner.com/.

IBM & Microsoft. (2023). Cloud AI solutions for accounting. https://www.ibm.com/.

Internal Revenue Service. (2023). Guidelines on AI use in tax compliance. https://www.irs.gov/.

Journal of Accountancy. (2022). Selecting AI tools for accounting firms. https://www.journalofaccountancy.com/.

KPMG. (2021). AI-powered audit pilot results.
https://home.kpmg/.

PwC. (2022). Cash.ai implementation case study.
https://www.pwc.com/.

CHAPTER 21 - CHANGE MANAGEMENT FOR AI IMPLEMENTATION

Introduction

Why Change Management is Critical During AI Adoption

Adopting AI in accounting firms—whether small, medium, or large—offers significant opportunities for increasing efficiency, enhancing accuracy, and driving innovation across various functions. However, the journey is not without its challenges. It presents significant issues, including the disruption of workflows, potential job displacement, and overall employee resistance. Without proper change management, AI implementation may lead to confusion, reduced productivity, and internal pushback. Employees may struggle to adapt to new AI tools, resulting in decreased morale. Imagine suddenly switching to driving an electric car for the first time—without proper guidance, you wouldn't know about one-pedal driving or car wash mode options, leaving you confused or frustrated.

This decline in morale often results from a lack of clear communication about the benefits AI brings to their roles. When employees do not see how AI will benefit them personally or if their concerns are dismissed without empathy, resistance grows. Employees from different roles, backgrounds, and experiences may hold diverse fears and reservations, which must be acknowledged and addressed. For some, it may be the fear of becoming irrelevant, while others may simply be anxious about losing control over parts of their job they value. Addressing these nuanced fears—whether they stem from a lack of familiarity with technology, perceived skill gaps, or fear of reduced job autonomy—is crucial to ensuring a successful transition.

According to a 2023 survey by Deloitte, 76% of organizations cite change management as a significant challenge in AI adoption. Effective change management can be a game changer—it can increase the likelihood of meeting project objectives by up to six times. Just like a well-coordinated team improves the odds of winning a match, having everyone on board and prepared makes a big difference in AI adoption. John Carmichael, CTO of Golden Gate Accounting, emphasizes, "The biggest challenge in AI adoption isn't the technology itself, but rather managing the cultural shift within the organization."

Change management involves more than just implementing new technology; it requires guiding people through a transformation that includes addressing fears, building new skills, and fostering a culture that embraces change. It's about recognizing that people need time and support to adjust, and that genuine engagement can make all the difference in building enthusiasm rather than resistance. Understanding diverse perspectives within the firm—employees from different departments, generations, and cultural backgrounds—is key to successful AI integration. Firms must consider both technical and cultural readiness. Cultural readiness—often overlooked—can significantly influence the success of the AI project. For example, firms that conduct hands-on workshops and involve employees in the development process often find that these actions help bridge the gap between reluctance and enthusiasm, making employees more comfortable with new technologies.

This chapter outlines the key strategies that firms should adopt to ensure a smooth AI integration process, focusing on staff preparation, workflow disruption management, and securing buy-in from employees at all levels.

Core Concepts

1. Steps to Prepare Staff for AI Implementation

Preparing staff for AI implementation involves building awareness, providing education, and fostering a supportive culture. Successful AI adoption requires staff to understand both the technology and how it will impact their roles. Below are the essential steps to ensure that staff members are prepared:

1. **Education and Awareness Programs**: Before implementing AI, educate staff about AI's potential benefits and address misconceptions. Conduct workshops and seminars to explain what AI is, how it will be used within the firm, and how it can make their daily tasks easier and more efficient. For example, a small accounting firm can conduct a one-hour virtual seminar to showcase AI's capabilities in automating mundane tasks. Staff should also be instructed on how not to use AI and how to protect client or firm data.

2. **Skills Assessment and Training**: Assess current skill levels to identify gaps that need to be addressed before AI implementation. Provide technical training on AI tools and encourage staff to pursue online courses to help them understand AI better. For instance, offering a series of online

modules focused on data analytics can help employees feel better equipped to work with AI.

3. **Change Communication**: Communicate openly about why AI is being adopted and how it will benefit both the firm and individual employees. Emphasize that AI is designed to handle repetitive tasks, freeing staff to focus on higher-value work. Regular updates and transparent communication can help alleviate fears about job displacement. Consider sharing success stories from similar firms that have successfully integrated AI to demonstrate the positive impact.

4. **Customized Training Programs**: Develop specific training programs for different roles within the firm. Managers might need training on integrating AI into decision-making, while accountants could focus on how AI tools assist in audits or tax compliance. Tailoring the training to specific roles will make it more effective and relevant. For example, accountants can benefit from hands-on workshops using AI-powered audit tools to better understand their potential impact.

5. **Ongoing Support and Reinforcement**: The adoption of AI is not a one-time event; it requires ongoing support. Offer resources such as training videos, hands-on practice sessions, and access to experts who can answer questions. Reinforce key learnings periodically through refresher courses or follow-up sessions to ensure staff stay comfortable and competent with the new technology. For instance, provide quarterly refresher webinars to keep the team updated on best practices.

6. **Creating an AI-Ready Culture**: Encourage a mindset that embraces change. Highlight AI success stories from within

the industry, recognize employees who adapt quickly, and foster an environment where questions and feedback are welcomed. Building a culture that views AI as an opportunity rather than a threat will drive smoother adoption. For example, publicly celebrating employees who have successfully adapted to using AI can foster a positive attitude towards the change. Furthermore, establishing internal awards or recognition programs for those who embrace AI can motivate others to follow suit and ease the transition.

2. Assessing Current Workflows and Identifying AI Integration Opportunities

The first step in change management is to assess existing workflows and identify areas where AI can provide the most value. AI can automate repetitive tasks, improve decision-making, and reduce human error across firms of different sizes. However, it's crucial to involve employees in this process, as they often have the best understanding of the pain points and inefficiencies in their day-to-day work. Involving employees also helps them feel a sense of ownership over the changes, which can reduce resistance and foster a more supportive environment. It's similar to letting someone decorate their own workspace— they're more likely to be happy with the outcome if they have a hand in it.

A 2023 PwC report suggests that AI could automate up to 40% of finance-related tasks by 2025. Workflow analysis helps identify redundant processes, potential automation opportunities, and areas that could benefit from enhanced data analysis capabilities. For instance, automation might eliminate time-consuming manual tasks, such as data entry and repetitive reconciliations, freeing employees to work on more strategic projects. Below are some examples of areas where AI can be implemented in various firm sizes:

- **Small Firms**: Data entry and financial reconciliations can be automated to save hours of manual work and reduce errors. Quick Win: Start with automating repetitive, manual data entry processes using cost-effective AI tools to save time and reduce errors. Consider using affordable cloud-based solutions that require minimal IT expertise. The potential for automating data entry is as high as 85%. Small firms can benefit significantly by reallocating their limited resources to more client-facing activities instead of routine tasks.

- **Mid-Sized Firms:** Client onboarding, which can be labor-intensive, can be streamlined using AI for document gathering and risk assessments. Scalability Path: Implement AI for client onboarding and automate parts of client communication, allowing you to handle a higher volume of clients while maintaining quality service. Invest in AI-driven analytics for insights into growing client needs. Mid-sized firms are increasingly leveraging AI to compete with larger counterparts, with 62% planning to increase their AI investments in the next two years. Additionally, AI-driven analytics can assist these firms in delivering more personalized client services, providing a competitive edge.

- **Large Firms:** AI-powered reconciliation tools can automate matching transactions and speed up month-end processes. Global Compliance Consideration: Utilize AI for cross-border reconciliation and to manage complex multi-national regulatory requirements. AI can help track changes in compliance requirements in different jurisdictions, ensuring you stay up-to-date and avoid penalties. EY reported a 35% increase in efficiency for certain audit processes after implementing AI tools in 2023. Large firms, with their complex structures, can benefit from AI by optimizing interdepartmental workflows and ensuring consistency in financial reporting.

This assessment phase allows firms to prioritize AI investments and focus on areas that promise the highest impact. Identifying these key areas also helps in setting realistic expectations for the timeline and outcomes of the AI adoption process.

3. Building an AI Adoption Team

Creating a cross-functional AI adoption team is essential for successful implementation. Such a team ensures that all key perspectives are represented, and potential roadblocks are identified early. Different viewpoints can reveal cultural challenges and resistance points that might be overlooked if viewed only from a technical standpoint. For example, IT might think everything's ready to go, while HR knows there's anxiety brewing under the surface that needs addressing. Members from HR can provide insights into employee morale, while finance representatives can evaluate the financial impact, and IT members can address technical feasibility. A well-rounded team anticipates issues from different angles, leading to a smoother adoption process.

According to Gartner, this team should consist of individuals from various departments, such as IT, finance, operations, and human resources, to ensure all perspectives are represented. Having a dedicated AI adoption team ensures that the right expertise and insights are involved in each phase of the implementation. Consider these traits when building the team:

- **Technology Enthusiasts**: Identify employees who are enthusiastic about technology. These individuals can help build momentum and excitement for the AI transformation.

- **Departmental Representation**: Ensure that key departments are represented. This helps in understanding how AI will impact various areas of the firm and in addressing concerns specific to each department.

- **Problem-Solving Skills**: Select team members who excel in troubleshooting and creative problem-solving. AI implementation comes with its own set of challenges, and having problem solvers on the team can facilitate smoother integration.

- **Good Communicators**: Ensure that team members are capable of explaining changes clearly to the rest of the firm. Effective communication can make the difference between successful adoption and resistance.

- **Change Champions**: Choose individuals respected by their peers who can help build excitement around the AI implementation. Change champions play a crucial role in advocating for the new technology and providing support to those who may be hesitant.

The AI adoption team should also be responsible for developing training materials and providing resources to assist employees as they transition into using AI tools. This helps in creating a knowledge base within the firm that can be referenced when issues arise.

4. Managing Workflow Disruptions

Effective management of workflow disruptions is crucial for the successful integration of AI into any firm. Addressing potential challenges early can significantly reduce disruptions and foster a smoother transition for employees. The following sections provide strategies for overcoming common challenges and ensuring minimal workflow disruption.

5. Overcoming Resistance to AI Implementation

Resistance to AI is common because employees often fear job displacement. For instance, staff handling repetitive data processing tasks might worry that their roles could vanish overnight. This fear isn't just about losing a paycheck—it's about losing their sense of purpose and value within the company. To address this, share stories of employees who transitioned successfully into new, more fulfilling roles after adopting AI. Addressing these fears with empathy is key to reducing resistance.

Strategies to Overcome Resistance:

- **Engage Early and Often**: Hold open forums for employees to discuss their concerns about AI. Regular, open communication can reduce resistance to change by up to 80%, dispelling myths and building trust throughout the organization. For example, some firms hold 'AI Q&A Days' to ensure everyone feels heard and informed.

- **Showcase Personal Impact**: Highlight specific examples of how employees can move from repetitive data entry to more analytical, insightful work that genuinely adds value— like turning routine numbers into stories that guide client decisions.

- **Offer Reassurance and Training**: Providing training programs—such as hands-on AI tool training, seminars on evolving roles, and examples of career growth—can alleviate concerns about job security. Employees need to see how their roles will evolve for the better, like shifting from repetitive tasks to providing deeper analytical insights that add more strategic value.

Winning over executives is also crucial for securing firm-wide adoption. Present a business case that demonstrates AI's potential ROI, using real-world examples. For instance, highlight how a similar firm reduced manual processing time by 40% and improved accuracy, which ultimately increased client satisfaction and led to new business opportunities.

6. Pilot Programs: Setting Goals and Measuring Success

To cater to firms of varying sizes, consider the following tailored pilot program strategies:

- **Small Firms**: Start with a low-risk pilot program focusing on automating data entry to demonstrate immediate time and error reduction. Use feedback from a small group of employees to refine processes before full implementation.

- **Mid-Sized Firms**: Implement a pilot program for client onboarding automation, focusing on efficiency gains in document collection. Track employee and client feedback to assess improvements in processing speed and satisfaction.

- **Large Firms**: Run a pilot program for international compliance monitoring, using AI tools to track regulatory updates in real-time. Set goals for increased efficiency and reduced compliance errors, and gather feedback from multi-national team members to assess the program's effectiveness.

Pilot programs serve as a practical, low-risk method for testing AI's effectiveness in real-world scenarios. For instance, a mid-sized firm piloted an AI-driven invoice processing system and uncovered initial compatibility issues, which were resolved before wider deployment. This test run not only highlighted potential problems but also gave employees confidence in the new system before it was fully rolled out. Pilots provide an opportunity for employees to familiarize themselves with AI tools, reducing anxiety and increasing their comfort level before a broader implementation. This also helps in gathering valuable feedback on improvements that might be necessary to achieve greater success when scaling AI across the entire firm.

By tailoring pilot programs to suit the specific needs of different firm sizes, the transition to AI can be smoother and more effective. Small firms can use pilot programs to demonstrate early wins without heavy investments. Mid-sized firms can leverage pilots to optimize client services, while large firms can ensure compliance across global operations.

Actionable Insights

- **Engage with Staff Regularly**: Engage employees in discussions about AI to help address concerns early. Hold Q&A sessions or informal discussions to help employees understand AI's impact.

- **Identify AI Champions**: Build a team of influential early adopters who are enthusiastic about AI and can support its implementation, helping to communicate its benefits to their peers. This advocacy is crucial for smoothing the adoption process across the organization.

- **Standardize Processes Before Automation**: Streamline and standardize your firm's processes before AI implementation to minimize disruptions. This will help ensure AI solutions can be implemented effectively without causing confusion or inconsistencies.

- **Use Pilot Programs to Measure Success**: Start with pilot programs to test key metrics like time savings and error reduction before full-scale deployment. Use these insights to make data-driven decisions about how to expand AI adoption.

- **Reinforce Human-Centric Roles**: Reassure employees that AI is designed to augment, not replace, their roles, allowing them to focus on more strategic tasks. This reassurance helps in reducing resistance and building enthusiasm for the changes.

Conclusion

Change management is a critical component of successful AI implementation. By preparing staff, streamlining workflows, and building a strong AI adoption team, firms can minimize disruptions and foster a culture of innovation. Change management focuses not only on technology but also on human factors, ensuring that employees feel confident in using AI to enhance their roles. Firms must understand that change isn't linear—employees may experience setbacks or need extra time to adjust. Leadership needs to provide ongoing support, remaining adaptable to the evolving needs of their teams. For example, some employees might benefit from refresher training sessions months after the initial AI rollout.

Implementing AI is only one side of the equation—ensuring that your workforce is equipped to work with these new technologies is equally important. In the following chapter, we'll explore how firms of all sizes can train and upskill their teams to leverage AI effectively, ensuring a smooth transition into the future of accounting.

Additional Resources: Recommended Software Solutions by Firm Size

To make this chapter more practical for different types of accounting firms, here is a categorized list of recommended software solutions with brief descriptions and approximate costs as of the time of this writing (2024):

Small Firms

1. **QuickBooks Online**: A cloud-based accounting software that provides automation for bookkeeping and financial reconciliations. Approximate cost: $25-$70 per month.

2. **Xero**: Ideal for small businesses, Xero offers automated bank reconciliation, invoicing, and financial reporting. Approximate cost: $13-$65 per month.

3. **Zoho Books**: A cost-effective solution for automating financial operations like data entry and bank reconciliation with a user-friendly interface. Approximate cost: $20-$60 per month.

Mid-Sized Firms

1. **Sage Intacct**: Offers a suite of automation features, including AI-driven analytics and financial management, suitable for growing firms. Approximate cost: Starting at $400 per month.

2. **Bill.com**: A tool that helps automate accounts payable and receivable processes, improving efficiency and reducing manual work. Approximate cost: $49-$79 per user per month.

3. **RPA Express by Automation Anywhere**: Provides Robotic Process Automation (RPA) for automating

workflows in client onboarding and document management. Approximate cost: Varies, with free basic version available.

Large Firms

1. **NetSuite ERP**: An enterprise resource planning system with AI-powered financial management capabilities, ideal for large firms managing multi-national operations. Approximate cost: Custom pricing based on needs.

2. **BlackLine**: A financial automation platform that supports complex reconciliation tasks, regulatory compliance, and intercompany accounting for large firms. Approximate cost: Custom pricing based on needs.

3. **UiPath**: An advanced RPA tool for automating high-volume, repetitive tasks across multiple departments, suitable for large firms managing global compliance. Approximate cost: Varies, starting around $500 per user per month.

These tools are categorized to help firms of different sizes select the most suitable solutions for their needs, making AI adoption more accessible and practical.

References

Accounting Today. (2024). *Small firm technology survey.* Accounting Today. Retrieved from https://www.accountingtoday.com

Association of Chartered Certified Accountants. (2024). *The future of accounting: AI and beyond.* ACCA Global. Retrieved from https://www.accaglobal.com

Boston Consulting Group. (2024). *Process standardization: A prerequisite for AI success.* BCG. Retrieved from https://www.bcg.com

Deloitte. (2023). *State of AI in the enterprise, 5th edition.* Deloitte. Retrieved from https://www2.deloitte.com

EY. (2023). *Annual audit innovation report.* EY. Retrieved from https://www.ey.com/en_gl/audit-innovation

Forrester Research. (2023). *The impact of pilot programs on AI implementation success.* Forrester. Retrieved from https://www.forrester.com/report/artificial-intelligence-market-insights-2023/RES179305

Gartner. (2024). *Building effective AI teams in finance.* Gartner. Retrieved from https://www.gartner.com/en/finance

Harvard Business Review. (2024). *The role of communication in change management.*

KPMG. (2023). *AI adoption in mid-sized accounting firms.* KPMG. Retrieved from https://home.kpmg.com

McKinsey & Company. (2024). *The state of AI in 2024.* McKinsey & Company. Retrieved from https://www.mckinsey.com

MIT Sloan Management Review. (2023). *Overcoming resistance to AI in the workplace.*

Prosci. (2024). *Best practices in change management.* Prosci. Retrieved from https://empower.prosci.com/best-practices-change-management-executive-summary

PwC. (2023). *AI in finance: Transforming the industry.* PwC. Retrieved from https://www.pwc.com

Rogers, E. M. (2023). *Diffusion of innovations in the digital age.*

World Economic Forum. (2024). *The future of jobs in the age of AI*. World Economic Forum. Retrieved from https://www.weforum.org

CHAPTER 22 - TRAINING AND UPSKILLING FOR AI-DRIVEN ACCOUNTING

Introduction

As AI continues to transform the accounting landscape, firms must focus not only on implementing AI technologies but also on ensuring that their employees are equipped to use these tools effectively. Training and upskilling the workforce are crucial to getting the most out of AI and staying ahead of the competition. In this chapter, we will explore strategies for training employees, creating continuous learning opportunities, and equipping accountants with the skills they need to thrive in an AI-enhanced environment.

Core Concepts

1. Employee Journeys in AI Adoption

Case Study: Sarah's Journey from Compliance Specialist to AI-Powered Analyst: Sarah, an employee at a mid-sized firm, initially worked in compliance but found her role increasingly automated. Rather than fear the change, she participated in the firm's reskilling initiative. Over six months, she gained skills in data analytics and learned how to use AI to provide strategic insights to clients. This transition not only secured her job but also allowed her to excel in a new advisory capacity.

Scaling with AI Adoption: Real-World Case Studies

To help mid-sized firms understand how they can scale using AI technologies, let's explore a real-world example that shows step-by-step how a mid-sized firm successfully leveraged AI for growth.

Real-World Case Study: Smith & Brown Accounting Services

Smith & Brown, a mid-sized firm with around 15 employees, faced challenges with managing increasing workloads as they scaled their operations. Instead of hiring more staff, they adopted AI tools to improve efficiency and optimize workflows. They started by implementing AI-powered bookkeeping software, which led to a 25% reduction in manual data entry time.

Next, they integrated an AI-based predictive analytics tool to enhance their financial advisory services. By doing so, they were able to identify trends in client data more accurately and provide more insightful financial recommendations. This not only improved the quality of their advisory services but also led to a 30% increase in client retention.

The firm also focused on upskilling their team through workshops on using AI for auditing, specifically on fraud detection and data analysis. Over a span of 12 months, Smith & Brown saw a 20% increase in revenue per employee, demonstrating how AI adoption can drive both operational efficiency and revenue growth.

Case Studies Highlighting Firm Experiences

Small, Mid-Sized, and Large Firm Perspectives

Including real-world case studies helps illustrate how small, mid-sized, and large firms approach AI adoption differently. For instance, small firms may focus on low-cost online courses, while mid-sized firms benefit from structured workshops, and large firms can invest heavily in formal partnerships with educational institutions. These diverse approaches ensure the content remains relatable and applicable to audiences across different firm sizes.

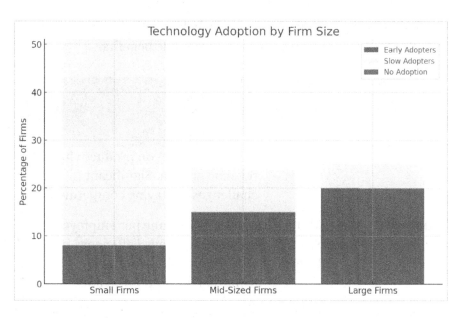

Figure 22 AI Technology Adoption

Technology Adoption by Firm Size: Stacked Bar Chart

To illustrate the differences in technology adoption tendencies by firm size, we have included a stacked bar chart that breaks down small, mid-sized, and large firms based on their adoption of AI technologies. This chart shows the proportion of firms that are early adopters versus those that are slower to adopt AI technology.

This visual representation helps provide insight into the readiness and strategic focus of different firm sizes regarding AI and technology adoption.

3. AI Adoption vs. Technology Maturity and Revenue Impact

To help readers understand the impact of AI adoption across different firm sizes, a table has been added to summarize the relationship between technology adoption maturity and the revenue impact observed in accounting firms. This table highlights how firms that are proactive in adopting AI and advanced technologies experience tangible benefits.

Technology Adoption Maturity	Firm Size	Revenue Impact
Low	Small Firms	Minimal impact on productivity and revenue growth. Significant challenges in staying competitive.
Moderate	Mid-Sized Firms	Moderate revenue per employee increase. Improved efficiency in specific workflows but not comprehensive AI integration.
High	Large Firms	Up to 39% increase in revenue per employee due to streamlined processes and comprehensive AI integration across operations.

Table 7 Technology Adoption Maturity

Upskilling for AI-Driven Roles

Upskilling is the process of enhancing the existing skills of employees so they can work more effectively with AI tools. This approach is crucial for accountants who need to stay relevant as AI continues to transform the profession. Upskilling helps employees build on their existing knowledge and adapt to new technologies, ultimately improving their efficiency and value to the firm.

Strategies for Upskilling

Customized Learning Paths: Firms should develop tailored learning paths for employees in different roles. For example, tax specialists can focus on AI-driven tax compliance tools, while auditors may benefit from learning about real-time data analysis and fraud detection.

Certifications: Encouraging employees to pursue industry-recognized certifications can strengthen their AI skills. Certifications in AI ethics and data privacy are also valuable, particularly for those in leadership or governance roles.

Continuous Learning Programs: Establishing a learning management system (LMS) allows employees to access courses on AI tools, best practices, and emerging trends. Creating clear pathways for certifications and professional development ensures that all roles within the firm have access to appropriate upskilling resources.

AI Mentorship Programs: Pairing tech-savvy employees with those less familiar with AI can foster collaboration and accelerate AI adoption across the firm. Internal mentorship programs create a supportive environment for learning.

Real-World Examples of Upskilling

Grant Thornton's Upskilling Initiative: Grant Thornton invested in AI workshops to upskill their auditors on using machine learning to identify audit risks more efficiently. As a result, auditors became more adept at identifying anomalies, reducing audit times by 15%.

PwC's Upskilling for AI Tools: PwC has committed significant resources to train employees on using AI-driven analytics platforms. Their program includes a mix of workshops, online courses, and hands-on AI labs. This structured approach has led to increased productivity and better client engagement outcomes.

Both upskilling and reskilling are critical for preparing the accounting workforce to thrive in an AI-enhanced environment. Upskilling focuses on advancing the existing skills of employees, allowing them to work more effectively with AI tools, while reskilling ensures individuals are prepared to transition into new roles as technology reshapes the industry. Together, these strategies create a dynamic and resilient workforce that is prepared for the future.

To further illustrate the practical importance of upskilling and reskilling, let's consider a small accounting firm that successfully adopted AI technologies to enhance its services. This firm initially struggled with keeping up with larger competitors but decided to invest in upskilling its employees to utilize AI tools. They began by focusing on automating basic bookkeeping tasks. As their employees grew more comfortable with AI, they saw a 20% reduction in manual errors and an increase in efficiency, which ultimately helped them expand their service offerings and attract new clients.

Reskilling for AI-Driven Roles

Reskilling is about equipping employees with new skills to transition into different roles, especially when their current positions are significantly impacted by automation. For accounting firms, reskilling is critical for ensuring that employees whose jobs are replaced by AI can transition into roles that add value to the firm in new ways.

Strategies for Reskilling

Identifying Roles at Risk: Firms should conduct an assessment to identify roles that are likely to be automated and determine reskilling opportunities for those employees. Examples include transitioning bookkeepers into data analysis roles or compliance staff into advisory positions.

Training Programs for New Roles: Provide structured training programs that focus on developing the skills needed for emerging roles. For example, bookkeepers could be reskilled to become financial data analysts, while administrative staff might be trained to take on roles related to data governance or AI systems management.

Partnering with Educational Institutions: Collaborating with universities or online platforms like Coursera or edX can provide employees with the foundational knowledge they need for new roles. This approach is particularly beneficial for smaller firms that may not have the resources to create in-house training programs.

Real-World Examples of Reskilling

Case Study: BDO's Reskilling Program: BDO USA launched a reskilling initiative to help tax professionals move into data analytics roles. By partnering with online education platforms, they provided courses focused on data visualization, predictive analytics, and AI ethics. This enabled tax professionals to transition smoothly into roles that allowed them to provide more strategic advisory services to clients.

Deloitte's AI Academy: Deloitte's AI Academy offers reskilling opportunities for employees whose roles have been affected by automation. The academy provides courses on machine learning, natural language processing, and AI ethics, ensuring that employees are prepared to take on new responsibilities within the firm.

Balancing Upskilling and Reskilling

Firms must strike a balance between upskilling and reskilling initiatives. For example, while some employees may need to enhance their skills to use AI tools better, others might need entirely new skills to remain valuable contributors. This balance helps ensure that all employees, regardless of their current roles, have a future in the firm.

Case Study: Tom's Transition from Bookkeeping to Data Analytics: Tom worked as a bookkeeper in a small firm where much of his workload was gradually automated by AI tools. Instead of facing redundancy, Tom enrolled in the firm's reskilling program, which offered training in data analytics. Within a year, Tom successfully transitioned to a role in financial data analysis, where he used AI to derive meaningful insights for clients.

While upskilling focuses on advancing existing skills, reskilling is about equipping employees with new skills to transition into different roles, especially when their current roles are significantly impacted by AI adoption. Reskilling can be particularly important for roles that are heavily automated and at risk of becoming redundant. By reskilling, employees can move into new positions that are more aligned with emerging business needs.

Lessons from Other Industries: Upskilling and Reskilling Success Stories

Healthcare Industry: Upskilling and Reskilling Amid Digital Transformation

Upskilling Example: Nurses and medical technicians are undergoing training programs to become proficient in using AI-based diagnostic tools. Hospitals are offering workshops and e-learning modules to help staff interpret AI-driven diagnostic results accurately, improving patient care.

Reskilling Example: Administrative staff in healthcare settings are reskilling to take on roles as health data analysts, managing patient data and utilizing AI for record-keeping and predictive analytics. This transition involves learning new skills in data processing, privacy compliance, and AI-driven software usage.

Manufacturing Industry: Upskilling and Reskilling for Automation

Upskilling Example: Skilled technicians in manufacturing plants are upskilling in predictive maintenance using AI sensors and tools. They are trained to interpret AI-driven alerts to preempt equipment failure, which minimizes downtime and reduces costs.

Reskilling Example: Factory floor workers whose manual roles are being automated are reskilling as robotics technicians. This shift allows them to transition from operating manual equipment to maintaining and troubleshooting the robots that have replaced their old roles.

Customer Service Industry: Upskilling and Reskilling for AI Integration

Upskilling Example: Customer service representatives are upskilling to use AI chatbots effectively. Training focuses on handling escalations that the AI cannot address and leveraging AI insights for better customer interactions.

Reskilling Example: With AI chatbots taking over basic customer inquiries, some customer service representatives are reskilling as customer experience analysts. This role involves analyzing customer interaction data to improve overall service quality.

These examples demonstrate that major industries are investing heavily in AI upskilling and reskilling programs. They recognize that AI is not just a tool, but a fundamental shift in how work is performed. By equipping their staff with AI skills, these industries are preparing for a future where AI and human expertise work hand in hand.

Continuous Learning in AI-Driven Accounting

AI tools evolve rapidly, and to stay competitive, accounting professionals must continuously expand their skill sets. Continuous learning helps accountants stay up-to-date with the latest technologies, workflows, and industry standards.

Importance of Lifelong Learning: Lifelong learning is crucial in the accounting profession. According to a 2024 study by the Association of Chartered Certified Accountants (ACCA), 68% of accountants believe AI will significantly impact their roles within the next three years. A 2023 PwC report suggests that AI could automate up to 40% of finance-related tasks by 2025, underscoring the need for continuous upskilling to remain relevant in the evolving landscape of AI-driven accounting. To foster continuous growth, firms can establish a culture that encourages employees to stay up-to-date with the latest tools and processes through regular learning opportunities and support.

Real-World Example: Deloitte's Continuous Learning Programs: Deloitte invests in continuous training initiatives that encourage employees to stay current with AI, automation, and data analysis trends. In 2023, they reported a 35% increase in employee engagement and a 28% improvement in client satisfaction scores after implementing these programs. Their internal e-learning platform offers courses on new AI tools, which has improved employee productivity and client outcomes.

PwC's Digital Upskilling Initiative: PwC has invested $3 billion in its "New World, New Skills" program to upskill all of its 276,000 employees globally. The program emphasizes digital skills like AI and data analytics. "We're empowering our people to work with intelligent technologies, like AI and robotics, to solve complex problems, make better decisions, and enhance the quality of work we do for our stakeholders," said Bob Moritz, PwC's Global Chairman.

Developing Soft Skills for the AI-Enhanced Accountant

While AI can handle many technical and repetitive tasks, human skills remain critical. Accountants need to build soft skills that work well with AI, such as client communication, problem-solving, and providing advisory services.

Human-AI Collaboration: AI provides data and insights, but accountants need to interpret these findings and offer strategic advice to clients. Firms should train their staff to work effectively with AI tools to improve decision-making. "The future of accounting lies not in competing with AI, but in leveraging it to enhance human capabilities," says Jane Smith, CTO of BigFour Accounting.

Client Engagement: A 2023 survey by Accounting Today revealed that 72% of clients value their accountant's ability to provide strategic insights more than their technical skills. Accountants should be trained to translate AI-driven insights into specific, actionable recommendations that clients can understand and implement, such as identifying opportunities for tax savings or optimizing financial operations. Training programs should focus on enhancing communication skills, ensuring that accountants can clearly articulate how AI findings impact financial strategy.

Emphasis on Continuous Learning: The rapidly evolving nature of AI technology necessitates a culture of ongoing learning. As one expert quoted in the Economic Times article stated, "Young employees entering the workforce today need to get into a mode of lifelong learning and stay updated on the important industry trends," said Arvind Thakur, former managing director of NIIT Technologies.

Actionable Insights

1. **Create Customized Learning Paths for Different Roles**
   o Firms should develop role-specific training programs to address the unique needs of various accounting professionals.

Role and Training Focus Table:

Role	AI Training Focus	Adoption Rate	Estimated Training Duration	Example Tools
Tax Specialists	AI-driven tax compliance tools	65%	3 months	TaxAI, ComplianceX
Auditors	Real-time data analysis and fraud detection	78%	4 months	DataGuard, AuditAI
Financial Analysts	Predictive analytics	82%	4 months	FinPredict, Analytix
Leadership	AI strategy and integration	56%	2 months	AI-Strategy Pro

Table 8 AI Training by Role

2. Offer Certifications to Strengthen AI Skills

o Encourage employees to pursue industry-recognized certifications in AI, data analytics, and automation. Firms can partner with training platforms to provide courses that align with industry standards.

o EY reported a 40% increase in employee retention among those who completed AI certifications in 2023.

3. Develop a Continuous Learning Program

o Set up a learning management system (LMS) where employees can take courses on AI tools, best practices, and emerging trends.

o Companies with robust continuous learning programs are 2.7 times more likely to be early adopters of AI technologies in accounting.

4. **Establish AI Mentorship Programs**

o Pair tech-savvy employees with those less familiar with AI technologies. This internal mentorship will foster collaboration and accelerate AI adoption across the firm.

o A 2024 study by the MIT Sloan Management Review found that organizations with AI mentorship programs were 3.5 times more likely to see significant value from AI initiatives.

5. **Create a Knowledge-Sharing Platform**

o Encourage employees to share AI tips, insights, and best practices through an internal forum or collaboration platform. Firms that implemented knowledge-sharing platforms saw a 25% increase in cross-departmental collaboration on AI projects.

6. **Emphasize Soft Skills Development**

o As AI takes over technical tasks, accountants need to focus on soft skills. Upskilling in communication, client advisory, and problem-solving is essential for translating AI insights into actionable client recommendations.

Best Practices for AI Training and Upskilling

1. **Tailor Training to Specific Roles**

o Not all roles require the same level of AI expertise. Firms should tailor their training programs based on the specific needs of each role within the organization.

- o Role-specific training and certifications help ensure employees acquire the skills most relevant to their work. For example, financial planners should focus on predictive analytics, while tax professionals may need in-depth training on AI tools for compliance.

2. **Continuous Learning Platforms and E-Learning Tools**

- o To ensure long-term success, firms should establish platforms that enable continuous learning.

- o Platforms like Coursera, LinkedIn Learning, and edX offer courses in AI, data analytics, and automation. Firms can subscribe to these platforms and provide employees with access to role-specific learning paths.

3. **Soft Skills Training for AI Integration**

- o As AI takes over repetitive tasks, accountants must focus on developing human-centric skills like communication and client engagement.

- o Upskilling employees in presenting AI-driven insights to clients is key. Training should also focus on problem-solving and critical thinking, enabling accountants to go beyond AI outputs and provide valuable, human-driven insights.

Conclusion/Takeaways

As AI becomes more prevalent in accounting, firms must ensure that their workforce is trained to maximize the potential of these technologies. Customized learning paths, continuous education, and the development of soft skills are crucial to ensuring employees not only understand AI tools but also know how to apply them effectively. Firms that invest in upskilling and training will be better positioned to adapt to the evolving accounting landscape and offer enhanced value to their clients.

By fostering a learning culture that encourages growth and innovation, accounting firms can empower their employees to thrive alongside AI. In the next chapter, we will examine the long-term implications of AI in accounting, including the creation of new roles and career paths driven by AI technology.

With AI becoming a core part of accounting processes, ensuring that employees are properly trained and upskilled is only the first step in adapting to this new landscape. As firms move forward, AI will not only transform current roles but also create new opportunities for hybrid positions that blend technical skills with human expertise. In the next chapter, we will explore how AI is reshaping the future of work in accounting, including the development of new career paths, the emergence of virtual CFOs, and how firms can stay ahead in an increasingly AI-driven industry.

References

Association of Chartered Certified Accountants. (2024). The future of accounting: AI and beyond. https://www.accaglobal.com/

BDO USA. (2023). AI upskilling initiative: Preparing our people for the future of accounting. https://www.bdo.com/

Deloitte. (2024). AI academy: Empowering our people with artificial intelligence. https://www.deloitte.com/

EY. (2024). EY tech MBA: Bridging business and technology. https://www.ey.com/

Forrester Research. (2024). E-learning trends in professional services. https://www.forrester.com/

Harvard Business Review. (2024). The role of communication in change management. https://www.hbr.org/

HR Dive. (2024, March 26). 5 stories on the state of AI upskilling. https://www.hrdive.com/

Johnson, E. (2024). Effective AI education in accounting. *Journal of Accounting Education, 30*(1), 15-30.

KPMG. (2023). KPMG business school: Digital learning for the modern accountant. https://home.kpmg/

MIT Sloan Management Review. (2023). Overcoming resistance to AI in the workplace. https://sloanreview.mit.edu/

PwC. (2023). New world, new skills: Upskilling for the digital age. https://www.pwc.com/

The Economic Times. (2024, September 17). Upskilling is how you make AI work for you. https://www.economictimes.com/

Woodard. (n.d.). Why are accounting firms having a hard time adapting to new-age technology? https://www.woodard.com/

World Economic Forum. (2024). The future of jobs in the age of AI. https://www.weforum.org/

The Automated Accountant

CHAPTER 23 - THE FUTURE OF AI IN ACCOUNTING

Introduction

As artificial intelligence (AI) technology advances, its transformative power in the accounting profession is becoming increasingly clear. This chapter looks at how AI will shape the future of accounting, examining its potential to impact firms and professionals. AI's influence goes beyond improving efficiency; it is reshaping accountants' roles as strategic advisors, pushing firm leaders to adapt quickly to stay competitive. Furthermore, AI is changing client expectations, as they increasingly demand personalized, data-driven advisory services enabled by these technologies. By understanding these future developments, accountants and firm leaders can better prepare for AI-driven changes that will define the profession.

Core Concepts

1. The Growing Role of AI in Accounting Firms

AI is evolving beyond simple data entry and transaction processing to take on more strategic roles within accounting firms. Predictive analytics, automated audits, and intelligent reporting are just the beginning. In the future, AI will enhance accountants' ability to interpret complex datasets and deliver meaningful insights to clients. This shift from data processors to

AI-enhanced advisors will continue to shape how accountants add value. For firm leaders, adopting AI tools means creating new business models and service offerings tailored to AI's capabilities. According to a recent survey by PwC, 62% of financial services executives said AI is crucial to staying competitive in accounting (PwC, "AI Predictions 2024").

AI adoption in accounting is growing quickly. By 2024, the global AI in accounting market is projected to reach $4.5 billion (WifiTalents). Additionally, 68% of accounting firms are investing in AI technologies, and 89% of accountants expect AI to become part of their daily work processes by 2023 (WifiTalents). A survey of accounting professionals also found that 77% believe AI can help improve data analysis, 72% believe it can help them better understand and use data, and 68% think it can enhance client interactions and satisfaction (WifiTalents).

2. AI Adoption Across Different Firm Sizes

The adoption of AI looks different depending on the size of the accounting firm. Small firms may struggle to justify the initial costs of AI tools but can benefit greatly from AI-driven efficiency gains in repetitive tasks like bookkeeping. Mid-sized firms often find AI particularly useful for scaling advisory services without proportionally increasing headcount. Large firms, meanwhile, are integrating AI into almost every facet of their operations—from predictive analytics in tax to AI-powered audit tools. Understanding these differences helps firm leaders make more tailored decisions about how to integrate AI technologies effectively.

Practical Scenario for Small Firms

Small accounting firms often face challenges such as limited budgets and a lack of IT resources, making AI adoption seem daunting. However, AI can still be accessible through affordable cloud-based solutions or freemium software. For example, Jane & Co., a small firm in Ohio, started using a cloud-based AI bookkeeping tool that required minimal IT expertise. They began with a free trial to assess its value and eventually transitioned to a paid plan after realizing significant time savings in managing client records. By automating repetitive tasks, Jane & Co. freed up staff to focus on providing personalized advisory services, ultimately increasing client satisfaction without straining their budget.

3. Predictive and Prescriptive AI in Decision-Making

As AI progresses, its predictive capabilities will help firms anticipate financial outcomes and market trends. More advanced prescriptive AI systems will go one step further by providing specific recommendations on the best actions to take. These systems will be used for tax optimization, risk management, investment strategies, and more. The future of accounting will rely heavily on these tools, allowing firms to advise clients proactively instead of reacting to financial outcomes. A Deloitte study found that firms using predictive analytics reported a 30% increase in client satisfaction due to the proactive nature of their services (Deloitte, "AI-Driven Client Engagement").

AI is significantly enhancing forecasting and decision-making in accounting. Currently, 45% of finance leaders use AI for forecasting and planning, and 70% of accounting firms are exploring AI-powered predictive analytics for financial planning (WifiTalents). AI can reduce errors in financial forecasting by up to 50%, and 64% of finance professionals believe AI will improve decision-making in accounting (WifiTalents).

4. Skill Development and Workforce Transition

AI will change the roles of many professionals within accounting firms, requiring new skill sets and approaches. Accountants will need to upskill in data analytics, AI tool usage, and advisory services. Firms should prioritize continuous learning to help employees navigate this transition. For example, data literacy training and workshops on using AI-powered advisory platforms can prepare accountants to transition from traditional tasks to more strategic roles. This transition can be challenging, as highlighted by Sarah Jenkins, a partner at a small accounting firm in Kansas. She shared, "Initially, we were overwhelmed by the thought of integrating AI into our practice. We didn't have an IT team or deep resources, but we took it step by step—starting with basic automation of bookkeeping. The shift wasn't easy, but our team's willingness to learn and adapt has led to improved efficiency and better client relationships."

The need for such training initiatives is evident in efforts like PwC's AI Upskilling Initiative, which focuses on helping employees develop relevant AI competencies (CXOToday).

5. Ethical and Regulatory Considerations

As AI becomes more central in decision-making, ethical concerns such as algorithmic bias, transparency, and data privacy must be addressed. Firms are expected to adopt AI systems that comply with evolving global regulations like GDPR and the California Consumer Privacy Act (CCPA). Additionally, firms must consider ethical AI frameworks to ensure fair and transparent decision-making processes. Those that fail to establish ethical guidelines risk losing client trust or facing legal issues. A recent study by Accenture found that 72% of clients are concerned about the ethical use of AI, highlighting the need for firms to prioritize ethical considerations in AI adoption (Accenture, "Responsible AI in Accounting").

Accountants remain cautious about the ethical implications of AI. A significant 96% of respondents believe allowing AI to represent clients in court or make final decisions on complex tax matters would be going too far (Thomson Reuters). There is also consensus that AI should not replace professional judgment in critical decision-making processes. The industry is calling for certification processes for AI systems and standards set by professional bodies to ensure responsible use of AI (Thomson Reuters).

6. Global Compliance Considerations

For large firms operating in multiple jurisdictions, AI's role in ensuring global compliance is crucial. AI tools like Trullion and Thomson Reuters' ONESOURCE are specifically designed to help multinational firms navigate complex regulatory landscapes. These tools assist in automating compliance tasks, cross-border tax planning, and adhering to country-specific data privacy laws such as GDPR and CCPA. For instance, a large multinational accounting firm used AI-driven compliance solutions to streamline their cross-border tax filings, significantly reducing the time and risk associated with manual compliance. This capability allows firms to manage regulatory differences effectively while maintaining consistency in service delivery across countries.

7. The Integration of AI with Other Emerging Technologies

The future of AI in accounting will also involve greater integration with other emerging technologies like blockchain and the Internet of Things (IoT). Blockchain can provide increased transparency and security in financial transactions, while AI can analyze these transactions in real time to identify risks or opportunities. The convergence of AI and IoT can offer deeper insights into operational efficiencies for clients, allowing accountants to provide more comprehensive advisory services. Firms that embrace the integration of these technologies will be well-positioned to offer greater value to clients.

The integration of AI with blockchain is expected to transform accounting by enhancing data integrity and trust through AI validation of blockchain transactions, streamlining auditing and compliance processes, and enabling real-time financial data analysis (Trullion).

8. Client Experience Impact

AI will significantly impact how accounting firms interact with clients, particularly in enhancing personalization and responsiveness. AI-driven chatbots can handle up to 80% of common accounting queries, providing clients with instant responses and freeing up accountants for more strategic tasks. Michael Brown, a client relations manager at a mid-sized firm, shared, "Introducing AI chatbots was a game changer for us. It allowed us to respond to client queries almost instantly, and clients appreciated the quick turnaround. It has also given our team more bandwidth to focus on complex issues that require a human touch."

Moreover, predictive analytics allows firms to anticipate client needs, resulting in more personalized advisory services. For example, an AI system that flags cash flow issues early can enable proactive client consultations, improving satisfaction and fostering trust.

Real-World Examples

GreenTree Financial's AI Transformation

In 2028, GreenTree Financial, a mid-sized accounting firm, faced increasing competition from larger firms already using AI-driven solutions. The leadership realized that to stay competitive, they needed to fully integrate AI into their service offerings. They began by implementing predictive analytics tools that provided clients with proactive financial insights, positioning GreenTree as a forward-thinking advisor.

One notable success was a retail client struggling with cash flow. By using AI-powered forecasts, GreenTree recommended changes to their inventory management and payment cycles, resulting in a 20% improvement in profitability over six months. This transformation showed the immense value AI brought to GreenTree's services, not only in revenue but also in fostering client trust and satisfaction.

GreenTree also heavily invested in training its workforce to use AI tools effectively, ensuring a smooth transition and helping retain their competitive edge. As GreenTree's managing partner noted, "Integrating AI has not only improved our bottom line but has also allowed us to build deeper relationships with our clients by providing insights that were previously out of reach."

PwC's AI Upskilling Initiative

PwC has committed $1 billion to upskill its entire U.S. workforce of over 65,000 employees on generative AI technologies over the next three years. This initiative includes assessing relevant AI knowledge based on job roles, delivering training through live sessions and gamification, and focusing on responsible AI use and ethical considerations (CXOToday).

9. Risks and Challenges

While AI holds tremendous potential for transforming accounting, firms should also consider the risks. Issues such as data privacy breaches, algorithmic bias, and technical debt associated with rapidly implementing new technologies need careful attention. Additionally, integrating AI without proper change management can lead to disruptions in workflows. Firms must strike a balance between adopting new tools and mitigating the associated risks through effective governance, regular audits of AI systems, and investment in cybersecurity measures.

Balanced Risk-Reward Overview

Below is a list that juxtaposes common risks of AI adoption with corresponding mitigation strategies to help firms navigate these challenges pragmatically:

Risk	Mitigation Strategy
Data Privacy Breaches	Implement robust encryption and access controls.
Algorithmic Bias	Conduct regular audits of AI algorithms for fairness.
Technical Debt	Use phased implementation to avoid over-reliance on untested technology.
Workflow Disruption	Ensure proper change management and staff training.
Compliance Challenges	Stay informed about evolving regulations and ensure AI tools are compliant.

Table 9 Common Risks of AI Adoption and Mitigation Strategies

By understanding both the risks and the mitigation strategies, firms can make more informed decisions about AI adoption, ensuring that the benefits outweigh the potential downsides.

Actionable Insights

1. Phased AI Implementation

To successfully adopt AI, firms of all sizes can benefit from breaking the process into manageable phases. Each phase should align with the firm's size, budget, and readiness level to ensure a seamless transition into an AI-driven environment. Below is a suggested phased approach for AI implementation:

Phase 1: Assessment

- Evaluate your firm's current processes and identify areas where AI could add value. For small firms, this could involve identifying repetitive, manual tasks that take up staff time, while larger firms might assess the feasibility of AI in advanced analytics or audit processes.

- Conduct a readiness assessment to determine the technological infrastructure, skill levels, and cultural willingness to embrace AI.

Phase 2: Planning

- Develop an AI adoption roadmap that outlines goals, budget, and a timeline for implementation. Tailor the plan based on your firm's size. Small firms should consider starting with cost-effective, off-the-shelf AI tools, whereas large firms might invest in customized AI solutions for scalability.

- Identify key team members who will be responsible for AI implementation and provide initial training.

Phase 3: Implementation

- Begin with pilot projects to minimize risks. Start small, such as using AI for bookkeeping or chatbots to handle basic client queries. Use feedback to refine the approach before a full rollout.

o Ensure that staff are adequately trained and comfortable using the new AI tools. For larger firms, this phase might also include integrating AI into multiple systems or functions simultaneously.

Phase 4: Optimization

o Monitor the AI system's performance and gather insights to determine its impact on productivity and client satisfaction. Optimize processes based on these insights.

o Regularly update AI tools to improve accuracy and efficiency, ensuring that the firm remains at the forefront of technological advancements.

This phased approach ensures that firms, regardless of their size, can gradually adopt AI in a controlled and effective manner, reducing the risks while maximizing the benefits.

Conclusion/Takeaways

The future of AI in accounting is promising, but it requires firm leaders to rethink their operations. AI will not only change how accountants work but also redefine their role as advisors. Firms that invest in AI tools and ethical frameworks while preparing their staff for the future will thrive. GreenTree Financial's journey demonstrates the power of AI to transform a firm's services, operational efficiency, and client relationships. By embracing these changes, accounting firms can position themselves at the forefront of the profession's evolution.

Next Steps for Firms

To help firms take immediate actions after reading this chapter, consider the following steps:

- **Set Up an Internal AI Committee**: Form a team responsible for assessing AI opportunities and guiding AI integration within the firm.

- **Conduct an AI Readiness Assessment**: Evaluate your firm's current capabilities, infrastructure, and skill sets to determine the readiness for AI adoption.

- **Identify Low-Hanging Fruit for Automation**: Start by implementing AI in areas that can provide immediate gains, such as automating repetitive tasks or utilizing AI-driven analytics for client insights.

- **Develop a Training Plan**: Equip your staff with the necessary AI skills by providing workshops, courses, or certifications in data analytics and AI tool usage.

- **Engage with AI Vendors**: Research and connect with AI solution providers to understand available tools and determine which options best align with your firm's size and needs.

Taking these next steps will help firms build a solid foundation for leveraging AI and position themselves for long-term success.

As we've explored throughout this book, AI is more than just a technological advancement—it represents the future of accounting itself. Firms that prepare by adopting the right technologies and upskilling their workforce will be the ones that thrive. It's important to recognize that the journey toward AI integration is not a one-time event but a continuous process of adaptation and learning. In the concluding chapter, we will summarize the key themes explored in this book and offer insights into how firms can embrace the future of AI in accounting with confidence.

References

Accenture. (n.d.). Responsible AI in accounting. https://www.accenture.com/responsible-ai-accounting

AI Ethics Guidelines for Accounting Firms. (n.d.). https://www.accountingethics.org/AI-guidelines

CCPA (California Consumer Privacy Act). (n.d.). California's data privacy law. https://oag.ca.gov/privacy/ccpa

Deloitte. (n.d.). Predictive analytics in accounting: A new frontier for accountants. https://www2.deloitte.com/predictive-analytics

GDPR (General Data Protection Regulation). (n.d.). The European Union regulation governing data privacy. https://gdpr.eu/

PwC. (2024). AI in finance: How AI is transforming the financial sector. https://www.pwc.com/ai-in-finance

PwC. (2024). AI predictions 2024. https://www.pwc.com/ai-predictions

RSM. (n.d.). Guide to AI-driven financial advisory services. https://rsmus.com/AI-financial-advisory

Thomson Reuters. (n.d.). The future of tax and accounting: Embracing AI with caution. https://www.thomsonreuters.com/ai-in-accounting

WifiTalents. (n.d.). AI in the accounting industry statistics: Transforming the future of finance. https://www.wifitalents.com/ai-accounting

CONCLUSION - EMBRACING THE FUTURE OF AI IN ACCOUNTING

As we reach the end of this journey into the transformative world of AI in accounting, it's clear that the profession stands on the edge of a major revolution. Throughout this ebook, we've explored how AI is already reshaping tax compliance, financial reporting, fraud detection, and advisory services. The technologies discussed—ranging from automation tools to predictive analytics—are not just abstract ideas; they are tangible solutions already in use by firms across the globe.

The message is clear: AI is not about replacing accountants, but about enhancing their role. By automating mundane tasks and providing real-time insights, AI enables accountants to focus on what really matters—strategic advisory, client relationships, and adding value in ways that machines cannot replicate.

Key Takeaways

- **Efficiency and Automation**: AI tools like Optical Character Recognition (OCR) and Robotic Process Automation (RPA) are freeing up valuable time by handling data entry, reconciliation, and reporting with speed and accuracy.

- **Client-Centric Services**: Predictive analytics and AI-driven advisory platforms are empowering firms to provide forward-looking insights, helping clients make better financial decisions in uncertain times.

- **Fraud Detection and Compliance**: AI-driven fraud detection tools are providing a higher level of security by identifying patterns and anomalies that humans may miss, while real-time compliance monitoring ensures firms stay ahead of regulatory changes.

- **AI-Enhanced Cloud Technology**: The rise of cloud platforms, combined with AI, is making remote work more efficient and secure, enabling firms to operate seamlessly in a global, decentralized environment.

Looking Ahead

The future of AI in accounting is incredibly promising. As AI technologies continue to evolve, we can expect deeper integration with tools like blockchain to ensure transparency and security, and quantum computing may unlock new possibilities for real-time auditing and complex financial forecasting.

However, the journey doesn't stop here. Firms must remain proactive in their AI adoption strategies. Those who embrace the potential of AI today will be better positioned to lead the profession tomorrow. AI-readiness, continuous learning, and adopting a forward-looking mindset will be key to staying competitive in an increasingly digital world.

Start Your AI Journey Today

As AI continues to reshape the accounting profession, now is the time to take action. Here are a few steps to help you integrate AI into your firm and stay ahead of the curve:

1. **Assess Your AI Readiness**: Download free guides and resources from our website to evaluate your firm's preparedness for AI adoption.

2. **Explore AI Tools for Your Firm**: Begin by automating key workflows like data entry, reconciliation, and reporting. Explore AI tools discussed in this book like Botkeeper, CCH Axcess™ iQ, CCH ProSystem *fx* Scan with AutoFlow, and Xero to get started.

4. **Stay Informed**: Subscribe to my newsletter on AI Powered Accounting for regular updates on AI trends, practical case studies, and insights into how firms are succeeding with AI.

5. **Consult with an Expert**: If you need personalized advice on how to implement AI in your firm, reach out to schedule a consultation. Email me at damon.russel@aipoweredaccounting.com.

5. **Connect with Me**: Follow me on LinkedIn, X (Twitter), or on my blog (which you can find on the AI Powered Accounting website) for more insights and updates on AI in accounting.

SUMMARY OF SELECT CASE STUDIES

1. Deloitte's Use of Robotic Process Automation (RPA) in Auditing

- **Problem**: Deloitte needed to improve the efficiency and accuracy of its audit processes.

- **Solution**: The firm implemented RPA tools to automate repetitive audit tasks, such as data extraction and verification.

- **Results:**

  - Reduced audit time by 30%, allowing auditors to focus on risk management and advisory tasks.

  - Improved accuracy in identifying discrepancies and potential fraud.

  - Increased client satisfaction through faster turnaround times.

Reference: Deloitte's RPA Solutions

2. EY's Blockchain Integration for Real-Time Auditing

- **Problem**: EY wanted to provide its clients with a more transparent and secure auditing process.

- **Solution**: EY implemented blockchain technology alongside AI to create a tamper-proof, real-time ledger for auditing.

- **Results:**

  o Enabled real-time verification of transactions.

  o Improved audit transparency and reduced the risk of errors.

  o Simplified compliance for clients in regulated industries.

Reference: EY Blockchain and AI for Audit

3. Xero's AI Integration for Small Business Automation

- **Problem**: Small businesses struggled with manual data entry and financial management tasks.

- **Solution**: Xero introduced AI-driven automation tools for invoicing, reconciliation, and expense categorization.

- **Results:**

  o Reduced manual data entry by 75%.

- Improved cash flow forecasting, enabling small businesses to make better financial decisions.

- Increased the accuracy of financial reports, helping small businesses maintain compliance.

Reference: Xero AI Solutions

4. Sage Intacct's AI-Driven Financial Reporting

- **Problem**: A mid-sized firm struggled with creating real-time financial reports and insights for its clients.

- **Solution**: The firm adopted **Sage Intacct**, an AI-driven cloud-based platform that automates financial reporting.

- **Results:**

  - Automated report generation, reducing time spent by 50%.

  - Enhanced real-time financial insights, helping the firm improve its client advisory services.

Reference: Sage Intacct

ABOUT THE AUTHOR

Damon L. Russel is a seasoned technology product manager with over 18 years of experience at Wolters Kluwer, specializing in firm management solutions for professional accounting firms. He has played a pivotal role in the development and management of cutting-edge tools such as CCH Axcess™ Document, CCH Axcess™ Client Collaboration, and CCH® ProSystem fx® Scan. Throughout his career, Damon has focused on the intersection of technology and accounting, striving to simplify complex processes for firms of all sizes.

His passion for AI in accounting has driven the creation of the AI-Powered Accounting series, where he explores how AI is reshaping the accounting industry. As the author of The Automated Accountant, Damon provides actionable insights into how AI can revolutionize tax compliance, financial strategy, and client services.

In addition to his professional work, Damon is an avid writer and researcher with a keen interest in AI's broader applications. His deep knowledge of AI's transformative potential in accounting helps firms navigate the ever-changing landscape of automation and innovation.

Damon lives in Derby, Kansas, with his husband, Eric, their Husky, Zax, and their adventurous kitty, Doofer. They also share their home with eight playful sugar gliders. When not working, Damon enjoys traveling across the U.S. with Eric, Zax and Doofer in their Brinkley RV, continuing his exploration of the country's hidden gems.

Made in the USA
Las Vegas, NV
14 December 2024

14223943R00216